'The world today is experiencing a massive proliferation of dest[...] political, terrorist, commercial, self-help, healing, recovery and r[...] use deceptive recruitment tactics and coercive control of members. [...] help those leaving cults, Dr. Jenkinson adds this comprehensive and essential volume. Having herself traversed the daunting path from traumatic abuse in a cult to freedom and recovery, Dr. Jenkinson offers the reader decades of wisdom gleaned from her therapeutic work with survivors, distilled into this eminently readable and usable volume. Both survivors and therapists alike will welcome and treasure this essential and urgently needed addition to the cult recovery literature'.

Daniel Shaw, *psychoanalyst and author of* Traumatic Narcissism: Relational Systems of Subjugation *and* Traumatic Narcissism and Recovery: Leaving the Prison of Shame and Fear

'Gillie Jenkinson has provided former members and those who counsel them with a unique gift, which will profoundly impact the recovery field. After leaving cult life's cognitive and emotional confusion, Dr. Jenkinson uses the perfect grounding metaphor of a physical journey (with illustrations) to give former cult members a step-by-step 'psychological roadmap'. Like the best kind of guide, she offers wisdom gained from her own cult experience and her years as a therapist in the cult recovery field. With each step forward, as the 'fog' of cult life begins to clear, former members can finally arrive at a place where they gain their authentic identity with a wide range of feelings and a clearer sense of reality. This workbook is a remarkable achievement'.

Lorna Goldberg, LCSW, PsyA, *Past President, International Cultic Studies Association and Director, Institute for Psychoanalytic Studies*

'Dr. Gillie Jenkinson is one of the most thoughtful and insightful clinicians in the cultic studies field. In this book, she applies her personal experience and many years of research and clinical work to construct a practical workbook for people leaving cultic groups. This is not simply an explanation of why people join and leave cults. The book provides what would be called 'homework' in some counseling approaches. It is interactive and asks 'participants' (they are much more than readers) to think and write, to complete forms, to wrestle with their memories, thoughts and goals for the future. 'Participating' in this handbook could be worth thousands of dollars in consultation time. The book is a wonderful resource, especially for those former members who do not have the resources to travel and pay for professional consultation. I recommend it highly'.

Michael D. Langone, PhD, *formerly Executive Director, International Cultic Studies Association*

'This is a unique book and should be essential reading. It was forged in the fire of painful experience and refined by a keen mind. Gillie offers a clear pathway enabling others to make their own choices and find their own freedom. It is a remarkable story of personal transformation and hope'.

Alistair Ross, *Associate Professor, Psychotherapy, Oxford University*

'Dr. Gillie Jenkinson is a professional I know and trust. Her work has helped in the education, awareness and healing of countless people'.

Steven Hassan, PhD, MA, MEd, LMHC, NCC, *Freedom of Mind Resource Center, Inc.*

'This valuable book is a sensitively written, practical guide to cult recovery. Based on her own experiences, first as a former member and then as a therapist specializing in cult recovery,

Dr. Jenkinson shares her knowledge and offers guidance for the difficult process of integrating into the non-cult world in a healthy way'.

Alexandra Stein, PhD, *visiting research fellow, London South Bank University*

'There is a new tool to help former cult members and other survivors of abusive groups and relationships, and I will be recommending it to every former cult member who consults with me. In this ground-breaking book, Gillie Jenkinson literally takes her readers on a step-by-step journey to recovery. She doesn't use jargon and she doesn't list aspirational goals and leave the 'how' to the reader's imagination. Instead, she offers clear exercises and examples that untangle the process of recovery. The whimsical illustrations help the reader to visualize the recommended steps and invite the reader to participate. I recommend this workbook without reservation'.

Bill Goldberg, *clinical social worker and psychoanalyst, formerly Program Supervisor for Rehabilitative Services for Rockland County, New York (retired)*

Walking Free from the Trauma of Coercive, Cultic and Spiritual Abuse

This is an interactive self-help workbook and psychological road map to enable survivors of coercive, cultic and spiritual abuse to find healing, recovery and growth.

This book provides a comprehensive guide to recovery, based on a tested model of post-cult counselling, and years of research and clinical experience. It is designed to help survivors of diverse abusive settings, including religious and spiritual, political, gangs, business, therapy and wellness and one-on-one relationships. The reader follows a beautifully illustrated journey through four Phases of recovery and growth, one Milestone at a time, to make sense of what has happened to them, learn how to walk free from psychological control and find resources for healing. The author includes stories from her own experience, detailing her path towards recovery and how she learned to come to terms with and overcome what happened to her.

Written in accessible language, this workbook serves as both a self-help book for survivors and former members, and a guide for therapists working with them.

Gillie Jenkinson, PhD, is an accredited psychotherapist, international speaker and a director of Hope Valley Counselling. For over 25 years she has specialised, as a therapist, researcher and trainer, in the challenges faced by those who have experienced coercive, cultic and spiritual abuse.

Walking Free from the Trauma of Coercive, Cultic and Spiritual Abuse

A Workbook for Recovery and Growth

Gillie Jenkinson
Illustrations by Camilla Charnock

Routledge
Taylor & Francis Group

LONDON AND NEW YORK

Designed cover image: Illustration by Camilla Charnock

First published 2023
by Routledge
4 Park Square, Milton Park, Abingdon, Oxon OX14 4RN

and by Routledge
605 Third Avenue, New York, NY 10158

Routledge is an imprint of the Taylor & Francis Group, an informa business

© 2023 Gillie Jenkinson

The right of Gillie Jenkinson to be identified as author of this work has been asserted in accordance with sections 77 and 78 of the Copyright, Designs and Patents Act 1988.

British Library Cataloguing-in-Publication Data
A catalogue record for this book is available from the British Library

Library of Congress Cataloging-in-Publication Data
Names: Jenkinson, Gillie, 1952- author. | Charnock, Camilla, illustrator.
Title: Walking free from the trauma of coercive, cultic and spiritual abuse :
a workbook for recovery and growth / Gillie Jenkinson ;
illustrations by Camilla Charnock.
Description: Abingdon, Oxon ; New York, NY :
Routledge, 2023. | Includes bibliographical references. |
Identifiers: LCCN 2022053952 (print) | LCCN 2022053953 (ebook) |
ISBN 9781032305882 (hardback) | ISBN 9781032305875 (paperback) |
ISBN 9781003305798 (ebook)
Subjects: LCSH: Psychological abuse victims—Rehabilitation. |
Ritual abuse victims—Rehabilitation. |
Ex-cultists—Rehabilitation. | Self-help techniques.
Classification: LCC RC569.5.P75 J46 2023 (print) | LCC RC569.5.P75 (ebook) |
DDC 616.85/82—dc23/eng/20230202
LC record available at https://lccn.loc.gov/2022053952
LC ebook record available at https://lccn.loc.gov/2022053953

ISBN: 9781032305882 (hbk)
ISBN: 9781032305875 (pbk)
ISBN: 9781003305798 (ebk)

DOI: 10.4324/9781003305798

Typeset in Sabon
by codeMantra

For all who have been through the trauma of coercive, cultic and spiritual abuse, and their families and therapists.

Does this book apply to me?

Walking Free is for those:

- who have suffered coercion and abuse in groups or relationships of all types: religious, spiritual, counselling, coaching, self-realisation, wellness, domestic and family relationships, business, pyramid schemes, political, gangs and more
- whose lives were dominated or taken over by a leader, a group or a relationship, cutting them off psychologically and maybe physically from mainstream society
- whose thinking and emotions have been suppressed and confused
- whose identity has been changed, controlled, formed or re-formed
- who struggle with life and relationships, perhaps with depression, anxiety, addiction or a sense of cultural and spiritual dislocation, and are starting to connect these struggles to their coercive and abusive experience
- who think they are weird because they grew up in or joined a coercive, cultic and/or spiritually abusive group or relationship
- who think they are less than others or that they are stupid because they got taken in, duped and betrayed
- who just wanted to make the world a better place but ended up coerced and exploited
- who barely recognise themselves anymore
- who want to make sense of what happened, understand and be understood
- who want to recover and grow from these experiences and are looking for a roadmap to navigate the terrain in order to heal
- who are therapists in need of a navigation tool to help survivors of coercive, cultic and spiritual abuse to heal

This book is for you!

Contents

Acknowledgements

I want to thank my family first and foremost. Tony, my husband and editor extraordinaire, for his love and all-round support over the years, it has been invaluable in more ways than I can begin to say – thank you! Hannah and Esther, my beautiful creative daughters, thank you for being you and always contributing wisdom and love to my life and this project – I am so proud of you.

Thank you to my many friends (you know who you are!) and Martin, Emma and Rod for cheering me on and affirming that Mum and Dad would be so proud. Sheila Mudadi-Billings, your insight, friendship, wisdom, sisterhood, challenge and honesty mean the world to me. My therapist, Janet Hawksworth, who faithfully sat with me, helping me emotionally heal with her kindness, compassion and understanding. Thank you to my supervisor, Louise Porteous, for your consistent ongoing support and encouragement – you were there at the beginning of the Post-Cult Counselling journey and your input has been invaluable. My ICSA friends, Lorna and Bill Goldberg, Michael Langone, Gina Catena and too many more to name, who have welcomed me into your circle and have contributed so much love and insight into my life. Thank you to Wellspring Retreat and Resource Centre for the opportunity to intern with you, I never forget all you have done for me. I also want to acknowledge those who have 'passed': Dr Paul Martin, Dr Betty Tylden and Lady Daphne Vane, all heroes in their time.

Thank you to Camilla Charnock for her beautiful illustrations, and Lydia Lapinski at thoughtsmakethings.com for the graphic design, it has been a dream working with you both. I want to thank all my clients who had the courage to enter into Post-Cult Counselling – I hope you learned as much from me as I learned from you – and those who participated in my research and generously gave of their time and their story. And finally, thanks to the therapists who attended the Certificate in Post-Cult Counselling and dared to try out my Recovery Workbook with their clients and found it helped!

Part One

Setting the scene

I live in a beautiful rural area of England, by a road that was used for hundreds of years by traders using packhorses to take their merchandise from one town or village to another. Here and there, it is still possible to see ancient milestones telling the traveller how many miles they have walked from the last town and how far they still have to go to the next. Often they must have thought the way was long and slow, but each milestone meant real progress and a sense that their destination was that bit closer.

I see the process of recovery and growth after a coercive, cultic or spiritually abusive experience as a journey. It takes time and effort and we need a roadmap as we navigate across bumpy terrain and around some roadblocks, but there is a way through and a destination worth seeking.

I have made this journey of recovery and growth myself and sat with many clients as they have made their own journey. I have discovered that, although we all come from different types of abusive and coercive groups or relationships, many aspects of our journeys follow a similar course, and we need to pass the same milestones, one step at a time.

Before we start, I will give you an overview of the book and the Walking Free journey by introducing you to the Roadmap and a summary of what is to come.

DOI: 10.4324/9781003305798-1

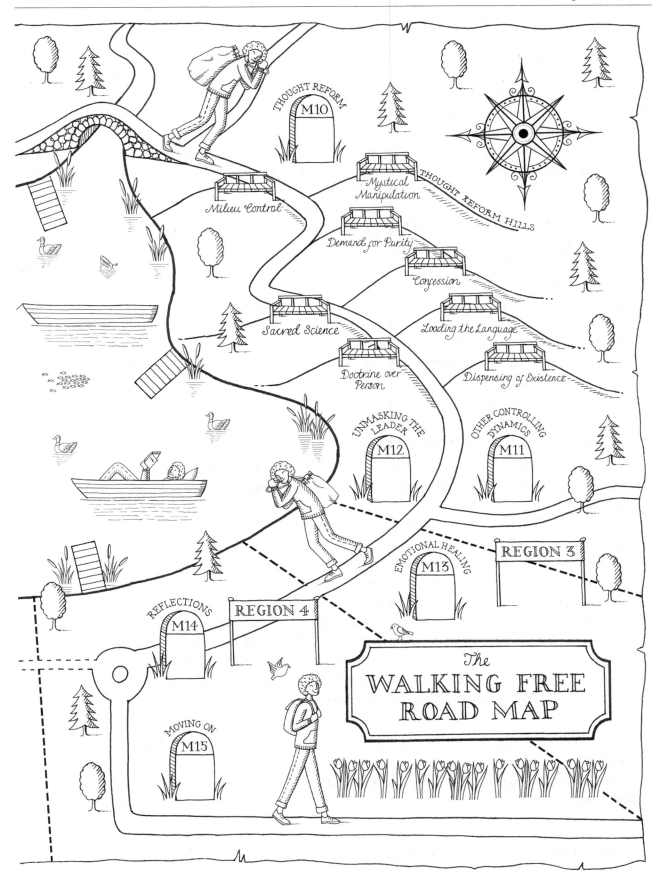

P1.1 Introducing the Roadmap

If you are in the process of leaving, or have left, a coercive, cultic and/or spiritually abusive group or relationship, you may be wondering how to move forward in your life. As a result of your membership, you may feel confused, distressed, lost and that you are carrying a lot of heavy baggage. You want to feel better and recover from your difficult experiences but don't know which way to go to process and empty out your baggage.

The Roadmap illustrates a journey that you can take, passing through four Regions and by 15 Milestones. Each Milestone is an opportunity to explore an aspect of your experience, unpack some of your baggage and move on, feeling a little lighter.

You will see there is a wooden hut with the sign saying 'self-care packs and maps here' – I will say more about self-care later, but it is really important to take care of yourself while on this journey. That is why the road stays close to the edge of Oasis Lake, which is there to give relief and a 'Safe Enough Space' to retreat to whenever you need to. You can take a break and rest by, or on, the lake at any point of the journey.

I will say more about navigating the Regions and Milestones in P1.6 below.

If you have experienced a coercive, cultic or abusive group or relationship, you know what it is like to have your choices restricted. Although I have set out the journey in a way that I believe is logical, and has helped former members, you can choose differently if you wish! On the Roadmap, you will notice that there are some side roads leading in other directions, so if you feel the need to leave the route at any time, you can!

P1.2 What else is in this Workbook?

In this Part One, we are 'Setting the Scene' for the rest of the book, and I introduce you to some important topics that will arise, and things you might like to equip yourself with, in order to complete the journey.

In Part Two, 'Who am I?', I introduce myself and tell a little of my life story, so you know who you are engaging with!

Part Three is 'Preparing for the Journey', where I encourage you to be ready to look after yourself on this journey by creating a 'Safe Enough Space' and by considering some grounding and journalling tips. There are also some areas to reflect on before setting off.

Part Four is 'The Walking Free Journey' that follows the Roadmap.

Part Five provides some guidance about 'Seeking Therapy', for those who would like to do so, and Part Six is 'Advice for Therapists' who want to support clients in their Walking Free journey.

I hope you benefit from and enjoy this Workbook and that it helps you Walk Free from your coercive, cultic and/or spiritually abusive experiences.

> In this Workbook, the Parts will usually be referred to as P1, P2, etc., and sections within the Parts as P1.1, P1.2, and so on.
>
> The Milestones within Part Four are referred to as M1, M2, etc., and sections within the Milestones are M1.1, M1.2, and so on.

P1.3 Why this Workbook on this subject?

Why a Workbook on this subject? Well, as an experienced therapist who specialises in counselling former members and survivors of coercive, cultic and spiritual abuse, and as a former cult member and survivor myself, I recognised there was a serious lack of specially designed recovery resources.

Recovery and growth involve a complex and often baffling journey, and former members (and their friends, family and therapists) can feel in the dark as to what to do next after leaving. This can be both thrilling and frightening.

It took me 15 years between leaving an abusive cult and really starting to understand the psychological effects. During that time, I suffered from depression and anxiety which I put down to other causes. I also found myself drawn to other high demand groups that turned out to be abusive because I didn't understand what had happened to me. It was a massive shock when I realised that I had been in a coercive cult and had been spiritually abused, and even more so to discover how significantly that experience had changed my identity, and the way my thinking and emotions worked.

Although this was a devastating moment, it was also the start of my own journey to recovery and growth. I left the church where I was partially repeating my cult experience, and began to research trauma, abuse, cults, coercive control, spiritual abuse, religious trauma and their consequences. As a result, I realised that I needed to *understand* the experience in order to be able to Walk Free of its effects.

It is now over 40 years since I physically left the coercive and spiritually abusive cult, and over 26 years since I began that process of leaving psychologically. I have trained and qualified as a counsellor and psychotherapist, working with clients of all types, but my heart has always been in helping those who have been subject to coercive, cultic and spiritual abuse. I have researched what helps former members recover at Master's and then Doctoral (PhD) levels, but my best teachers have been my former member clients who have let me accompany them on their recovery journeys.

Some may ask why something specific is needed for survivors of coercive, cultic and spiritual abuse. There are many self-help books on dealing with trauma and overcoming anxiety, depression and so on, and many therapists who can help with such things. But one thing that my personal experience, research and clinical practice have made clear is that there are some fundamental differences in the coercive, cultic and spiritually abusive experience which are not addressed in general self-help books. Also, foundational trainings for mental health professionals and therapists seldom, if ever, address these issues and so therapists generally lack the necessary knowledge. Traditional therapy, including trauma therapy, is, therefore, often not enough when working with former members (Jenkinson, 2016). (I address this further in P6 for the benefit of therapists using this book.)

As a result of this lack of specialised training, it is difficult for the thousands of former cult members; for those who have experienced coercive control in groups or in one-on-one relationships; and for survivors of spiritual and religious abuse, to access knowledgeable therapeutic support and the information needed to aid recovery and growth.

> To avoid repeating 'coercive, cultic and spiritually abusive groups or relationships', I will usually just refer to **'cultic settings'** from now on, and those who have been there as **'former members'**. If you define your situation differently, I hope you will still consider how the material fits with your experiences.
>
> Similarly, when I refer to **leaders or leadership,** this may include single or multiple leaders and abusive partners in relationships.

Former members may have spent many years being unduly influenced (maybe a whole lifetime) and those who have left have 'baggage' – issues from their past – which may affect their current life, causing untold pain and grief.

Many try to forget their abusive experiences and get on with their life – they just want to throw the baggage in the rubbish bin. This rarely works: it usually comes back to 'bite them' later! Although ignoring the baggage may seem like a good strategy at the time, it is important, in order to move forward, to reflect on their experiences and sort through and address them, however challenging that may seem to be – when the time is right for them, of course! To ignore such a significant part of their life is to ignore and dissociate from their experiences – and authentic identity.

This Workbook is here to help sort through the baggage that is weighing or dragging them down, to 'chew it over', and decide what to keep, such as friendships or things learned along the way (more on this at M14), and what to get rid of.

An advantage of this Workbook is that former members can go at their own pace, and use it on their own as a self-help guide; or they can go through it with a safe friend or therapist. It can also be used by couples or in recovery support groups for former members.

> Throughout this book, there are various references to and quotes from other writers, denoted by names and dates in brackets. The full references are listed in a separate section at the end of the book. These are a way of seeing who said what but are also a clue as to what else you might like to follow up to read in addition to this book.
>
> You will also see quotes with just a first name and no other reference. These are from former members whom I interviewed as part of my Doctoral research, and who generously gave their time and the benefit of their own experiences. Their names have been changed.

In this Workbook, I offer various ideas, theories and perspectives and it is important that you chew over and apply what is relevant to your experiences. I have no agenda in relation to faith and spirituality. I want to help those who want to have a spirituality or faith, to chew over and keep what fits for them and discard what does not. I also want to support those who have decided they want to move on from faith and spirituality.

I will now say a bit more about the evolution of this Walking Free Workbook.

P1.4 Based on 'Post-Cult Counselling'

This Workbook is an expanded version of the 'Recovery Workbook' I use with former member clients, and an integral part of the model of counselling I have developed, 'Post-Cult Counselling'. This evolved slowly but surely out of my personal experience of being in a coercive, cultic and spiritually abusive group; leaving, recovering and growing; over 25 years of training and practising as a therapist; receiving personal therapy; two internships at the Wellspring Retreat and Resource Centre in Ohio, USA (now sadly closed); learning from others' research; regularly attending International Cultic Studies Association conferences; my Master's and Doctoral research; and my experience of counselling hundreds of former members.

A major aspect of Post-Cult Counselling is *psychoeducation*. This is information about a particular subject to help you better *understand* that subject. In this case, psychoeducation is delivered through this Workbook. It is designed to help you make connections between your personal experience of coercive, cultic and/or spiritual abuse, and psychological theories which help to explain how that abuse took place, to address its after-effects, and to heal. As a result, you develop your own psychological skills and put building blocks in place for your recovery and growth.

In Post-Cult Counselling with former members, I usually talk them through the Worksheets, but here I have included in the text much of what I say in the sessions.

This Workbook is also designed to help you highlight and understand how your identity was changed (re-formed) if you joined as an adult, and how your identity was formed if you were born and/or raised there.

One effect of being in a coercive, cultic and spiritually abusive setting is the adaptation to the coercive environment and the resulting formation of what has been referred to, by myself and others, as the 'pseudo-identity' (Jenkinson, 2008; West and Martin, 1994). This identity goes deep but is in part made up of all the things you 'must', 'should' or 'ought' to be – you must be obedient, perfect and nice, you should smile and pretend you are happy even if you are not, learn to empty yourself of yourself, do what the leader tells you, follow the rules and swallow your feelings – that sort of thing!

While a member, many do not realise they are being coercively influenced, and some are happy with their cultic identity, content to comply as they believe all they are told is true. The problems often emerge on leaving, or considering leaving, as the individual begins to view their experience from a different perspective.

At the heart of the recovery process, therefore, is highlighting this 'pseudo-identity', formed as a result of the membership constraints and in order to be a member – and, crucially and equally importantly, developing and getting in touch with your authentic identity or your 'real me'.

If you were born, or raised from an early age, in a cultic setting, you may feel that it is impossible to separate what is really you, your authentic identity, and what is your cultic pseudo-identity. This is understandable since your early years, when you formed much of your understanding of yourself and society, were spent in that setting. However, I have worked with many clients who were born and/or raised, and as we have explored this together they have recognised elements of themselves that feel authentic, a true part of who they are, and other elements that feel imposed, like intruders. Disentangling these elements has helped them to Walk Free from their cultic experience.

I often think of the process of understanding our authentic identity as like a jigsaw puzzle in the wrong box. The picture on the box is, say, a black-and-white-city scene with high-rise buildings (the pseudo-identity), but when you put the pieces together you realise the actual picture is quite different, perhaps a country cottage with a garden full of flowers (the real you)!

A main aim of this Workbook, therefore, is to give you an opportunity to highlight and 'chew over' your pseudo-identity. I imagine the pseudo-identity being layered over your authentic autonomous identity (your 'real me'), like asphalt or tarmac over a seed deeply buried within, but waiting to break through, grow and blossom in the right conditions. Autonomous means being free and independent, with the freedom to make your own decisions and act in your best interests.

The Workbook provides a way of removing these layers, one Milestone at a time, to help you discover the real you buried underneath. This is a hopeful concept, filled with the promise of being fully yourself, who you authentically are, not bogged down by identification with the coercive, cultic and/or spiritually abusive setting and who you had to be there. We will return to this, and you can reflect in more depth on your identity at M6.

When you have *understood* the abusive dynamics (and *understood* what is not you and not your fault) and started to discover your authentic autonomous identity, then you are well on the way to recovery and growth and to Walking Free from your coercive, cultic and spiritually abusive experiences!

Let's look at what you need, to equip yourself for this journey.

PI.5 Equipping yourself

Every journey requires some sort of preparation. If we are walking, we need a bag or rucksack to carry everything in, including a map, but we also need the right hiking boots, socks, sunscreen, snacks, a compass, etc. We need to pace ourselves and take care of ourselves. This is the case for this journey but what we need here is a little different (although you will definitely need lots of snacks along the way!). There are some things I suggest you consider before you set out.

First, I suggest you get a **notebook or journal** to use in addition to the Worksheets. This is so you can make your own notes and track your journey to recovery and growth.

There are many journals on the market: pretty, plain, large and small. It is important to choose the right one to suit you – and making this choice can be a helpful step in thinking about what you like and what your preferences are, as this helps you to know yourself better.

Or you may prefer to find another way of keeping notes or reflections, for example, a loose-leaf folder, computer, special software or an app.

Whichever method you choose, I will refer to it as writing in your 'journal' from now on, but please use the one that suits you best.

I also suggest you date all the entries, as it can be annoying to look at notes later and not know when they were written!

In P3, I introduce you to Tips for Journalling.

Second, you might like to have some **creative materials** to hand. For some, creativity, including drawing or painting, can be more helpful than trying to express ourselves in words. It can help us grow and develop as we connect to our authentic ideas and identity in a different way.

If you are one of those people, you could consider buying art paper, felt tip pens, wax crayons, coloured pencils or paints. You could use stickers, glitter or card, or cut out pictures from magazines that express what you are thinking and feeling. Or you may prefer to create using a digital device, specially designed software or app.

I love the idea of experimenting because it is creative and opens our minds to new ideas as we find out what suits us best. This is important because we build our authentic identity as we make decisions about what we like and what we don't like, as we make choices for ourselves which help us to know ourselves better.

Whatever suits you!

Third, you might like to **colour in** the drawn roadmap and illustrations which are scattered throughout the book. Many find colouring grounding and soothing.

If you decide to colour in the map, you might:

- colour one milestone at a time
- reflect your mood while doing it
- do it to track your progress
- simply do it for fun, or to make your book more colourful

Colouring is playful and has been shown to be helpful to many – including adults! Being playful is important, especially if you never had much opportunity to play as a child (in which case you will be learning a new skill by doing this!). It can help relieve stress, lets you nurture your inner artist, lets you create a world of your own and can even help with silencing a negative critical voice because you are concentrating on something else (Achwal, 2019). It may not do any of these for you, but you could experiment with colouring and see if it helps – it is certainly worth a try! (There are lots of colouring books with intricate designs on the market if you find it helpful and want to do more!)

We will now look at how to navigate the Workbook before considering some challenges that might arise.

P1.6 Navigating the Workbook

In this Workbook, we are embarking on a journey, Walking Free from the trauma of coercive, cultic and spiritual abuse one step at a time.

Walking is therapeutic, it slows us down, is good for us physically, gives us space to think and reflect; it takes us to new places, and we begin to see things differently and from new perspectives. If we walk around a hill, for example, we begin to know it in different ways. If we approach it from the North, we will view it differently from approaching it from the South. It is the same geographical phenomenon but we know the whole of it more clearly after seeing it from different angles. We will be exploring the coercive, cultic and spiritually abusive experience from different angles. As you get to know it and raise awareness of it, my hope is that you will begin to unpack the baggage and Walk Free of it.

When walking in a new place, a map provides a visual representation of the roads and landscape, making it easier for the traveller to navigate their way to their desired destination. In government or business, a 'roadmap' defines a route to the desired outcome, and provides a clear plan, with important steps along the way.

This Workbook is a *psychological roadmap* leading towards a destination which I have called 'recovery and growth'. You have an opportunity to reflect on how you would describe your own personal chosen destination in P1.17 below.

I have introduced you to the need for a Roadmap to guide you, one Milestone at a time, as you unpack your 'baggage', but this journey also goes through different **Regions**. The Regions are based on a finding from my Doctoral research – that the recovery journey usually goes through four Phases of recovery and growth. For some people, the Phases may overlap, but most found that they worked through them in the same order.

I imagine each Phase as a Region on the drawn Roadmap and they provide a structure and guide for the recovery journey, as follows:

Region 1 – leave physically so you can begin to recover psychologically

To really recover and grow, we need to physically leave the confines of the coercive, cultic and/or spiritually abusive setting. Often, this is the Phase where we begin to 'wake up' to the control and abuse. We need to step out into the fresh air, light and space outside. It is usually difficult to leave psychologically before we have left physically.

Region 2 – wake up and leave psychologically by understanding what happened to you

Here, we continue to leave psychologically. We do this by understanding the dynamics of the coercive, cultic and/or spiritually abusive setting, and what happened to us there. This helps us unlayer our pseudo-identity and begin to get in touch with our authentic identity (our 'real me'). This Region takes up the largest part of the Roadmap.

Region 3 – heal emotionally

This is where we access our authentic feelings (our feelings that belong to our authentic identity and not the pseudo-identity) and talk about emotional healing for the effects of the painful abuse and post-traumatic stress we may be suffering. We also address pre-membership vulnerabilities, and how and why we joined (for those who did). In this Region, it can be especially helpful to access therapy to process our feelings and emotional pain alongside the Workbook.

Region 4 – recognise what you have learned and move on

Here, we identify and recognise when we are recovered – or recovered enough to move on in our life. We might also realise we have grown through, and in spite of, the experience of being in that setting and leaving it. This is sometimes referred to as post-traumatic growth.

Within each Region, there are one or more **Milestones**. At each Milestone, we will sit and reflect on specific psychoeducational areas, with Worksheets designed to help you relate the theory to your own personal experience. This will help you to pull out certain baggage and have a good look at it. As you begin to *understand* what you are dealing with and why you still carry it, you increase your choices. You can put down some of the baggage, let go of it, heal from it, stop blaming yourself, leave behind what you do not want or need and keep what you do.

The Worksheets are *tools* to help raise awareness, highlight blind spots and point you along a road that facilitates healing, recovery and growth – and even thriving! This means focussing on your experiences, 'chewing them over' and understanding more clearly what happened to you, so you can stop blaming yourself for things which are not your fault, and heal from your experiences more fully.

You can complete and make notes on the Worksheets, or you may prefer to photocopy some and write on the copy. Some suggest writing about your experiences, which you may prefer to do in your journal.

Please complete the Milestones and Worksheets in the way that is most helpful for you – and do it as creatively as you can. Experiment and see what works best for you. This helps you develop an internal dialogue and discussion within yourself, which assists critical thinking and raises awareness of your experience.

You may like to:

- read the explanations at the Milestones silently to yourself
- read the explanations out loud to yourself
- read and record the text on your phone or other device and play it back to yourself
- ask someone else to read and record the descriptive text for you, and then listen to it
- go through the Milestones with a trusted friend or therapist (I find that reading the Workbook aloud with clients helps – we often alternate who reads)
- draw answers using creative materials, paints, coloured pencils, software or app
- come up with your own creative and experimental ways of approaching the Worksheets!

The first time you go through the Workbook I encourage you to follow the Roadmap as it is set out, and go one Milestone at a time, because there is a logical progression that has helped others and may help you – and you will find the later Milestones refer to earlier ones. Once you have a clear overview of the whole journey, I encourage you to revisit the Milestones and Worksheets whenever and as often as you need to.

P1.7 Telling your story into the Workbook

I encourage you to tell your story *into* the structure of the Milestones and Worksheets. Reading the text and doing the exercises will raise your awareness of your unique story and experience – and at the same time, you will gain more understanding about what coercive, cultic and spiritual abuse is and how it affected you.

Finding concepts, images and words that describe your experience is an important part of:

- increasing your understanding
- making sense of what happened to you
- challenging blind spots
- unpacking your baggage
- 'chewing over' and unlayering your 'pseudo-identity'
- understanding and managing your trauma-related symptoms and
- telling your story by creating a clear and coherent narrative

Understanding will help you to externalise and describe your story, and I hope you will find that this will help validate those experiences. It will also help you to untangle your experiences like untangling a mass of different coloured wool – each area will become clearer as you go through the Walking Free Workbook!

We will now look at some of the challenges and triggers that may arise from the Workbook and Worksheets.

P1.8 Challenges and triggers

One general challenge of writing a book like this is that it is virtually inevitable that some suggestion, or language used, may be a trigger and reminder of difficult memories and associations from the past. A 'trigger' is a reminder in the present of a difficult memory which you have not purposefully tried to recall.

For example, the idea of journalling can be 'triggering' for some, as can reading information sheets. The suggestions might remind you of practices from the abusive setting, such as reading holy texts like the Bible, or a group's literature. It may also remind you of negative experiences at school. You may have been taught to be wary of any new 'teachings' or ways of looking at things. You may have been told that seeking help was wrong.

What I am suggesting you do, as you work through this book, is different from reading texts when you were in your coercive, cultic and/or spiritually abusive setting, where you were probably learning by rote or taking in and introjecting the beliefs without chewing over the ideas. I understand that triggers and reminders can be difficult to stand up against, but I encourage you to work through them, use your critical thinking and tell your story as it was for *YOU*. (More about 'introjects' and 'critical thinking' at M5.)

If any suggestion I make is particularly challenging or triggering, then see if you can use some of the other ideas, or come up with creative ways of going through the Milestones until you get used to them.

If you are strongly affected by *purposeful remembering* or by triggers, you could check out the Safe Enough Space exercise, and tips for grounding and journalling in P3. Also, I explore the effects of traumatic stress on your body, feelings and mind at M7. These can help you to regulate yourself and cope more easily with the effects.

An idea: If it is hard to apply your own story at any stage, you could start by finding another former member's story and apply that. This will familiarise you with the psychoeducational theories, but objectively and at a distance. There are many published former member stories which can be sourced online or in books.

P1.9 If the Milestones don't seem to fit

If a Milestone or Worksheet doesn't initially seem to fit or seem relevant, I encourage you to still work through it because I have found all are (usually) applicable in some way. It is always interesting to me if someone says that something is not relevant, and I have found that exploring it anyway can still enhance understanding. Not recognising the relevance of an issue may be an indication of a blind spot, and so rather than moving on from it, you may find spending more time on it productive.

For example, one former member client told me that there was nothing special about the language they used in their group (see 'loaded language' at M10.6), but when they started talking, I found I didn't understand a good deal of the words they were using. When I pointed this out to them, they suddenly burst out laughing and realised that it had been a huge blind spot! We spent a good deal of time after that looking at the clichéd language used in their group.

P1.10 All coercive, cultic and spiritually abusive settings

This Workbook is intended for those who have been in all sorts of 'coercive', 'cultic' and 'spiritually abusive' groups and relationships. This includes families, for example, those with narcissistic parents; high demand coercive and cultic groups; spiritually abusive groups and relationships; and one-on-one relationships including narcissistic psychopathic control from a partner. It also includes some businesses like multi-level marketing and pyramid schemes; 'therapeutic' groups and relationships, including abusive 'encounter groups'; and some boarding schools and teen programmes.

There are lots of different terms that attempt to describe, define and name abusive groups and relationships and their effects. Some of them are coercive control, cult, sect, new religious movement, high demand group, authoritarian group, spiritual abuse, religious abuse, religious trauma, radicalisation and fundamentalism.

Different terms have different meanings to different people, and meanings also vary in different countries. Some have clear definitions and are used in specific ways. In this Workbook, I am not going to try and define all the terms, or discuss how they are different. Most of the material in this book applies to all sorts of coercive, cultic and spiritually abusive groups and relationships, and learning gleaned from one can inform and possibly be applied to others.

One thing that surprised me when I started working in this area, and still fascinates me, is that former members who have been in very different types of groups or relationships turn out to have similar experiences and outcomes. I sometimes run therapeutic recovery courses, bringing together individuals who have been in a range of situations with different purposes, beliefs and practices. As they talk, they discover that the underlying dynamics and the way that their lives were controlled were similar – and that the Recovery Workbook is applicable to them all. Although cultic settings based on various forms of religion, politics, therapy or one-to-one control may seem very different from the outside, the ways in which they create and maintain control, and affect people, tend to be much the same. This means that most former members and survivors of cultic settings can follow the same, or a very similar, route to recovery.

You will be able to 'chew over' and clarify the definitions of a cult, spiritual or religious abuse and coercive control, and to reflect on whether one or all applies to you, at M3 – and this might help you to settle your mind as to whether it was a 'cult' or 'spiritual abuse' or not, as the words we use can be important too.

As you go through the book, you may wonder why I do not name particular groups or abusive individuals. This is in part because some are highly litigious – they like to sue critics! It is also because some groups are more abusive in certain locations than in others, so it is not always possible to generalise. If you want to know if a particular group or leader has been called cultic then it may be possible to check them out online. I tend to search for the name of the group or leader and put the word 'cult' at the end, and I usually find my way to information. I then approach that information with a critical mind, because not all online sources are reliable and accurate!

What matters as you consider how to label your group or relationship is *your* experience and what happened to *you*. It is important that you think about and chew over how the psychoeducational information applies to *your* personal experience of *your* group or relationship, whatever anyone else says or thinks.

P1.11 All generations

There are different 'generations' of former members, and I have written Walking Free for those who were born and/or raised in a cultic environment *and* those who joined as an adult. There are some important differences, so I will say if some aspect is more applicable to one or the other. You can reflect on this further in P3.2.

P1.12 Others' stories to help you recognise yours

In this Workbook, I give examples from my own life story, composite, anonymised examples from client work (with permission) and other former members' stories. I also use quotes from interviews that I undertook for my Doctoral research, using a first name, which has been changed for this purpose, for each participant. I include all these so that you can begin to recognise your own story at each Milestone.

It is a challenge to illustrate all the different cultures, beliefs, language, rituals, leaders and so on, because each individual's experience is different, even if they were in the same group. But I hope the examples and quotes will help you to make connections to your own story and challenge any blind spots.

P1.13 Take your time and pace yourself

It is important on any long walk to take your time and pace yourself, and the same is true as you Walk Free.

I suggest you don't attempt to rush through the Milestones or do a lot in one sitting! If a particular Worksheet is too upsetting, then give yourself a break and perhaps return to it later, or visit another one – they all interact with each other.

Please eat well, exercise, have fun, enjoy nature, see friends, take regular breaks, have holidays, read novels, watch fun TV, listen to music, watch a good movie or whatever YOU love to do. It is an important part of the recovery process to identify things you love to do that are good for you – and it is not selfish or a waste of time – it is essential!

P3 gives further opportunity to concentrate on looking after yourself in more depth including setting up a 'Safe Enough Space', journalling tips and grounding tips.

> I have learned over the years to let the Workbook do its job, to let each Milestone and psychoeducational area do its work. Each one builds on the last, and ultimately helps us build a picture, one jigsaw piece at a time. Once you reach the end, I hope you will see what I mean!
>
> And so, please be patient with yourself – and keep going – because this process is like travelling a road when it is shrouded in early morning fog. To start with, we cannot see anything much, other than the road just in front of us. The landscape is obscured, and the trees and houses are dark shapes, as are the people. As we go along, walking past the different Milestones and areas of the Workbook, the fog starts to clear, and we begin to recognise which voices belong to which people, where the trees and houses are located and we make more sense of what happened to us. Eventually, one step at a time, the fog lifts and we can see all around us. We have a clear perspective on the coercive, cultic and spiritually abusive experience behind us, and the way forward to healing, recovery and growth in front.

P1.14 A word about emotions

Although the main focus of this Workbook is on psychoeducation and understanding, you will experience emotions or feelings as you go through this process – and that is normal. But, before focussing on that aspect of your recovery, and purposefully getting in touch with your emotions, I think it is essential for you to *first focus on cognitively understanding and making sense* of what happened in the coercive, cultic and spiritually abusive setting.

This is important because feelings can come from different places within us. Some of what you feel may come from the pseudo-identity, the person you had to be in the cultic setting. If you are not aware of what belongs to the abusive experience, you may try to heal feelings that come from your pseudo-identity and the cultic experience, rather than from your authentic autonomous identity, the real you. You will be trying to heal feelings that are not genuinely and authentically yours (more about this at M5 and M6).

You may, like many former members, also struggle to understand the difference between your thoughts and feelings. You are likely to have suppressed your feelings throughout your time as a member, or worked hard to try and suppress them. It may be difficult for you to regulate your feelings when they come up – you may be out of practice or you may have never learned in the first place.

In most cases, feelings are not dangerous in themselves, but the cultic environment may have made them appear so, or made you believe they are. For example, if you were told that anger is wrong, then facing your angry feelings may be very challenging. We will look specifically at assertive anger at M8.

It is still important to explore your emotions (when you are ready), and there is an opportunity for you to do this at M13, after you have understood the dynamics of the group or relationship. Meanwhile, if strong feelings come up (and they likely will), remember there are resources in P3.

I am not suggesting you suppress feelings as you go through the Workbook, but we won't *focus* on them until near the end of the journey.

P1.15 What if you need support?

If you are doing this work by yourself and it gets too hard, or if you feel concerned about your feelings, or they become overwhelming, you could speak to your doctor or mental health professional, or find a therapist. An ethical trained professional therapist can be particularly helpful because emotional healing and processing feelings usually require a relationship in which to heal. You could have a look at P5.

If you don't want to go through the Workbook alone, you could find another former member who is prepared to go through it with you, in a safe, supportive and non-judgemental manner.

Let's now look at what recovery looks like, as I have suggested that is our destination.

P1.16 What does recovery look like?

I imagine you are interested in this Workbook because you want to 'get over' your experience and 'recover'. But what does recovery look like? Is it that you never feel awful again, or never remember the bad experiences, or never cry about it again?

I don't see it in these all-or-nothing terms. This is what some former members have said:

> For me it's overcoming something that is damaging, that has damaged me. I am overcoming that handicap, that impairment, you know, the damage that the cult has done to me. [Matt]

> [Recovery is] moving towards healing from traumatic and difficult experiences. [Cheryl]

> Recovery means no longer believing they are right. [Joe]

> I think [the word] recovery is helpful because people are very down on themselves when they've been wrong, SO wrong, and to think of yourself as a wounded person who is in recovery is, it's a very gentle analogy. You come out wounded but you can be healed and this is what recovery is. You could call it a process of healing. [Marjorie]

Recovery is not without emotion or memory. I have found this in my personal experience and clinical counselling with former members, that painful feelings related to memories of difficult and challenging incidents do emerge, but this does not necessarily mean we are not recovering or recovered.

Recovery means we are able to face memories and painful feelings and be curious about them. But also we can *withdraw* from them, without getting stuck in them. We don't go down a 'rabbit hole' or get stuck in 'fight and flight' or 'freeze' modes – as often!

There have been times when I think I have processed something and then it seems to come back, sometimes with more baggage because difficult memories are triggered, or there is still more to process. This can seem overwhelming and disheartening, but I have learned to welcome this with *curiosity* (most of the time!) rather than fight it. I think of it as new information about myself and so embrace it as part of my life story. This is not always easy, but I hope you will be able to do the same.

Reminder: It is okay that we need to process things – few things are ever perfectly sorted, and we cannot get rid of our memories or of what has happened to us – nor should we!

I think recovery means we have completed the journey and Walked Free because:

- We have looked at and unpacked the baggage, 'chewed it over' and got rid of it (or some of it), one Milestone at a time.
- We have raised awareness of the experience.
- We have done the psychoeducation, so we understand the experience for what it was.
- We are able to remember and feel the pain of the experience (rather than suppressing it).
- We are able to cry about it with *compassion* for ourselves.
- We are able to withdraw from it (eventually).
- We start to see it (a bit more) objectively.
- We are not stuck in our memories, symptoms, thoughts and feelings, although we are aware of them.
- We are not constantly plagued by and pushing away memories.
- We can engage with those memories, be curious about them, grasp them, process them and move on from them.
- We are realistic, and aware that this is a process that is likely to take quite some time, and maybe we will always be working on it in some way.
- We are beginning to integrate (bring together) the scattered polarised parts of ourselves (as Gloria says, we realise: '*I can be a whole person!! I AM A WHOLE PERSON!*').
- We can tell the difference between feelings and thoughts.
- We are aware of and have chewed over the pseudo-identity and are left with our authentic identity (our 'real me') – or we are working on it!
- We realise that we have developed a new life and purpose, and have grown from and out of those experiences, rather than being defined by them for the rest of our lives!

Gaining understanding and (to some degree) facing the feelings make up the journey to recovery, that we will go on together as you Walk Free by following the Roadmap.

When you have completed this Walking Free Workbook journey, I hope you will find you have more hope and have built your resilience, which is the capacity to manage, confront and recover from stressful and traumatic events – and the ability to bounce back.

Let's look next at *your* chosen destination.

P1.17 Your chosen destination

I have suggested that the endpoint of this journey is 'recovery and growth'. Having moved through the pain and found a place of understanding, many move on from the coercive, cultic and spiritually abusive experience and live a satisfying, independent, autonomous and connected life (connected to others and their authentic identity), in spite of their experience.

You may prefer to think about your destination in different terms or have more personal objectives in mind. In Worksheet P1.2, you have an opportunity to describe, as specifically as possible, what you would like your focus and aim to be in going on this Walking Free journey – what you want your destination to look like.

Your focus and aim may change and evolve as you journey on. You can return to and update this at different stages along the way, and when you have nearly finished the journey, at M14, you have an opportunity to check back and see if you have achieved your aims.

Before considering this, it may help to notice what baggage you are carrying. Worksheet P1.1 provides an opportunity to identify this by labelling the shapes on the bag. There is also space around it if you want to write more. For example, you may want to resolve fear or rage or depression, and you can write those in the shapes; or you may label specific incidents which you want to understand, address and resolve more fully.

Worksheet P1.1: Describe what you carry in your baggage

Date _____

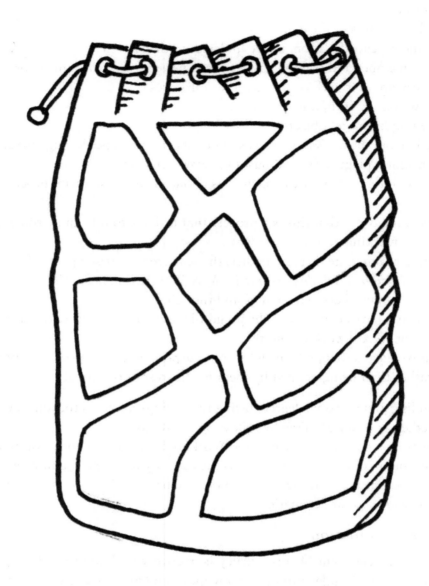

Now that you have thought a bit about your baggage, can you put into words what it is:

- you want to Walk Free of
- you want to achieve on this Walking Free journey
- you want your destination or aim to be

In Worksheet P1.2, you have an opportunity to reflect on this. Examples might be that you want to feel better about yourself; you want to understand what happened to you; or you want to feel you are allowed to express your 'anger' (or other feelings) more. You might like to add your own aims or destination to Worksheet P1.2 or in your journal.

Worksheet P1.2: Can you describe your chosen destination?

Date _____

Your aims or destination you would like to reach by the end of the Workbook journey – you can return to this and revise it as often as you want to.

I will now say more about myself in Part Two before we prepare for the journey in Part Three.

Part Two

Who am I?

Before you start on this Walking Free journey, you may like to know a bit more about me. Nowadays, I am an experienced counsellor, psychotherapist, researcher, writer and trainer, but before all of that, I am a former member and a survivor of coercive, cultic and spiritual abuse.

As you go through the Workbook, I will sometimes use my story to illustrate aspects of the recovery process and psychoeducational theory, in the hope that you perhaps recognise aspects of your story in mine. Former members often say it helps to hear other former members' stories and to know that others have been through, and got through, similar experiences.

I would, however, recommend not thinking too much about whether one person's experience was 'worse' than another's, or your own. In telling my story, I hope you might recognise something of your own experience in my feelings and reactions, and in the thought reform environment that I was in. But often former members say to me "my story is not as bad as other people's", and my response to this is, "If I break my arm in one place and you break your leg in 10 different places, our different experiences have no impact on each other – I cannot feel your pain and you cannot feel mine – your pain is your pain, and my pain is my pain and both need acknowledging as such". Please remember this as you read my life story.

DOI: 10.4324/9781003305798-2

I will share my story under the following headings: joining; life in; leaving in stages including my recovery journey; and life now. I have changed most of the names of the persons mentioned. Just a warning that there are some details which you may find distressing.

P2.1 Joining

If I had not joined what became a cultic group, I would not have embarked on this journey, and so, in some respects, it started when I became a 'born again' Christian in 1971, and two years later joined what evolved into a spiritually abusive cult. I changed from a fun-loving young woman to an intense, self-righteous fundamentalist!

I had long thick auburn hair and wore long hippy dresses when I first encountered evangelical Christianity in 1970 aged 18. I had not been seeking certainty, or anything! I had few ambitions other than to marry a British Lord! I was in contact with many titled people through a family friend and a distant relation, and this was my main aspiration. I had left a British boarding school the year before and was attending The Queen's Secretarial College – a staple for 'posh' girls who had not been instilled with academic ambition!

The Christian message that Jesus loved me and would give me eternal security was seductive and moved me deeply. I was born in Uganda, East Africa, in 1952, and (unusually at that time) my parents divorced when I was six. The many life changes, including the sense of abandonment, living with other families, and attending boarding school, left me insecure and vulnerable to the loving message.

Liza, who recruited me into evangelicalism, had to work hard initially to keep my interest, I was more interested in smoking and partying. But when I finally gave in and became 'born again', I grasped certainty, self-righteousness, Christian fundamentalism and rigidity wholeheartedly – I became radicalised – and did not let go for another 25 years. Even at this early stage following my conversion, and before I joined the cult, my family observed an obvious change in me as I gradually left behind the fun-loving, boy-seeking, glamorous young woman that I was, and became what they described as very 'earnest', serious and intense, overly focussed on God and church. I didn't even wear make-up anymore! I had started to develop a pseudo-identity, which I will say more about later.

As my involvement increased, it became apparent there was more to the message than I first realised. I was told that whilst God did love me, he also wanted to 'break' me, and I learned that I should 'deny myself' and 'lay down my life' for others, surrender all. It also became apparent that the church was more important than my family, who needed to be 'saved' as they were 'going to hell'; the implication being that they had nothing of great value to offer me, nor did any outsiders.

As a child born in the 1950s, I had learned compliance and respect for authority figures, intensified by five years at boarding school. Whilst the first churches I belonged to were not cults (by the definition I will use in M3), I was, even at this early stage, too deeply involved to feel I could challenge the elders and pastors, their teachings, the expectation of obedience to their authority as God's representatives and the resulting fear. This laid the foundations and ensured I had a rationale for later abuse.

My conversion, therefore, resulted in my becoming narrowly focussed on church and put me on a path that led to my joining what I will refer to as the 'Fellowship' in 1973. I learned of the Fellowship because the founder, whom I will call Brian, offered counselling, which was unusual in the evangelical church in the 1970s. I had hit a crisis and was unsure if I was depressed, infested with demons (something I had been told), or if my conversion wasn't genuine. I was living elsewhere but a friend told me about Brian. Together with an occasional member, Simon, he counselled me. I was appalled to learn years later that they only had half a day's counsellor training!

They told me I wasn't, after all, genuinely 'born again', apparently answering my previous dilemma. This style of Christian counselling assumed that I should rely on them to tell me what was right and true for me. This crisis, and being geographically distant from my family, increased my vulnerability to their suggestion that God wanted me to join them. I was flattered, it felt like they were doing me a favour as I had no permanent home, and in 1973, I moved into the first of what eventually became seven community houses, and which became my 'home' for the next seven years.

Within a year the Fellowship evolved from an outward-facing and creative charismatic evangelical fellowship, with a desire to model New Testament radical Christianity, into a coercive and abusive live-in community cult. I will refer to this as 'the Community'.

P2.2 Life in

I was clearly different to everyone else as I did not speak with the broad local accent, being from the south of England. Perhaps they felt my international upbringing brought some kudos – also implying that they had a wide reach. In the early days, we enjoyed a shared 'vision', were creative and had camping trips and fun times. Most members (although not the leaders!) went out to work, and most of the time, I was working in the area as a secretary. All our earnings went into a 'common purse', which we were taught was a Biblical practice, reflecting the life of the early Christians. God would look after me as I did His work. I also worked as an unpaid 'housemother' for two years.

Despite some counselling being offered, emotional problems were not recognised nor really understood, and displays of emotion or upset were treated either as 'sin' or lack of commitment, which were to be 'repented' of, or demonic influence which was to be exorcised. This was devastating for me as I increasingly suppressed my childhood issues, depression and grief (which had not been resolved by joining), fearing my feelings and the consequences of expressing them, but often not being able to contain them.

There was no structured leadership initially, although it was assumed that Brian, and perhaps half a dozen others who were older and apparently more mature and capable, were the leaders. (I was never a leader!) The focus under Brian had been to recruit new members and was outward-facing. In 1974, Simon appeared to have special insight into a difficult situation that arose, and as Brian was exhausted from the years building the Community, Simon began a slow but sure process of taking over. The focus became more inward-looking. The Community became more structured under his leadership as we modelled ourselves on other communities in the UK and the USA, where members lived together and shared everything. This resulted in two years of intense personal 'counselling' and reshaping of the Community's lifestyle, in order that it would look good to outsiders. We often worked late into the night, including decorating the community houses after our regular jobs.

Image was of paramount importance to Simon and was seen as evidence of our success and blessing from God. Our changed image increased our attractiveness to outsiders and resulted in a good reputation with some churches and potential members. We changed from dowdy evangelicals and, unbeknown to the churches, were taught that James Bond was an example of an ideal Christian man, as Simon tried to model our life, in some respects, on him! This included drinking Martinis (shaken not stirred of course!), and it became acceptable for any man and woman to have a casual date together and sexual contact (but not full intercourse as that would be a sin!).

Both Simon and Brian lived off the earnings of the other members, believing their status entitled them to special treatment. I accepted this without question, as I was convinced it was God's will that divinely appointed leaders should be afforded special treatment. I believed that Brian and Simon were called specially by God to lead the Community. Whilst I did not view them as Gods, I believed they were God's representatives. I became terrified of them because of the power they wielded within the Community, and their punitive practices, particularly in the later years. They were successful for a long period of time in maintaining physical and psychological control over us, through threats, bullying, gaslighting, manipulation and fear.

In 1976, Brian decided that we needed to increase our level of commitment and he wrote a 'New Covenant', which we read together every morning in our prayer time before work. I have retained a copy which I replicate because it illustrates the cultic mindset, control and brainwashing, or 'thought reform' (Lifton, 1989):

> I, of my own free choice, covenant myself to you my brethren, for today and eternity. I identify myself with the New Covenant between the Lord Jesus and the Father, and trust the Spirit of Jesus to keep me so that I may fulfil it completely. I lay down my life for the Lord Jesus and for each one of you my brethren; this includes giving up my rights, my family, my possessions, my career, my all for you. My goal in life is to be your servant and your friend, so that you may grow and mature in the Lord Jesus so that this community will be truly seen to be the city on a hill. My one desire is to be with you and that together we may obey God's commandments and love one another even as He has loved us.

Repeating this continued to cement us as a community, reiterating daily that we were committed, dependent, cut off from our families, special – and in it for life. I recognise, looking back, that this brainwashing was effective because the repeated verbal promise ensured that we were more likely to honour that commitment (Cialdini, 2001).

The most terrifying time was the first four months of 1978: a surprisingly short period when I look back, but which felt like years. The singing group returned from a church visit and they were perceived as having let the Community image down. Simon and Brian decided that they must be punished by physical beatings and that the current punishments (being 'rebuked' – shouted at and criticised) were clearly not working. A time of increased terror began. Physical beatings quickly spread around the Community. The reason for the punishment was usually 'sin', which could mean anything whatsoever, but particularly letting the image down.

I was first beaten because Brian, who was the leader of my community household, had arthritic pain in his hand. He said it was a 'sign of sin' in the household. In my terror, I confessed to resentment, which resulted in 40 lashes with a bamboo cane, stripped naked to the waist in front of all the ten members of our household. This was carried out by another member, a muscly strong man, under threat of being beaten himself. Brian and Simon usually coerced other members into carrying out the beatings.

I was tricked a few times into further beatings, by Brian. He would ask me an outright question quite randomly, and I always seemed to give the wrong answer. I still believed that God wanted to break me, that all suffering was worthwhile, and that the punishment was justified because I was a bad sinful person – it would make me a better person. Simon, in particular, seemed to relish people being beaten and I learned years later that he would gather all his household members together for a report on who had been beaten that day, and laugh about it (they hated doing this but were too frightened to say so).

Over this period, we were criticised daily and I was frozen and dissociated (split off from myself), hoping no one would notice me. We were expected to read ten chapters of the Bible a day (or we would be beaten). At one stage, Brian read a section from Deuteronomy, in the Old Testament of the Bible, which sets out curses and punishments for sin. These were terrifying, as I took them literally and believed they were happening to me. For example, if you disobey, "the Lord will send on you curses, confusion and rebuke in everything you put your hand to, until you are destroyed and … will plague you with diseases" (Deuteronomy 28:20–21).

After being broken down over the years, I had no resources within myself to argue against this terrifying logic, believing that my dark and painful feelings were proof of my sin and the reality of these curses, and that God was going to kill me. There was a powerful dissonance between reality and the implied 'sin', and I became frozen and increasingly afraid to speak or act.

Simon began to fear that the beatings would leak out to the press or the police. A few people left at this time and spoke to local church leaders, several of whom questioned Simon. He lied outright, categorically denying the beatings had happened. We were told that the 'Blood of Christ' wiped away the past, including all evidence of the beatings. We had to pretend to ourselves, and others, that they had not happened. This silencing tactic was extremely effective with me, and I did not speak of the beatings to anyone but my husband Tony (whom I met in the Community), for many years; my family did not know until relatively recently.

This punishment phase served to increase conformity and dependency through fear. I believed this fear was a true fear of God ('fear of the Lord leads to life', Proverbs 19:23). The rationalisation was that I was so sinful and evil that I deserved the punishment. I did not, therefore, perceive any of this as wrong, nor that it was abuse, and I considered it to be necessary to mould me into the person I needed to be to do God's work.

I had no conscious doubts or thoughts of leaving for years, until, in 1979, my father invited me to visit him at his home in Belize, Central America. I would not have dreamed of going without permission, but Simon allowed me to go – I think it fitted with his James Bond, jetsetter, image! The short break from relentless fear and pressure, being with my father, and exposure to a normal life, allowed me to begin to think for myself – a bit. I wrote to Simon asking to change households but had a reply by return of post saying how hurt and angry he was that I would betray the household members in such a way and to return as soon as possible. Although I had asked for very little, he exerted his control and the terror returned. Sadly, I did not tell my father. The Covenant and the fear had done their work, as had the continued rationalisation and belief that God wanted to break me, which had never been challenged.

P2.3 Leaving – in stages

From 1979, the grip of control was slowly beginning to loosen: the trip to Belize had helped me, and generally, there seemed to be a bit more space to think for ourselves about things, although we were still afraid and often threatened. In October 1980, unbeknown to me, the women in Simon's community household challenged him, having finally dared to speak to each other about the abuse. This resulted in the Community splitting overnight into two camps: for and against Simon.

After some deep heart-searching, panic and fear, I joined the 'against' faction, along with Tony, whom I was close friends with and liked. I had not dared to allow myself to think about him as a boyfriend, because many potential partners and married couples had been separated: Simon seemed to view 'exclusive' relationships as a threat. Tony and I left together and were married the following spring. That part of the nightmare, my time in the Community, was finally over.

There is, however, a big difference between leaving physically and leaving psychologically, as this book, Walking Free, illustrates. The Community itself started to fall apart following the split and everyone went their separate ways over the next year or two. But the effects of the control continued for many years in our minds and our lives.

Although Tony and I understood that we had been tricked, abused and hurt in the Community, we still had a mindset that assumed we should commit ourselves utterly to God's work, to changing the world, 'laying down our lives' as part of a church. Over the following 15 years, we found ourselves drawn to a series of radical churches which had grandiose ideas of their mission and importance, often with leaders who believed they had a special calling to lead and the right to direct the members' lives. We believed that these leaders had the right and the superior wisdom to tell us how to live and what we could and could not do. They were only too happy to have compliant, dedicated people joining their cause.

The last of these churches was also the least healthy, and whilst it was not a cult (using the definition in M3), there was subtle but harmful spiritual abuse. The internal pressures started to build in us, as new traumas were added to the underlying post-traumatic stress, which was never recognised or addressed after leaving the Community. We became increasingly aware of the cognitive dissonances in our lives (see M11.2). For example, we were encouraged to take leadership positions but slapped down if we acted in a way that the main leader did not like, or that threatened him. We were trapped because we believed God had told us to be part of that church and that leaving meant we would be spiritually 'lost', but we were hating every minute of it. I could see no way out, I wanted to die; not suicidal but trapped with no other way out.

Our conditioning made it difficult to look outside the church for help, but I was becoming depressed and desperate. I spoke to my doctor who was warm, kind and accepting and pointed out my 'all-or-nothing' thinking. I saw a television programme about cults and recognised the same dynamics in the Community and some of the churches since. I called a cult information centre, and Tony and I went to see an 'exit counsellor'.

This was the beginning of us leaving psychologically as he explained the cultic dynamics, and helped me put words to the experience – I began to diagnose the Community and 'call a cult a cult', which was very helpful. He explained that my personality had been forced, through abuse, fear and manipulation, into a 'pseudo-identity', an identity I had to exhibit in order to be a member. My thinking had been 're-formed' and I had lost sight of my authentic and pre-cult identity. Unfortunately, whilst helpful with the information we needed, the exit counsellor did not provide the space for us to find our own way forward, and suggested we stay in the church and change it from within. This was bad advice and caused us more months of abuse, building to a traumatic crisis before we could make the crucial step of leaving physically.

I had been involved in counselling while within the church, but this was far from the safe, ethical process that I now see as crucial. It was considered as unnecessary, and indeed dangerous, to go outside the church for training in counselling because this might not accord with 'correct' Biblical doctrine. In any case, God would guide our counselling sessions so what more did we need? Any problem could be resolved in one or two long sessions, dependent only on the client's and counsellor's faith and openness to God's intervention. The effects were sometimes damaging, but this could always be explained away as a lack of faith on the part of the one being counselled.

The experiences of untrained counselling in the Community and the churches, and with the exit counsellor, motivated me to undertake proper professional training, to become accredited by a national counselling association, to find myself an ethical therapist and supervisor, and to speak out about the potential harm that can occur to former members when they consult untrained counsellors who have no clear ethical code, supervision or accountability. I also decided that, whilst I was most interested in the issues of former cult members, I should obtain experience with a wide range of clients before becoming too specialised.

I trained first as a pastoral counsellor, with a Christian theological college, where I discovered Christians who encouraged me to think for myself, were ethical, respectful and supportive. This contributed to my leaving psychologically. Some years later, I undertook a Masters in Gestalt Psychotherapy, and eventually a university Doctorate. At each stage, I found myself learning much, not only about counselling but about myself and the effects of my own experience; and my specialist research focussed on what helps former cult members recover.

I worked with schoolchildren, bereaved clients and most notably in a Rape Crisis Centre. At the same time, I saw a wide range of private clients before increasingly specialising with former members.

In the absence of specialised services in the UK, I visited several organisations in the USA which specialised in helping former members, to learn what I could from them. In 1998, I started attending International Cultic Studies Association (ICSA) conferences and have travelled the world learning and speaking. I interned twice at Wellspring Retreat and Resource Centre in Ohio. I owe much to Wellspring, which sadly no longer exists, and its late Director, Dr Paul Martin, for enabling me to learn about the recovery journey of former members and the 'thought reform model'.

P2.4 Life now

People often ask if I am still religious. I am not – but I respect others' beliefs, if they are healthy! I like to think of myself as openly spiritual and I take this stance because I never want to become rigid in my thinking again, I want to be open to the beauty and mystery of life without labelling it or tying it down.

I love to walk every day in the beautiful Hope Valley in England where I live. I am an avid reader of novels, mainly at bedtime and on holidays. I love my work and if I won the lottery would do it anyway! I love to travel and have been to many different countries in the world, both as part of my exciting adventures learning about the cultic studies field, and visiting family.

My story is of course my own, and yours will be different, but there may be elements that chime with you if you have, like me, suffered harm in a coercive, cultic and/or spiritually abusive group. Perhaps you have left physically but not yet left psychologically, a shadowy and foggy place where I spent 15 years. Maybe you are on the path to recovery and growth, or maybe that still seems out of reach. I hope that this book will help you Walk Free, as I have!

In Part Three, we will look at what you need to equip yourself before you embark on the journey in Part Four.

Part Three

Preparing for the journey

Before setting off on any journey, it is important we prepare ourselves, and this is true for this Walking Free journey. At P1.5, I suggested you equip yourself with a notebook or journal and creative materials. Here, we will address other issues to consider before setting off in Part Four, including: looking after yourself; reflecting on which generation you are; creating a family tree; drawing up a history of your cultic setting; and creating a personal timeline.

P3.1 Looking after yourself

We start this section by reflecting on some strategies to help you look after yourself as you go through the Walking Free journey.

As you Walk Free, you will be *purposefully remembering*, and this may include difficult things, both from your time in the coercive, cultic and/or spiritually abusive setting and from life since leaving. This may at times leave you feeling overwhelmed or numb.

You may also find you '*trigger*' more often. A trigger is a reminder in the present of a difficult memory which you have not purposefully tried to recall. As a result, you may have similar reactions in the present (physical or emotional) as you did when the original incident that is 'triggering' you happened.

DOI: 10.4324/9781003305798-3

These can be draining and tiring, and so, as we journey on, we all need:

- to take a break sometimes – to just sit and rest before carrying on
- to be able to soothe ourselves when we feel wobbly and churned up (overwhelmed and stressed or frozen and numb)
- to be able to find a 'safe enough space' where we feel rested, calm, stabilised and safe enough – in our body and our life
- to be able to express what we are feeling
- to be able to 'ground' ourselves

In this section, I introduce you to three related exercises to help you look after yourself as you Walk Free: the Safe Enough Space exercise; tips for grounding; and tips for journalling. You could start by familiarising yourself with these, and then experiment and try them out for yourself.

On the drawn Roadmap, looking after yourself is indicated by the lake in the centre, an oasis you can retreat to whenever you need. An oasis is a fertile green area surrounding a pool of water in a desert, a place that provides relief, a pleasant contrast to the surroundings, a refuge. You will see that the road winds around Oasis Lake and you can access it from every Milestone. On the lake, you can see the people looking after themselves, reading a novel in the boat, rowing with a picnic, fishing with their dog and relaxing on the island. You may not be able to do these things literally, but think about what helps you feel relaxed and safe. You could colour in the images on the Roadmap.

You might like to put together a **self-care pack** containing all you need for the journey, as this can also help you to soothe yourself. This could include such things as: this book; your journal and notes; creative materials, including coloured pencils; and things that will help you to soothe and ground yourself such as scented oils (more ideas below). You could create an attractive personalised container to keep these things together – and keep it close by.

You are not alone in the struggle to leave this kind of trauma and abuse behind, there are many others who have travelled this road, including myself. Everyone's experience is different, but I hope it helps to remember this and even imagine us travelling with you as you Walk Free.

To be aware of: Before exploring the Safe Enough Space exercise, grounding techniques and journalling tips, please note that some of the ideas listed may be triggering, or some words may remind you of cultic language. If this happens, I suggest you be curious about them, if you can. If you struggle with any of these ideas, please miss them out.

While most of the suggestions below are benign, if you suffer from any serious health issues, please avoid any that might make your condition worse.

P3.1.1 Safe Enough Space exercise

First, I introduce the Safe Enough Space exercise. This is adapted in part from Shapiro, who describes creating an "emotional oasis" (2018, pp. 117–118), a 'safe enough space' for yourself to find relief and refuge when you need it.

It is common for former members, and survivors of abuse, to struggle to identify what it is like to feel calm and 'safe enough', both emotionally and in terms of their physical reactions. This exercise and the suggestions below are designed to help with this.

Note: I use the term 'safe *enough*' and not just 'safe', because feeling 100% safe is unrealistic and hard for anyone to achieve.

You can return to this exercise whenever you need to support yourself to feel at least some level of safety.

Please be as creative as you like as you do this exercise! You could reflect on these points in your journal; draw; find a photograph of a person, place or thing; write a story; use software or an app; or whatever suits you!

So let's create a Safe Enough Space by going through these numbered steps:

Step 1

Can you connect with yourself, and focus your thoughts on something positive that generates feelings of calm and safety, and which you can return to whenever you need?

You could start by thinking whether you ever had anyone or anything in your life that you could escape to and feel better with (relieved and/or comforted by), either from your time as a member, before joining or since leaving.

However rare this experience may be for you, is there someone or something you can think of? You could try to remember as clearly as possible those 'kernels' (seeds) of a place, experience, object, animal or person (more options listed below) that might have given you a sense of safety, however small, in spite of the difficult experiences. **That is the feeling I want you to grasp and amplify.**

Here are some ideas of things or people that *might* give this feeling of being safe enough. I recognise you will have been harmed by things and people, so it is important to only identify those who were helpful and not those who ever harmed you. In relation to people, this is about finding someone who was good to you, kind to you, understood you and who you wanted to be with.

Do any of these fit your experience?

- a non-member grandparent or relative (even if you only had occasional contact)
- a sibling
- a friend
- a teacher
- a kind and accepting therapist
- a pet
- a soft toy
- escaping into nature
- being creative, like knitting, studying, drawing and painting
- fun playing with friends, for example, memories of playing in the snow

The experience of being 'safe enough' may not exist for you, or may have been so rare that you cannot remember it clearly. I am sorry for that, and if that is the case, I want to support you to try to **create a safe enough space for yourself in your creative mind in the present.**

Some examples of creating a Safe Enough Space:

When I started speaking publicly, I lacked confidence because I felt terrified of being criticised or 'getting it wrong'. My trusted therapist gave me a plastic model of a horse, which I kept in my pocket. Whenever I felt wobbly, I would hold it (no one knew!), and this helped to ground me and gave me a feeling of safety, because I remembered my therapist's support and kindness.

Someone else I know returns to the children's book, Winnie the Pooh, which they remember reading in their warm safe bed as a child in the cultic group, and this helps them connect to one experience of feeling safe enough growing up.

What we want to achieve here is **a safe enough space that 'grounds' you, as you think of something that associates you with a sense of well-being.**

To assist, Worksheet P3.1 is a list of ideas: you could choose a few different options or add your own. You may find that certain ones work better in different circumstances. If anything on the list is triggering, or reminds you of the cultic setting, then please ignore it – **it is important you only use the ones that help you feel safe enough.**

You could write in the spaces provided or in your journal.

 ## Worksheet P3.1: Identify something that helps you feel safe enough

Date _____

Imagine a Safe Enough place, experience, object, animal, person, etc.	What do you want to say about this, and which will you use?
a beautiful fantasy land like a fairyland or somewhere in outer space	
a real specific place e.g. a house, beach, mountain, wood, town or city	
beauty in nature e.g. another country, countryside, seaside, mountains, the sky, sunshine, flowers, the moon, the sun	
a wild animal e.g. protective dolphin, tiger, elephant	
a pet animal	
a particular memory e.g. playing in snow with other kids, laughter	
a person	
a treasured object such as a teddy bear or doll	
a view from a window	

Now you have thought about some options, could you say more about what you have chosen as your Safe Enough Space, and why? See if you can describe it clearly, what colour is it, what shape is it, what do you love about it?

_____

_____

_____

_____

Step 2

Could you reflect on what you have chosen, and focus on the positive physical sensations and emotions that imagining it conjures up, listening out for those bodily sensations or feelings that are comforting, relieving, calming and soothing, and those that express kindness and compassion towards yourself?

How about you write these sensations and feelings down in Worksheet P3.2 or your journal, so you can return to them?

Worksheet P3.2: Identify the sensations and feelings associated with your Safe Enough Space

Date _____

_____

_____

_____

_____

_____

_____

_____

_____

_____

Step 3

It may help to think of a *word or short phrase* to describe and associate with your choice, so you can easily access it – such as 'teddy bear', the name of a character from a storybook such as 'Pooh Bear' or 'Piglet' (from the Winnie the Pooh stories), the name of the safe person, object, pet, etc., or a positive word such as 'safe', 'serene', 'calm', 'happy' or 'light'. You could write this word or phrase in Worksheet P3.3 or your journal.

Worksheet P3.3: Note down the word or short phrase associated with your Safe Enough Space

Date _____

_____

_____

_____

_____

You could also consider *carrying an object* that reminds you of your choice and helps you easily access your Safe Enough Space, as I did with the figure of a horse (above).

Step 4

I suggest you practise accessing this Safe Enough Space as often as possible (a few times daily if you can), even when you feel okay. This will help you find it more quickly when you feel stressed, down, numbed, unsafe or wobbly about anything.

Step 5

I suggest you return to this exercise throughout the Walking Free journey, whenever you need to.

> It will take time and practice to start to feel safe enough each time you feel wobbly, churned up and unsafe. That is normal, and my hope is that, once you have completed the whole Walking Free journey, you will have increased this sense of well-being and feeling 'safe enough' in your body and with your feelings. For now, I suggest you use this as an oasis and refuge along the way.

Because feeling unsafe can be such a physical experience (flight and fight and freeze), I will introduce you to the tips for grounding next. These are designed to help you return to a more 'grounded' and rested place in the present.

P3.1.2 Tips for grounding

When I was growing up in Africa, we had a lightning conductor on our house. This was a metal rod sticking up above the roof, and it was 'grounded' into the earth. When lightning struck, instead of destroying the house, it would move through the rod and dissipate in the ground, causing no harm. The same idea of grounding can help dissipate the harm of emotional shocks.

The aim of these grounding tips is to notice how you are feeling (physically and emotionally) and to carry away the emotional and physical charge caused by purposefully remembering or being triggered. It is important to remind yourself of what you came up with in the Safe Enough Space exercise so you *recognise* you are safe enough – and then to ground yourself. It can be helpful to remind yourself that the incidents you are recalling are not happening now but are in the past. They are "just a memory" (Fisher, 2021, p. 32), so you can return to the present.

These can be done anywhere and no one needs to know!

Like the ideas in the Safe Enough Space exercise, these grounding techniques take practice and become easier over time – you could experiment with some of these ideas so you are prepared and practiced at doing them when you feel ungrounded or unsafe.

You will probably need to keep returning to this section as it will help you to stay in the present, reduce stress, tolerate feelings better and help you think and feel at the same time.

We will look at a number of grounding tips, some of which may be helpful for you to adopt. There is an opportunity to identify a few for yourself that you find easy to use in different situations. As a reminder, you could write them down and put what you have written in your pocket or bag – and looking at them will probably be grounding in itself!

Reminder: Grounding tips help shift our focus and 'ground' us back into the present, the here and now.

Important point: As you do this exercise, can you notice your thoughts and feelings with *curiosity and compassion*, not judgement? Curiosity brings acceptance, as does compassion.

So you remain aware of everything that's going on around you, it can sometimes help to keep your eyes open while you are grounding yourself. I suggest you notice what it is like doing these, and you could make a note in your journal.

To help ground yourself, you could

- Imagine the energy of remembering difficult incidents moving through your body, into the ground and away from you, like the electric current of lightning dispelling through the lightning conductor and into the earth.
- Sit in a chair and gently push both feet into the ground. Notice the sensations in your legs and back as you are pressed back against the chair. Experiment with finding just the right amount of pressure, or stomp your feet instead of pushing.
- Sit comfortably; take a breath in for 4 seconds (through your nose if possible); hold that breath for 2 seconds; release your breath, taking 6 seconds (through your mouth if possible). You can vary the length of the breaths to suit you.
- Replicate this breathing exercise but on the out-breath gently utter "vooo" (make a sound like the wind) and sustain the sound throughout the exhalation (Levine, 2018, p. 20).
- Replicate this breathing exercise but with your hand on your heart.

It can be helpful to ground ourselves using all our five senses – sound, touch, smell, taste and sight. You might like to think about what you find helpful under these headings. In Worksheet P3.4, I have added a few examples to get you started, and have provided space so you can add your own, or you may prefer to use your journal.

Worksheet P3.4: What helps you 'ground' yourself?

Date _____

Tick what helps you connect with the present	Your grounding tips
Sound • Radio, TV or podcast • A piece of music or a special song • Bells • Birdsong or nature sounds • Talking to someone safe enough • Reading something out loud **Touch** • Being wrapped in a warm soft blanket • Popping some bubble wrap (plastic wrapping with air bubbles in it!) • Putting your hand under lukewarm running water • Taking a warm shower • Rubbing your hand over a soothing surface and noting the texture • Patting or cuddling a pet • Touching a soft toy **Smell** • Using essential (aromatherapy) oils that remind you of your Safe Enough Space, and enjoying the fragrance • A fragrance you love e.g. lavender, frankincense, patchouli or rose geranium • A scented candle • Flowers • Pine trees or grass • Fresh bread or cake **Taste** • A soothing drink • Savouring smooth chocolate • Lemon or lime • Your favourite meal • Peppermint • Herbal teas **Sight** • Looking around the room and finding ten blue things or eight yellow things, etc. • Counting all the pieces of furniture around you • Putting on your favourite movie or TV show • Escaping into a comforting book • A lovely picture or photograph • A candle flame **Other** • Stretching • Walking or running • Dancing • Looking out of the window and noticing the weather • Moving to another room for a change of scenery • Finding a quiet place • A comfortable chair in your home • Solitude	

We will now look at some tips for journalling.

P3.1.3 Tips for journalling

Another way of supporting ourselves emotionally and mentally is by expressing thoughts and feelings through journalling. An advantage is that it doesn't need to involve anyone else!

Journalling includes reflecting on your day, writing a stream of consciousness and writing yourself encouraging statements. It can help to sort out what you are thinking and feeling, and you can express high emotional states, which can bring relief. It is an opportunity to express yourself, raise awareness, reflect and support yourself.

> **For example:** Jimmy, who was born and raised in a cultic group, had never heard of journalling, but was intrigued as I explained one way of approaching it – which is that you simply buy a journal and then start writing whatever comes into your head. He found that he loved doing this, and would express his thoughts and feelings, which helped to ground him. It also helped him to work out his own thoughts about many issues, including where he had been told what to believe. He filled quite a few journals by the time we finished our Post-Cult Counselling together!

The unsent letter

There are numerous journalling exercises, but one that I think is particularly useful is the 'unsent letter'. This can be especially helpful if you are struggling with strong feelings towards someone, but it is difficult or inappropriate to confront them directly.

For example, those born and/or raised in the cultic setting often struggle with challenging feelings towards their parents who brought them up there, and perhaps allowed them to be abused; but they don't want to hurt them by telling them what it was like for them growing up. As a result, they are left with a mass of thoughts and feelings that they cannot seem to get rid of or resolve. A letter written to their parents, but not intended to be sent, expressing how they feel can be cathartic (which means it provides relief through the open expression of strong emotions).

It can be helpful to write several versions. The first version may be 'saying it as it is', messy, sweary and rageful. Then as you work through each version, you may find that you process your feelings, until it fits what you could actually say. The purpose of this is *for you*, not them, although some people sometimes do send the letter – but I advise caution about sending an unfiltered letter as it may cause more problems than it resolves!

You can also write an unsent letter to:

- someone who has died, to resolve issues, express what is unsaid and process grief and/or rage
- a 'god' or higher spiritual being who has ruled over your life, letting them know what you think about them
- the leader/ship
- to yourself – yourself in, yourself after, at a certain age, to your body – the possibilities are endless!
- to anything or anyone that you think it might be helpful to communicate with, but that you can't or don't necessarily want to have contact with.

Guidelines for effective journalling

These general guidelines, adapted from books by Kate Thompson (2011), Kathleen Adams (1990) and Tristine Rainer (2004), may be worth keeping in mind when journalling:

1. Forget what you were taught at school about handwriting, grammar, spelling and structuring a piece of writing. None of these matter here.

2. Work out what means of writing feels most comfortable for expressing personal thoughts: what sort of paper, pen, pencil or computer. This may be different from what you use, say, for your work.

3. You don't need to plan it or know where it is going. Just let it flow, or jump around from one idea to another. You could try writing quickly or very slowly.

4. Remember it is just for you, so you can be completely honest about all your feelings.

5. Don't judge or criticise yourself for what you write. (It may be the cultic voice that you are hearing if you do!)

6. Read through what you have written with curiosity, and consider what is striking, surprising, emotional or worth revisiting.

7. Decide whether you will keep what you have written or destroy it. For example, it may be helpful to have a ritual burning or shredding. But it may also be helpful to keep it and read it again in the future. If you keep it, make sure it is secure and private.

We will now look at some other things to consider before you set off on the Walking Free journey in Part Four.

P3.2 Consider your starting point before you set off

Before starting on a journey, it can be helpful to think about how we come to be where we are. You might like to consider:

1. Which generation you are
2. How your family history affects you
3. The history of your cultic group or relationship
4. Your personal timeline

P3.2.1 Which generation are you?

In this section, we are going to look at which 'generation' of former member/survivor you are. This is important because it has an impact on your identity and how you understand your own story. Many aspects of the coercive, cultic and spiritually abusive experience impact different 'generations' in different ways.

I will refer to three broad categories (although they can overlap):

*   'First generation' were recruited or joined as adults (usually referred to in this Workbook as 'joined')
*   'Second generation' were either born in the setting or joined at an early age, and have parents who joined (usually referred to as 'born and/or raised')
*   'Multi-generation' have at least one parent who was born and/or raised, and maybe up to five or more generations (usually referred to as 'multi-generation' (Aebi-Mytton, 2021) or 'born and/or raised')

A crucial difference is that first generation have substantial life experience from before joining, and an identity to return to after leaving. They may have joined because they were 'love bombed' and made to feel loved and special; or they may have been tricked into joining what they thought was an organisation that was trustworthy and presenting itself accurately; or they may have been in the wrong place at the wrong time.

Those who joined may also have vulnerabilities to joining from their life before. I will give you an opportunity to reflect on this, if it is applicable, in M13, when I address emotional healing needs. I recommend leaving the question of any pre-membership vulnerabilities on one side for now, as it is important first to *understand the dynamics* and issues addressed in the first part of the Walking Free journey.

Since those who were born in the setting did not join, they have no previous identity to return to after leaving. Those who joined as children have only a partially formed previous identity. Their parents who joined were exposed to life outside, and so have some previous identity to return to. In some cases, second generation may, therefore, have had some exposure to mainstream society through their parents, or personally if they joined as older children or teenagers, which might possibly help on leaving (Aebi-Mytton, 2021). However, many will have little or none.

There are also some who joined as children, usually teenagers, without their parents. Their experience often involves a mixture of first and second generation aspects, and will vary according to circumstances. This will also apply to some who were sent away to a cultic abusive boarding school or a teen rehabilitation programme.

Multi-generation have no previous identity to return to, nor did their parents and sometimes grandparents (Aebi-Mytton, 2021). Many are, therefore, unlikely to have been exposed to mainstream society in a normal way. The cultic setting holds more influence and control over their thinking than any other setting, so if the family leaves the group together, the parents may be as lost and vulnerable as the children. All are likely to have been taught to dismiss anything within 'the world' or mainstream society, and may have many fears and even phobias about it (see M5 for more on introjects and phobias).

All leavers may feel they are aliens in a foreign land, but many multi-generation may have particularly overwhelming feelings of being deeply different and weird, culturally dislocated and even socially disabled.

Some former members 'cult hop' (as I did) and join multiple coercive, cultic and spiritually abusive groups or relationships, not recognising that they all operate with similar dynamics. Some may be 'born and/or raised' in one group and 'joined' in another. For example, Hari had told me he was first generation but as we were discussing this he realised his father had been a member of a different cult, and so he was actually a second generation who then joined another cult. He was rather shocked by this but it helped him understand more clearly some of his complex feelings, why he was vulnerable to being recruited in his 20s, and why he was struggling to recover.

If you have been involved in more than one setting, you can reflect on the different impacts in Worksheet P3.5.

We will look at identity in depth, and the difference between the identity formed as a result of cultic dynamics (which I refer to as our 'pseudo-identity') and our authentic identity or 'real me', at M6.

Worksheet P3.5: Reflect on which generation you are and the effects

You could consider these questions – there is space to answer them below, or you could use your journal. If you can't think of the answers now, you could return to this later when you understand more about your experiences.

The purpose of these questions is to help you raise awareness of the impact the generation you belong to has on your life story and recovery, in preparation for the Walking Free journey:

Date _____

1. Which generation (or generations, if more than one applies) are you?

   _____

2. What level of exposure to society outside did you have when you were a member?

   _____

3. If you were a member as a child, did your parents tell you much about society outside the cultic setting, or did they totally dismiss it?

   _____

4. As a member, did you feel like an alien and weird compared to outsiders?

   _____

5. Did you feel like an alien and weird on leaving?

   _____

6. Do you think the 'generation' you belong to influences how you feel about yourself, and, if so, how?

   _____

7. What has identifying the generation you belong to taught you about yourself, and what difference does that make?

   _____

Worksheet P3.6: Second and multi-generation – how did your family come to join?

If you are second or multi-generation, you might like to reflect on why your parents or ancestors joined. This exercise may be aided by the following two sections (create a family tree and draw up a history of your cultic setting) and you could return to this Worksheet when you have completed those investigations if that helps. You can write in the space provided or in your journal.

Date _____

_____

_____

_____

_____

_____

_____

_____

_____

_____

_____

_____

_____

_____

_____

To help you reflect on which generation you are, and your parents' or ancestors' involvement, I suggest you create a family tree and investigate the history of your cultic setting.

P3.2.2 Create a family tree

It may help to investigate your family tree or genealogy at some point on this Walking Free journey. This can help you know more about who you are, where you are from, and the kinds of people you are from.

Not knowing about your roots outside the group might leave you feeling as if you do not belong anywhere other than to that setting, that you have no roots elsewhere. But this is not the case. It may be a challenge to go back up a family tree when you do not know much about your ancestors, but we all come from somewhere before the coercive, cultic and spiritually abusive setting existed, even if our family was in the group for several generations.

Reminder: The cultic setting may want you to see yourself as entirely part of that setting, and to view any roots or family outside it as irrelevant or even harmful. That keeps you a member and controlled. Finding family and roots outside helps us to see ourselves as not simply defined by the cultic setting.

If you are multi-generation, you could think about how many generations have been members, and on which sides of the family. For example, some have a mother who joined and a father who is fifth generation. This makes a difference in how each side of the family sees things, and their closeness or access to non-member family.

Here is an example of a family tree for someone called James:

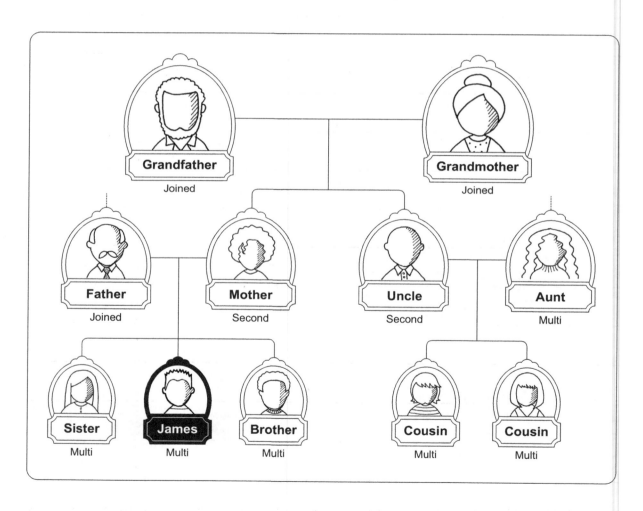

Worksheet P3.7: Create a family tree showing your family's involvement in the cultic setting

You could create a family tree for your family in this Worksheet, based on James's family tree, noting which generation each individual is. This exercise is to help you to understand where you, your parents and ancestors fit in.

Your Family Tree

Date _____

If you joined a cultic setting, it may still help to remember who you are through investigating your family tree. For example, I was told (in a so-called 'message from God' or 'prophecy') that God was telling me that my family was "like dusty furniture in an old Victorian attic" and that I needed to be 'cut off' from them in prayer. I felt ill when I was told this but was unable to disagree. Having my attachment 'cut off' from them 'spiritually' had a deep impact on my identity, disconnecting me on an emotional and psychological level.

After leaving, it helped me greatly to return to my family (who thankfully welcomed me) and to think about who my grandparents were, what they had done in their lives, who I was related to further up the family tree, etc. I discovered that it was possible to trace my family tree right back to an ancestor who invaded England with William the Conqueror in 1066 (long before the cult!). It was fun finding out and I felt much more grounded in myself after I had done this. I have returned to my family tree quite a few times to affirm who I am, my authentic identity and where I come from.

If you want to research this more deeply for yourself and your family, there are websites that investigate genealogy and family trees, and it may be worth having a look at those, if you feel this is a helpful exercise for you to do. If you do follow this up, it is important to check out the company that does these first. It is also important to be aware that some have discovered family secrets that were a shock and which they preferred not to know about, for example unexpectedly finding a half-sibling, or that their father is not their biological father.

Before creating a personal timeline of your own life, let us look at drawing up a history of your cultic setting.

P3.2.3 Draw up a history of your cultic setting

It can be helpful, along with understanding your parents' and ancestors' involvement, to look at the history of your group (or relationship, but as this applies mainly to groups I will refer just to them for the remainder of this section). This can help you to identify important characteristics of the group and to complete your personal timeline. For those born and/or raised, it may also help to understand what was happening, both in the cultic setting and society, when your parents or ancestors got involved, and what their experience may have been.

Many well-known cultic settings have been researched, and books written about them, often containing a history of the group. Some former members have published autobiographies of their experiences and these can be helpful in confirming what happened and when. It can also help to speak to other former members you know from your group, or to family who have left or never joined, if that feels safe for you.

Rebecca Stott (2017), in her book 'In the Days of Rain', mixes her investigation of her family's personal experiences and history, with the history of her group. Other former members of her group have told me that the book has been enormously helpful, partly because it helped them normalise their experiences and clarified what happened and when.

An investigation also needs to include the history of the founders or leadership. There is an opportunity to explore this subject further in M12.

While exploring your family tree, you might like to think about which country your group was founded in, and what sort of culture your family and ancestors came from. Many groups are founded in one culture and then move abroad or spread worldwide, perhaps expecting new members to take on the language and culture of the founders.

Some groups are influenced by historical events, and this can result in moving away from familiar cultures. For example, in her book 'Cruel Sanctuary' (2018), Christine Mathis-Rimes explains how she was born in England, but after her family joined they moved far away to Paraguay in South

America to avoid being conscripted into World War Two, because they refused to fight, as conscientious objectors. This move to a culture alien to the whole family had a major impact. Understanding what happened, and how this move came about, helped her make sense of her experience.

The investigation of the history of the group may therefore require an understanding of the society within which the group was founded, as well as the one that it moved to. Within groups with such a cross-cultural membership, many former members have parents from different cultures, so it is worth knowing about both parents' origins.

In Worksheet P3.8, you have an opportunity to reflect on some questions to help you draw up a history of your group. There is space to answer them below, or you could use your journal. If you can't answer now, you could return to this later when you understand more about your experiences.

Worksheet P3.8: Questions to consider when thinking about the history of your cultic setting

Date _____

1. In which country did the coercive, cultic and/or spiritually abusive setting originate?

   _____

2. If it was a group, who founded it?

   _____

3. What sort of culture did they create in the early days, e.g. was it an exciting time, was it repressive, etc.?

   _____

4. How did it evolve and what stages did it go through?

   _____

   _____

   _____

5. What influenced these changes e.g. did the founder die, did a new leader take over?

_____

_____

_____

6. If it was a group, what was happening in the central leadership when you were a member, and how did this influence your life?

_____

_____

_____

7. What was different in your time compared to other stages?

_____

_____

_____

8. What was different in your time compared to the founder's time?

_____

_____

_____

9. You could reflect on any other aspects that you can think of.

_____

_____

_____

In this next section, I suggest you consider creating a personal timeline.

P3.2.4 Create a personal timeline

Another thing that can be helpful is to create a timeline of your life experiences. This is a graphic or visual representation of what happened to you, which can help you better understand your own life history.

I find that former members often find it difficult to recall what happened when, and the timeline can help clarify when things happened, and in what order. It can bring a sense of clarity where there is confusion and can help clear the fog.

When we are feeling overwhelmed or in a frozen state, we cannot think *and* feel at the same time, and our sense of time can become distorted and seem somehow flexible. This is because trauma disrupts our ordinary experience of time (Stolorow, 2011). I say more about this in M7.

> I remember that, the first time I tried to create a timeline of my cult experience, I couldn't do it. I simply felt foggy and confused, almost dizzy. When I was finally able to do it for my Doctoral research, I was helped by a piece of unpublished research on my cultic setting, the Community, by another former member, which provided an overview of what happened when. I was lucky to find this because it included many incidents and dates. When I created my timeline, I realised that a particularly difficult period, which had seemed to last for years, was actually only about four months!

So what does a timeline look like? It can be:

- a fish skeleton with dates and information attached to each bone
- a ladder
- a river with rapids, deep water, bridges, tributaries, etc.
- a road
- a tree

The important thing is to visualise it in a way that suits your way of thinking. You can be as creative and colourful as you want with it.

A timeline can be created in your journal; on a computer, for example a Word or Excel file; or on a separate sheet of paper, large or small. I have provided a version below which you can use. You may like to photocopy this first, so you can reflect on different periods of membership, or create versions in your journal. You will see there are banners to complete, indicating the start and end dates of a particular period of time.

Worksheet P3.9: Your timeline

Date _____

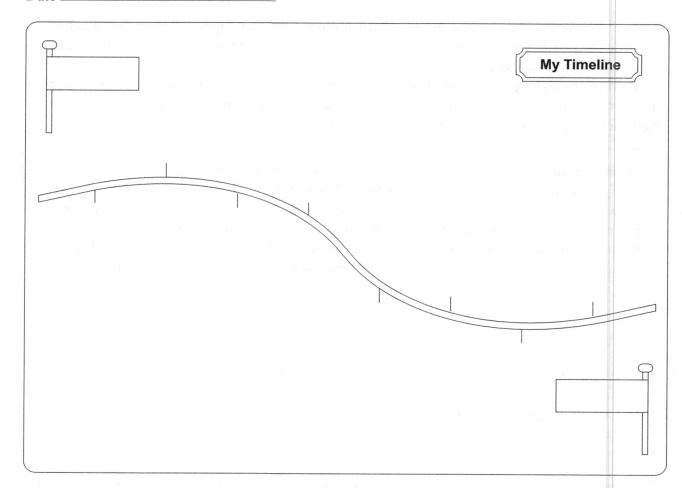

If you are struggling to identify an incident or a time to start from, you could work backwards from the present, or start with any date and work backwards and forwards from there.

If you are struggling to create a timeline while preparing for the journey, why not make notes of incidents and dates as they become clear to you at each Milestone? You could do this in a section of your journal. When you have enough clarity and information, you can then start creating or adding to your timeline.

You can return to this timeline whenever you have clarified or identified something that you want to add to it. You do not need to do it all now – in fact, you are unlikely to be able to complete it all at this stage.

We have completed our preparation and equipped ourselves! We will now proceed to Part Four and the Walking Free journey begins!

Part Four

The Walking Free journey

We are now ready to start Walking Free and the journey can begin! We have set the scene and completed the preparations, and have all we need to proceed.

We will be going through the four Regions, visiting each Milestone in turn, giving you the opportunity to unpack your baggage, and decide what to get rid of and what to keep. I introduced the Roadmap at P1.1 and explained the Regions and Milestones at P1.6. I suggest you keep referring to those sections as we proceed. **And, just as a reminder, please keep looking after yourself and returning to Oasis Lake and the Safe Enough Space exercise at P3.1.1 as often as you need to!**

It is important to leave both physically *and* psychologically to achieve recovery and growth – and reach the destination you chose at P1.17. This Workbook is mainly about leaving psychologically, but Region 1 and Milestone 1 consider the important first step of leaving physically.

DOI: 10.4324/9781003305798-4

Leave physically so you can begin to recover psychologically

In Region 1, we address the need to leave physically if you are going to recover psychologically. There is one Milestone in this Region.

If you have experienced standing on the threshold, on the way out of a coercive, cultic and/or spiritually abusive experience, you may have found it a challenge to work out which way to turn, which direction to go in that would be helpful and lead to recovery and growth.

Leaving is a huge step to face and the cost is therefore high – for everyone. This journey out towards recovery and growth can begin in many different ways as perhaps:

- you realise you are unhappy as a member,
- you realise you have doubts,
- you realise you are being abused,
- you dare to consider not attending anymore,
- you start to leave psychologically – whether you have been out for some time or are just leaving physically,
- you start the practical process of leaving or planning to leave,
- you are excluded, thrown out or shunned,
- you realise you need to heal from the after-effects of membership and of leaving – whether at the time of leaving or many years later.

Let's look at Milestone 1 and think about your and others' experiences of leaving physically.

DOI: 10.4324/9781003305798-5

Leaving physically

At this first Milestone, you have an opportunity to sit and unpack your baggage in relation to leaving. We will first learn about others' experiences and then reflect on your own.

If you have left a coercive, cultic and/or spiritually abusive group or relationship (usually referred to as a cultic setting), you will know that leaving is hard. What you may not realise is that you are not alone in this, just about everyone who leaves finds it challenging. I hope this will help you feel more 'normal' about your own leaving, and less isolated, guilty, confused or conflicted about it. This, along with the rest of the Walking Free journey, is a part of adjusting more easily to 'normal' life outside.

> One thing I have learned is that it is important not to compare our experience with others'. Our experience is our experience and how we feel about it is how we feel about it – that is normal for us. But we may learn from others' experiences and it can be helpful to refer to them.

It is hard to recover and grow if you are still in the abusive situation, or if you are neither in nor out. This is because you will continue to be influenced, perhaps in harmful ways that you are not necessarily aware of (I refer to these as blind spots). Some people talk about PIMOs (physically in,

DOI: 10.4324/9781003305798-6

mentally out) and POMIs (physically out, mentally in). As we Walk Free, we are aiming to leave both physically and psychologically – to be POMO – physically and mentally out!

In the next section, we will look at what to do if you haven't fully left physically, or if you returned and are considering leaving again.

M1.1 If you have not left physically or have returned

In view of the challenges of leaving, some people may physically remain in the cultic setting, but still wish to disentangle themselves psychologically. Others leave physically but struggle with life outside – maybe they miss family and friends who do not accept those who have left – and so return. It is your life and your choice and Walking Free may still help with certain aspects.

> **To consider:**
> You could reflect, in your journal, on the reasons for remaining or returning.
> You could reflect, in your journal, on ways that others have left, and see if their stories can help you to finally make that decision, if that is what you want.

Whilst it is, for most people, more difficult to leave psychologically and recover if you have not left physically, you can still follow the Walking Free journey. If, for example, you fear the group's doctrine is true, and you cannot tolerate the uncertainty involved in leaving, this journey should help you understand the psychological dynamics in your cultic setting. Some people have left after being exposed to some of the information in this book. You could return to this section and review where you are with your membership when you have completed the Walking Free journey.

> **Important:** If you are being abused in any way, including physically, psychologically, financially, sexually and/or emotionally, then I encourage you to question your decision to return or remain. You could seek help from other former members, agencies that provide impartial advice, and the authorities such as the police. If you feel you need to challenge doubts or fears you hold about the authorities, instilled in the cultic setting, I address this at M5.

I will now discuss what leaving looks like for many people, so you can normalise and/or recognise your own. Much of this arises from research for my Doctoral thesis (Jenkinson, 2016).

M1.2 What leaving looks like

There are many ways people leave, and you will have your own experience.

Leaving requires courage and resilience (the ability to bounce back) because it means you are moving away from the familiar and structured, though perhaps oppressive and highly controlled, environment of the cultic setting into an unfamiliar world outside. This is what two former members said about how it felt leaving:

> I felt like I had been beamed down to planet earth, you know, from this spaceship [the group], and I was now living with all these aliens and it was very scary and weird. [Marietta]

> They left because they were, let's say, standing on a precipice and didn't feel like they had any other options, there was nowhere to go, then all of a sudden, it's like being forced out into a foreign land by yourself. [Lavinia]

Leaving physically will mean different things depending on how the group or relationship is structured. It may mean leaving a house, community or compound which is run by the group or abuser. In other cases, it may mean stopping attending meetings, listening to the leader's teachings, or viewing particular websites or social media. Regardless of the setting, it means distancing yourself from the people who are abusing, influencing and/or controlling you.

Facing leaving:
Leaving may be freeing, and even feel exhilarating and a relief.
But it may also mean leaving many people you love.
And so leaving physically is easier said than done, and is rarely straightforward for anyone.

Some do not have anywhere to go, any non-cult family or friends.

Some do not have a support system to help them as they leave and try to adjust to life outside the group.

Others are deeply entangled in other members' lives as they leave together and struggle to find a way to stop being confluent and merged, and instead to become autonomous.

Some have to escape without telling anyone they are leaving.

Some secretly plan to leave, sometimes for years, saving money without anyone knowing.

Some find someone on the outside they can trust to help them leave.

Some are exposed to information about coercion, cults and spiritual abuse either in person or on the internet. They realise the nature of what they are involved in and leave.

Some are rescued in an intervention (sometimes called exit-counselling) by someone outside the group or relationship.

Sometimes the group disbands (as in my case).

Some are born in but leave with family in childhood and have no say in the matter.

Some are so depleted of energy, emotions and mental stability that they have no option but to leave for their own survival.

Some are thrown out, which may be a huge shock and adds to the challenge of adjusting to life outside. This is because they have no time to prepare psychologically as the choice is taken out of their hands: they lose control yet again, which in itself is traumatic.

Some are ostracised, shunned and rejected by those remaining in, including close family. They are, therefore, not only struggling to adjust to life outside the group but are also heartbroken at having lost their attachments to family, friends and all that was familiar in the culture they grew up in or have been a part of.

Some leave physically and psychologically but keep in contact with their family, who may work hard to get them back in, or who 'guilt trip' them to return. In this case, it is important to hold onto your authentic identity, to do what you want and what is best for you, to set boundaries with them whilst also having some contact if you want to – because they are your family after all.

Janice told me she struggles with whether to challenge her family who are still members, or whether to cut them out of her life altogether (which would be at great cost to her emotionally because she loves them and knows they are trapped there). This causes a difficult internal conflict for her, because staying in touch results in her having to appease her family and hide parts of her current life which would not be approved of. Every option, therefore, comes with its own psychological issues and making a decision (see M1.7 below), whichever way, is challenging and painful.

Many leave and do not dare to tell anyone in their new life about their experience, or they learn to lie about it. This is often because they feel ashamed or stupid (for having been a member), or they fear that they are weird, different and do not belong. As a result, they do not receive support for the very things they need help with. Often outsiders do not understand about the abuse and control that occurs in a cultic setting, making it challenging to find someone who 'gets it' – and it can be a real breakthrough when they find someone who is understanding and accepting.

There are many other scenarios, and you can reflect on the manner of your leaving physically in Worksheet M1.1 or in your journal. If you have not yet left physically, you could reflect on what might help you safely make that step.

Worksheet M1.1: How did you leave physically, or what will help you leave?

Date _____

1. How did you leave physically? Or what will help you leave physically?

_____

_____

_____

_____

_____

_____

2. Who can help you?

_____

_____

_____

_____

_____

_____

M1.3 Describing your experience of leaving

Former members use different metaphors or imagery to describe their experience of leaving. Some have described it as a 'rollercoaster' experience, others as having had "the rug pulled out from under my feet" or "like landing on another planet".

I wonder what metaphors or imagery you would use to describe your leaving? You could reflect on this in Worksheet M1.2 or in your journal:

Worksheet M1.2: Describe your leaving

Date _____

Can you describe your experience of leaving?

_____

_____

_____

_____

_____

_____

_____

_____

_____

_____

_____

_____

_____

_____

M1.4 Culture shock and feelings about leaving

You are likely to have strong feelings about leaving, and as a result of leaving. This may be in part down to 'culture shock'.

> **Reminder:** It is important to understand which feelings belong to your pseudo-identity and which to your authentic identity (see P1.4 and M6). I hope that once you have completed the whole journey, you will be better placed to understand the feelings you experienced when you left, and where they came from.

Culture shock for anyone (not just former members) occurs when you move between cultures or when you experience big changes in your life. It may include feeling disorientated; questioning your values, beliefs and identity; loneliness; loss of self-esteem; and depression (Jacobson, 2020). You may also feel under pressure because you do not know the rules of the new culture and what is expected of you, which can be destabilising, anxiety-provoking and confusing.

You may experience culture shock because the cultic culture is very different to 'the world' or society outside. If you left a commune or community, or moved from another country, you are likely to be disorientated and to have faced many challenges.

You may have left your family home or the only 'home' you have ever known. On leaving, you may have had to find your way in society, find accommodation and work out what people 'in the world' "wear, eat and do" (Kendall, 2016, p. 193). This can be especially difficult for some cult leavers who never had their own passport, money, choice of clothing or knowledge of how society works, such as riding a bus or operating a bank account. You may have left with little money, no employment and few qualifications that are recognised in society. So, you may have had to learn new skills, knowledge and information.

It is likely you were in some ways neglected but also developed skills and abilities required in the cultic setting. You may have only developed in areas where you were rewarded for being obedient, not in others which were regarded as 'wrong' or 'unnecessary'. You may therefore feel lost in the world outside.

Some former members are enthusiastic and fascinated by their new experiences after leaving, but as time goes on they experience burnout, isolation, anxiety and frustration (Zieman, 2020). The loss of the intense all-consuming purpose or vision, and of close relationships, may leave former members feeling empty and purposeless. Others may feel disenchanted on leaving, but adjust and feel better over time.

There is a strong connection between the stresses of adjusting to the new culture and mental health. Many former members suffer anxiety, depression, frustration, identity confusion, feelings of being on the margins or sidelines, and alienation. Some feel relief at leaving but also "guilt and fear due to them feeling like traitors" (Kendall, 2016, p. 195).

At M13, there is a discussion about feelings, and I suggest you return to focussing on these when we get there. The next 11 Milestones will help you *understand* what happened to you as a member, and will prepare you to address your feelings. This Milestone is about beginning to make sense of the experience of leaving, but I suspect it will take the whole Walking Free journey to finally achieve this.

M1.5 Finding your 'tribe'

Former members often overcome some of the challenges of leaving by finding their own 'tribe', who are also often other former members and survivors.

This is not another cultic setting (see M1.6 below). It is about connecting with those who understand your experience without you having to keep explaining; who have been through something similar; and who feel as 'weird' as you do! Many connect to other former members through websites or social media. This can really help (Ransom et al., 2021) so long as it is facilitated safely. It is important to find people with whom you are safe enough, feel you belong and are free to think for yourself.

You have an opportunity to describe your 'tribe' in Worksheet M1.3, or in your journal. If you have not found a tribe yet, you could think about who you would like to have in your tribe and how you might find them.

Worksheet M1.3: Describe your current 'tribe', or who they might be

Date _____

Who belongs to your tribe, or who would you like to belong?

_____

_____

_____

_____

_____

_____

_____

_____

_____

_____

MI.6 Beware of cult hopping

Amongst the important decisions on leaving, we need to decide which new relationships to make or organisations to join. This is an area of danger and vulnerability.

If we do not *understand* psychologically what happened to us, we may be in danger of 'cult hopping', which is moving from one cultic setting to another and repeating our history. Although other groups or relationships may look different from the setting we have left, perhaps with different beliefs and practices, they may have similar dynamics. For example, after leaving a political group, some may think it is safe to join a spiritual group because it looks so different, without focussing on how it operates. Or we may leave a cultic group and not realise that our new relationship entails the same dynamics but on a one-to-one basis, for example, domestic abuse involving coercive control.

I continued to 'cult hop' for 15 years after leaving the Community – my decision-making was still based on all I had learned in the cultic setting because I had not done the psychoeducational work needed to Walk Free.

So, I suggest you beware and be aware! You might like to check out these tips to help you keep safe after leaving.

MI.6.1 Tips for finding a safe organisation

When considering joining a new organisation, group or relationship, after leaving, it is vital that we keep ourselves safe. Here are a few tips which you might like to consider:

- Have a break from involvement in any setting similar to the one you have left, for as long as you need.
- Ask yourself if you are ready to join.
- Reflect on why you want to join.
- Reflect on what you want from a new organisation.
- Try out several different organisations, being careful not to commit yourself unless *you* are ready.
- Don't allow yourself to be pressured.
- Be curious and ask (lots of) questions!
- Remember it is always okay *not* to join.
- Notice if they are overly keen to have you join, or if they practice 'love bombing' – be very cautious if they do!
- Notice if they want you to get involved before you have had time to assess them.
- Resist pressure to take part in everyday tasks for them until you are ready – you are allowed to say no!
- Check if the leadership is respectful and facilitates choice and autonomy, or whether they are controlling and coercive – avoid them if they are the latter!
- Notice if the leadership is paranoid and thinks others are against them – avoid if they are!
- Notice if the leadership humiliates people – avoid if they do.
- Notice if the organisation respects others, including outsiders with similar aims, such as other churches or political organisations – avoid if they don't.
- Check how the money is spent – you should be able to access their accounts.
- Check out online if there are any reports of it being a 'cult' or abusive – avoid them if there are.
- Make sure there is a route out so you can leave at any time you choose.
- Talk to others who have left.
- Develop your decision-making skills: we will look at this next.

MI.7 Decision-making – on leaving or at any time

Leaving raises the issue of what to do next – with your life, how to earn money, what to do for a career, where to live and who to be with. These decisions can be difficult for former members and survivors at any time, but particularly at the point of leaving, with the rollercoaster of feelings and general confusion that can follow. The skill of decision-making is therefore important after leaving.

> You may need to go through this whole Walking Free journey before you feel able to make decisions for yourself, but for now, here are some thoughts to get you started. You could revisit this at the end of the journey, and see if decision-making is any easier then.

MI.7.1 Locus of control in decision-making

The 'locus of control' refers to where control of someone's life is positioned. Those with an internal locus of control are mainly in control of their life. They may take into account other people's views, but they are 'in the driving seat'!

Someone with an external locus of control has their important decisions effectively made by others. The cultic setting demands that the locus of control is externalised to the group, relationship or leadership. There is a power imbalance between the members and the leadership, and former members will have been more heavily influenced by others than by themselves. They are therefore in the passenger or back seat of the car, if not in the boot or trunk!

Making decisions is therefore likely to be a challenge because you probably had few opportunities to make important decisions for yourself.

MI.7.2 Decision-making as a member

When you were a member, did you have to make decisions by turning to the leadership or by praying to a higher being? If you were in a male/female-dominated setting, did you have to turn to the men/women for your decisions? Did this leave you assuming you did not have the right to decide for yourself, because any decision you made would be 'wrong' or faulty, and questioned and challenged by others? Did you learn not to trust yourself?

Did you believe that there was a 'blueprint' for your life, mapped out by a higher spiritual being, 'god' or all-knowing leader; or that fate or 'karma' determined the outcome of any decision, so there was no point in taking control of your life?

If you answered yes to any of the above, then the locus of control was with other people, not with yourself. I suggest that these beliefs and ideas need to be chewed over and challenged, as many will be introjects which are still holding you captive. (I explain introjects at M5.)

Given that making decisions for yourself in a cultic setting is virtually impossible, it is likely that your decision-making when you leave will also be affected. Some look back with regret at decisions they made, and I will address this next.

MI.7.3 Looking back at decisions

Many former members look back and question the decisions they made on or after leaving. These are not easy – those who were born and raised in a cultic setting may feel they never got on the right path for their life to start with. And those who joined may feel they have been taken off the path they thought they were on. But it is usually difficult just to resume an old path, or to find that 'right' path for the first time – and anyway the experience has changed us. At 18, I had no idea I would end up in a cult and then many years later as a psychotherapist helping former members recover – I had no inkling that this might be something I could or would do!

My friend, Gina Catena, mentioned below, is a nurse-midwife and clinical professor in the medical school at the University of California San Francisco, a writer and a former member. She tells me that when she left the group she grew up in, she made the decision to be a midwife. She sometimes questions herself as to whether she would be delivering babies now if she had not once believed she would be helping newly incarnated souls have a spiritual welcome to this existence!

Others have made career choices because someone else suggested it and they didn't know how to decide for themselves. Some question their choice of partner made just after leaving – but also reflect that they would not have their beloved children if they had not made that choice, so it is complex to say the least!

> We can only go on the information we have at the time we make the decision. What we have known and experienced before will influence our decisions in the present – this is one reason why we need to Walk Free of the group or relationship: so we can choose what we need for ourselves. I suggest we need to let ourselves off the hook (M13), and be understanding and compassionate with ourselves about the decisions we made.

So, going forward, how do we learn to make healthy decisions for the future?

M1.7.4 One way to help make decisions

Here is one way to make decisions (with thanks to Gina Catena (2021) for her thoughts on this):

1. Sit with a notepad or your journal – preferably at the beach or somewhere beautiful. (You could imagine you are on Oasis Lake!)
2. Clarify what is the decision you need to make.
3. Draw a vertical line down the page; on one side list pros (reasons why this might be a good decision); on the other side list cons (reasons why this might be a bad decision) (see Worksheet M1.4). The point of the pros and cons sheet is to remove the swirling thoughts from your mind and place them onto a page, where you can view them objectively.
4. *Nothing* is too trivial or too small to include. List every little pro and con, benefit or objection, and everything in your mind on the issue.
5. Then take a break from it and give yourself space and time to let it settle – have a long walk, a hot bath or shower, a meal out with a friend, another relaxing activity, or 'sleep on it' – anything to help your subconscious work in the background.
6. Once you have had some space, revisit your pros and cons list and see what you think and if the decision feels any clearer.
7. I suggest that this is a private exercise and for your eyes only, at this stage, and that you don't share it with anyone. This will help you take back the locus of control for yourself and put you in the driving seat. This is also because it is important to include any seemingly trivial or 'silly' thoughts (you can be as creative and outlandish as you like with this!) and by keeping it to yourself there will be no fear of judgement from another!
8. There is no pressure to come up with a solution immediately. This exercise is only to objectify your thoughts so your mind can cease spinning. Having removed the mind's hurricane and brought yourself to a point of mental rest, the answer usually becomes apparent.
9. If the decision does not seem clearer, then repeat the process, or rewrite or reorganise the pros and cons, until you get to some sort of clarity.
10. You will know when it is clearer because you may have a greater sense of what it is that *you* want to do.

11. If you decide you need to talk to a trusted friend or therapist about the decision, then that can certainly help – but I suggest you do so after going through the process above, and always retaining the locus of control. They are there to help you make your decision, not to tell you what you should do.

12. You decide whether to keep the list or tear it up and throw it away.

You choose the next step.

Gina says, "For myself, my heart usually settles on the answer as my writing nears the bottom of the page, after I removed the mire of conflicting ideas. Often the answer is not the one with the longest list of reasons. The mere act of removing the multitude of annoying thoughts from the mind, and placing them objectively onto a piece of paper, brings clarity."

Suggestion: If you are unsure if your decision will lead you into 'cult hopping' or into an unsafe place, *then* you might consider talking through with a trusted friend or therapist (P5) – but I suggest you only do this after completing the whole exercise!

You could try this out by completing Worksheet M1.4 or drawing this in your journal.

Worksheet M1.4: Decision-making pros and cons

Date _____

Decision to be made	
Pros	Cons

I hope this helps you make decisions for yourself, with an internal locus of control and you in the driving seat!

We have now completed Milestone 1! When you are ready you could move on to Region 2 and Milestone 2. You could follow your progress on the Roadmap.

Leaving psychologically

We have now entered Region 2 on the Roadmap. This is the largest Region, spanning Milestones 2 to 12. The whole of Region 2 is designed to help you *understand* your experience, leave psychologically and Walk Free, by addressing:

Milestone 2: Face your doubts.
Milestone 3: Diagnose your group or relationship.
Milestone 4: How confluent were you?
Milestone 5: Introjects, critical thinking and phobias.
Milestone 6: Who are YOU?
Milestone 7: Understanding traumatic stress.
Milestone 8: Boundary setting assertive anger – and rage.
Milestone 9: Healthy self-love.
Milestone 10: Thought reform.
Milestone 11: Other controlling dynamics.
Milestone 12: Unmasking the leader.

We will start with Milestone 2.

DOI: 10.4324/9781003305798-7

Face your doubts

In order to leave both physically and psychologically, it is important that we allow ourselves to face our doubts about the coercive, cultic and/or spiritually abusive setting. This includes doubts about its teachings and leadership, and the decision to leave. It is empowering to face doubts, and it activates something in us that helps us to stand up to others, assert ourselves, find a voice, and build our authentic identity (also see M6, M8 and M9). Milestone 2 provides an opportunity to sit and consider the baggage related to doubts.

M2.1 What are doubts?

The idea of 'doubt' has been discussed by theologians and philosophers for centuries. Jennifer Michael Hecht in her book *Doubt: A History* says, "Like belief, doubt takes a lot of different forms, from ancient Skepticism to modern scientific empiricism, from doubt in many gods to doubt in one God, to doubt that recreates and enlivens faith and doubt that is really disbelief" (2004, p. ix). She also talks about "the joy of doubt" (2004, p.484). Emmy van Deurzen (2022) has said, "Doubt is the source of all inquiry and knowledge. Listen to your inner doubts." In other words, it is healthy to doubt!

DOI: 10.4324/9781003305798-8

So what is doubt? Here are some definitions from *The Oxford English Reference Dictionary* (1996, p. 423):

- "a feeling of uncertainty"
- "an inclination to disbelieve"
- "an undecided state of mind"
- "lack of full proof or clear indication"
- to "feel uncertain or undecided"
- to "hesitate to believe or trust"
- to "call in question".

You may notice that 'uncertainty' and 'undecided' come up several times.

As a member of the Community, I did not doubt either what I was being told (the beliefs) or the leadership. I was certain about what I believed, where I was going when I died (heaven!) and that people who did not belong were doomed! When I left, I found the ever-growing sense of not knowing, of uncertainty about life and how I fitted in, painful and challenging, but ultimately freeing – I began to learn to doubt.

Former members may be faced with (at least) two sorts of doubts: those they had as members, and those they have on leaving. Although doubt is a big subject, for this Milestone I want to keep it simple and restrict the discussion to two questions:

- Did you doubt as a member?
- Have you sometimes doubted your decision to leave, and so doubted your genuine doubts about the cultic setting?

M2.2 Experiences of doubt as a member

We are looking at this because you may have suppressed any critical thoughts and doubts as a member. You may have been so controlled you had few doubts (like me), or it may be that doubts resulted in you finally leaving. Much of this section is adapted from my Doctoral research (Jenkinson, 2016).

René Descartes, a 17th Century philosopher, famously said: "If you would be a real seeker after truth, it is necessary that at least once in your life you doubt, as far as possible, all things." This goes against what most are taught in cultic settings that claim to be seeking (and to have sole access to) the 'big T' Truth, but who actually suppress members' doubts.

As a member it can therefore be risky, challenging and fear-inducing to face suppressed critical thoughts and doubts, because the implications are huge. Facing doubts may lead to change, including the individual deciding to leave or being expelled. It may also lead to conflict: either inner conflict or conflict with leaders and other members. Marjorie expresses a sense of panic about facing her doubts – what she calls an "unthinkable thought":

> That's the thought [slaps hand]. So, I think, 'I don't agree' - and then I might have to leave. I mean, you hardly dare think the thought. It's an unthinkable thought.

For some, the cultic mindset is totally closed to doubts, and, as Max says, it is like the individual member is encased in a *"marble edifice"*. Nevertheless, once even a small question or doubt becomes a thought, a *"crack"* may appear – and then spread as one question leads to another. This may lead to leaving. Once the member thinks the *"unthinkable thought"*, the marble edifice may crumble quickly. This is what Max has to say about facing doubts:

I have this idea, this sort of metaphor of the cult mindset, a cult member being in this marble edifice, which can't be cracked, there is no way in, and then at some point, there gets what I call a crack. And the crack is where you are able to at least ask a question. So this is very important for me. My own belief is if there is no crack nothing can be done. I myself had no crack for like 29½ of my 30 years [in the cult] - impervious. Once the crack is there very often the whole edifice crumbles down. The very first question that I just simply have is: 'Is there anything that, if it were proved, would make you question the guru or cult leader?'

Maribel put it slightly differently (see M11.2 for an explanation of cognitive dissonance):

Stuff that you don't wanna believe, and things that happen along the way that produce some cognitive dissonance, they go on the shelf and at some point the shelf gets so heavy it collapses and then you leave. You may not understand why you left, you just know it's no longer working and you leave.

For Jane, the suppressed doubts are like a *"drip, drip, drip"*, which are the unthinkable thoughts that she had as a member and that she repeatedly suppressed – but which kept returning until they built up into such a torrent they broke through the marble edifice.

Jane says that the impact can be likened to a *"reality breakdown"*, that is, the reality that has been maintained in the cultic setting breaks down. This may appear sudden, but because the drips have been dripping, and the *"stuff"* accumulates on the shelf, when the individual finally allows themself to make contact with their authentic identity and suppressed doubts, the shelf gives way and the cultic 'reality' collapses.

M2.3 Remembering your doubts as a member

What were your doubts when you were a member? In Worksheet M2.1, you have an opportunity to reflect on examples when you doubted in your cultic setting, how you dealt with these doubts, and what you think and feel now about facing doubts. To help you, here is an example:

Doubt as a member	How did you deal with this? Did you suppress it or address it?	What do you think now, and how do you feel about facing these doubts?
I noticed that the leader was cruel, but I was confused because I also believed they were the embodiment of love and/or a god.	I pushed the thought down because the implications were too awful to contemplate. OR I started to wonder if this was the perfect place I had thought it was. It was hard because it could mean all of life as I knew it starting to crumble, and having to start again.	I realise I was right to doubt but I understand why I could not face it then. OR It was the beginning of a scary but exciting process. I am glad I started to think this.

You could note down your own doubts in Worksheet M2.1 or in your journal.

Worksheet M2.1: Remembering your doubts as a member

Date _____

Doubt as a member	How did you deal with this? Did you suppress it or address it?	What do you think now, and how do you feel about facing these doubts?

M2.4 Facing doubts about leaving

The cultic setting you have left behind is likely to want you to doubt your doubts about them! That is, they want you to doubt your criticism of them, they want you to wonder if they were right after all. In fact, it is likely that you will doubt yourself sometimes, especially if you left alone or with only a few others. Since many members still believe, you may wonder if possibly you got it wrong. This may lead you to question and doubt your authentic thoughts and decisions, rather than questioning and doubting the cultic setting and its beliefs and practices.

I suggest it is, therefore, vital that you encourage your doubts about them and challenge the doubts you feel about leaving – the doubts about your doubts – as part of leaving psychologically.

For example, when Fred left his therapy cult, he remembered some of the helpful things the cult leader taught him, and that all the others had remained in the group, so he began to doubt his view of what had happened over the years. Then he remembered how the leader had split him up from his family and made him work for years for no pay as a modern-day slave, and the level of bullying and abuse he suffered. He realised that his doubts about the cult and leader were accurate; it was time to listen to them and allow himself to leave psychologically – and to no longer doubt himself.

You can think about any doubts you have, or have had, about leaving – your doubts about your doubts – in Worksheet M2.2. To help you, here are some examples:

Doubt about leaving	How can you challenge the doubt?	What do you feel about challenging these doubts? E.g. do you feel scared, excited, liberated, etc.?
Maybe I was wrong to leave because so many others have remained. Maybe they can see something I couldn't see.	What I know now is that those who remain members are unduly influenced, controlled and hoodwinked. I do not need to doubt my leaving.	I felt very scared because it seemed like a huge risk. What if they were right? What if I was going to hell for not following this person? Now I know this is rubbish and don't feel scared at all!
I thought I didn't believe it anymore, but maybe the pandemic/ war/ floods/ fires are signs that what I was taught about Armageddon and the end of the world was actually right.	There are so many other reasons for these things happening in the world. I need to consider these, look at the science from different perspectives, keep an open mind and remain grounded.	I feel so relieved that I am free to challenge these ideas and to see things more realistically!

You could note down your own doubts in Worksheet M2.2 or in your journal.

Worksheet M2.2: Facing doubts about leaving

Date _____

Doubt about leaving	How can you challenge the doubt?	What do you feel about challenging these doubts? E.g. do you feel scared, excited, liberated, etc.?

Now you have explored your doubts, hopefully, your baggage will feel a little lighter and you can continue your journey along the road to recovery and growth. The next Milestone 3 helps you to 'diagnose' your cultic setting and to apply what is relevant to your experience.

Diagnose your group or relationship

This Milestone gives you an opportunity to sit down and pull out the baggage in relation to what kind of group or relationship you were in. As you overcome any fear about critically appraising your experience, face the doubts (M2) and accurately name it for what it is, then you can continue the journey of truly understanding, recovering and Walking Free from your experiences.

In this Workbook, I have referred to 'coercive, cultic and spiritually abusive groups or relationships', or 'cultic settings' in short. Here at Milestone 3, we are unpacking just what this means.

M3.1 Types of groups and relationships included

Coercive, cultic and spiritually abusive settings can arise at all scales of human interaction: at the largest, entire countries (e.g., Nazi Germany); organisations and corporations; groups and families; right down to one-on-one relationships.

Abusive groups and organisations come in many different forms: religions; churches; spiritual centres; political movements; businesses, including some that offer therapy, well-being and yoga; multi-level marketing schemes; therapy groups; boarding schools and teen programmes; gangs. You can probably think of others. I know of a music group that became highly controlling, holding some members captive for years. In other words, anything can become coercive, cultic and, if it has spiritual aspects (and many do), spiritually abusive.

DOI: 10.4324/9781003305798-9

There are also one-on-one relationships (or 'one-on-one cults'), which have a dynamic in which "the more powerful partner asserts their superiority and leadership, often on a spiritual level" (Jenkinson, 2011, p. 4). This is a form of coercive control, and often includes domestic abuse, but effectively becomes cultic. These one-on-one coercive cultic relationships can occur in many contexts including couples; therapist and client; coach and client, including fitness, well-being and life coaches; and pastor or elder and church member. The abusing partner may make similar claims to other cultic leaders, for example, that they are specially chosen and insightful, they alone have access to the 'Truth' and must be followed. They may groom or 'love-bomb' the individual into trusting and following them, and they believe they can treat the other as they wish, manipulating, abusing and harming at will.

There are also families in which one family member, often (but not always) a parent, takes the role of an abusive leader. For example, this parent may be highly narcissistic, controlling the other members of the family, abusing and harming at will. This results in the others being weakened, dependent and unprepared for life outside.

Whilst coercive and cultic groups and relationships are predominantly abusive, that does not mean that other groups and relationships are perfect! Most are healthy in some respects and unhealthy in others: that is human nature. Let's have a look at this continuum.

M3.2 Continuum of 'safe enough' to abusive

Organisations and relationships can be seen on a continuum, from 'safe enough' and generally healthy, through to those that are a mixture of healthy and unhealthy, to those that are almost entirely unhealthy, closed, restrictive and abusive – a thought reform environment, as we will explore later at M10. I illustrate this in Figure M3.1. This can be applied to political, spiritual, religious, therapeutic and all types of groups and relationships.

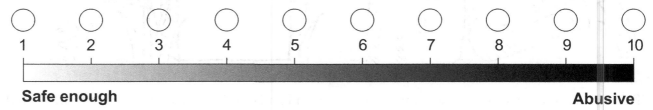

Figure M3.1 Continuum of safe enough to abusive

Some groups may be abusive throughout, whilst others are more abusive in a particular geographical location or part of the organisation. For example, Matt was a member of an international organisation that supported alcoholics. Most of the support groups were benign (somewhere in the middle of the continuum in Figure M3.1), but the one where he was a member became an abusive cult and controlled all the members (around position 9 in Figure M3.1); so his diagnosis of the group was different from some who were in different locations.

It can be helpful and liberating to 'diagnose' your group or relationship, to name it for what it was. When I interviewed Gloria, she said, *"you can't get a treatment if you don't have a diagnosis"*. I really like her analogy of needing to 'diagnose' our coercive, cultic and spiritually abusive setting because, as she says, when we get a diagnosis, we can access the right treatment! The diagnosis is not always obvious, so at this Milestone, you have an opportunity to reflect on *your* experience, chew it over and raise awareness, so you can apply your conclusions.

I will now look at the elements of 'coercive, cultic and spiritually abusive groups and relationships' separately, starting with 'cultic'; then spiritual abuse; and finally coercive control. Your experience may include elements of all or some of these.

As you reflect on these definitions, you can decide for yourself how you want to define your experience, and which elements are most applicable. There are Worksheets for each area and a final one at the end for the overall diagnosis of your setting.

Completing the Worksheets

Within each of the next three sections, there are Worksheets listing typical characteristics that may apply, with space to say how much each aspect applied to your experience, on a scale of 1–10 (1 not applicable and 10 very applicable). If numbering doesn't work for you, then you can just tick those that apply or write notes in the spaces allocated or in your journal.

If you were in more than one setting, please copy the Worksheet, or draw an additional column, or use your journal, so you can consider these points for each one. As some larger organisations may be abusive in some geographical locations and not others, I suggest you focus on the location(s) where you were most involved.

It is important to think about the language used in the definitions. If certain aspects do not quite describe your situation, then please change the wording as appropriate.

If there are a lot of high marks or ticks, this suggests a clear-cut diagnosis of a cult, spiritual abuse or coercive control, respectively. Some situations are more nuanced, with certain aspects marked down and others up. That is also useful information when considering your experience. Some aspects may not be relevant, for example, the points about children being harmed if no children were involved.

Reminder: It is important to think carefully about what you think applies, as you may have blind spots in relation to the severity of control and abuse you have suffered. A trusted friend, therapist (see P5) or another former member may be able to help you highlight blind spots.

Let's now look at 'cult'.

M3.3 Call a cult a cult

I learned from doing my Doctoral research that it is important to "call a cult a cult" – a bit like "call a spade a spade" – to accurately call our experience what it is!

The word 'cult' has several different definitions, but the relevant ones for the purposes of this Workbook are discussed below.

I realise some struggle with the term 'cult', which is often misunderstood or sensationalised. I have included 'coercive' and 'spiritually abusive' in this book to provide alternatives, and to include elements that may differ from the definition of a cult. However, there is a logic behind calling an experience a 'cult' to provide clarity, and because it leads to resources and help that are not available if you simply define the experience as 'abuse', 'spiritual abuse' or 'coercive control'.

Gloria told me how very lost she was after leaving her group, because she did not know how to describe that experience or where to go for help. One day she heard the term 'cult' and suddenly realised that was what she had been in. She put it like this:

I figured out 'OH IT'S A CULT, it was a CULT that's why my life is so ****ed up', excuse my French. I didn't have a diagnosis for what I was getting away from. I put 'cult' into Google and all this information came out, including sites exposing the group, including recovery needs and life issues, and I delved into that. Oh, it's just GREAT to have - you can't get a treatment if you don't have a diagnosis.

Maribel found something similar when she diagnosed her group as a cult:

> Well, if what I experienced was a cult, then I could study cults and come to understand what mind control, or thought reform, is.

Many struggle to label and diagnose their experience as cultic. Perhaps we do not want to believe that our spiritual group, religion, church, therapy group or political organisation could be a cult – it can feel like an insult or we feel foolish – and I understand, it is hard to face.

Some may have been told by the leader that it "wasn't a cult", or perhaps that it was a "good cult" – and this may still prevent us from diagnosing it accurately, or at all. (Probably no current member or leader admits to it being a "bad cult"!)

But if we can see our experience for what it was, we can start to process how it has affected us – the right diagnosis can help us to heal and Walk Free!

Below are two definitions of 'cult' for you to compare and see which best describes your group or relationship.

> "Groups that display three characteristics: totalistic or thought-reform-like practices, a shift from worship of spiritual principles to worship of the person of the guru or leader, and a combination of spiritual quest from below and exploitation, usually economic or sexual, from above." (Lifton, 1999, p. 11)

> "A cult is a group or movement that, to a significant degree,
>
> (a) exhibits great or excessive devotion or dedication to some person, idea, or thing,
> (b) uses a thought-reform program to persuade, control, and socialize members (i.e. to integrate them into the group's unique pattern of relationships, beliefs, values, and practices),
> (c) systematically induces states of psychological dependency in members,
> (d) exploits members to advance the leadership's goals, and
> (e) causes psychological harm to members, their families and the community." (Langone, 1993, p. 5)

You will see I have broken these down in Worksheet M3.1 and added a few points of my own, including some from my Doctoral research, to help you chew over and apply relevant aspects to your setting. There are spaces for you to add any aspects that you feel help to define a cult but are missing. Guidance on completing the Worksheet is at the end of section M3.2.

Worksheet M3.1: Was your setting a cult?

Date _____

	An abusive cult:	Scale 1–10
1	"exhibits great or excessive devotion or dedication to some person, idea or thing"	
2	"uses a thought-reform program to persuade, control, and socialize members (i.e. to integrate them into the group's unique pattern of relationships, beliefs, values, and practices)" (We will look at thought reform in detail later (M10), but for now you could just think about the effects of the group on its members.)	
3	"systematically induces states of psychological dependency in members"	
4	"exploits members to advance the leadership's goals"	
5	"causes psychological harm to members, their families and the community"	
6	uses "totalistic or thought-reform-like practices"	
7	involves "worship of the person of the guru or leader"	
8	combines "spiritual quest from below [by seekers or members] and exploitation, usually economic or sexual, from above [the leadership]".	
9	"engenders an 'us' and 'them' mentality, fear and rejection of the world outside the group" (Jenkinson, 2016, p. 84)	
10	(if children are present) allows harm to children's physical or mental health or development, for example, because group practices are more important than their well-being, or parents are not allowed to care for their own children, or parents are overly zealous and do not focus on their children's well-being	
11	is hard to leave – if you do well, you simply move to the next level within the cult rather than 'graduating' and leaving, as you would in healthy therapy or education, for example	
12		
13		
14		
15		

Having completed this Worksheet, are you able to draw any conclusions about the setting you were in, and whether it was a cult?

M3.4 Spiritual or religious abuse

Spiritual abuse (which includes religious trauma and abuse) can be present in some coercive control and one-on-one relationships, as well as in fringe spiritual groups, sects and cults. It also arises in mainstream religions, which may be assumed by society to be safe and moral spaces, for example, churches, temples and mosques. When spiritual abuse occurs in mainstream contexts, harmful abuse may be hidden behind practices and traditions that have been accepted for generations, and may therefore be overlooked, minimised or unacknowledged.

Spiritual abuse can occur when a leader takes advantage of their followers in a spiritual or religious setting. They are in a position of authority. Some have trained within, and were appointed by, a widely accepted organisation. Others are self-selected and believe they are a representative, or even an incarnation, of a 'god' or higher spiritual being. When the only route to 'god' or spiritual enlightenment is through the leader, the power imbalance can lead to followers being coerced to hand over their life, thinking and decision-making to that leader, and to become dependent on them.

Spiritual abuse can lead to sexual, psychological and emotional abuse, and has been "called a rape of both the soul and the mind" (Griffo, 2021, p. 1). It can destroy healthy spirituality. For example, an individual who had viewed God as benign and loving may be left feeling he is a monstrous presence in their life. Their sense of hope, spiritual identity or soul may be damaged or destroyed. Their aspiration to be good may be used and twisted, affecting the very essence of their being. Spiritual abuse can negatively affect an individual's sense of self and personal identity, resulting in a pseudo-identity (Jenkinson, 2008).

We will look at three definitions of spiritual abuse. If you were in a spiritual or religious group or relationship, you might like to see if your experience fits with these. You will see there are some similarities to the definition of a cult, although it is expressed somewhat differently.

Spiritual abuse can be difficult to identify in real life. I hope these definitions help you to recognise the differences between spiritual or religious abuse, and acceptable behaviour and practices.

> "Spiritual abuse is the mistreatment of a person who is in need of help, support or greater spiritual empowerment, with the result of weakening, undermining or decreasing that person's spiritual empowerment." (Johnson & VanVonderen, 1991, p. 20)

> Spiritual abuse "is coercion and control of one individual by another in a spiritual context. The target experiences spiritual abuse as a deeply emotional personal attack. This abuse may include: manipulation and exploitation, enforced accountability, censorship of decision making, requirements for secrecy and silence, pressure to conform, misuse of scripture or the pulpit to control behaviour, requirement of obedience to the abuser, the suggestion that the abuser has a 'divine' position and isolation from others, especially those external to the abusive context." (Oakley, 2013, pp. 21–22)

> "Spiritual abuse results when individuals are deceived and or otherwise manipulated in ways that cause detrimental changes to the manipulated individual. Spiritual abuse is especially acute when it harms core elements of the self, including a person's relationship to God, religious/philosophical beliefs, self-determination, and capacity to think independently. Though often associated with cultic groups, spiritual abuse may also occur in mainstream denominations when pastors or others misuse their authority or when individuals violate the ethical boundaries of proselytizing or other kinds of influence situations." (Spiritual Safe Haven Network, n.d.)

You will see I have broken these aspects down in Worksheet M3.2, and added some of my own, to help you chew over and apply relevant aspects to your setting. There are spaces for you to add any aspects that you feel help to define spiritual abuse but are missing. Guidance on completing the Worksheet is at the end of section M3.2. As we are considering spiritual abuse, the question here is whether each aspect occurs in a spiritual or religious context.

Worksheet M3.2: Was your setting spiritual abuse?

Date _____

	Spiritual abuse includes	Scale 1–10
1	The mistreatment of a person in need of help, support or greater spiritual empowerment	
2	Weakening, undermining or decreasing a person's spiritual empowerment	
3	Coercion and control of one individual by another	
4	Manipulation	
5	Exploitation	
6	Enforced accountability	
7	Censorship of decision-making	
8	Requirements for secrecy and silence	
9	Pressure to conform	
10	Misuse of scripture or holy texts to control behaviour	
11	Misuse of the pulpit/preaching to control behaviour	
12	Requirement of obedience to the abuser or leadership	
13	The suggestion that the abuser or leadership has a 'divine' position	
14	Pressure to isolate from others, especially those external to the abusive context	
15	A view of God or a higher spiritual being as punitive or monstrous	
16	Using this version of God as an excuse or reason to abuse and control	
17	Being deceived or manipulated in damaging ways	
18	Harm to core elements of identity	
19	Harm to someone's relationship with God and religious/philosophical beliefs	
20	Harm to self-determination (the ability to decide for oneself)	
21	Harm to the capacity to think independently	
22		
23		
24		
25		

Having completed this Worksheet, are you able to draw any conclusions about the setting you were in, and whether it involved spiritual abuse?

M3.5 What is coercive control?

In this section, we will look at 'coercive control'. This term is often associated with domestic situations and partner abuse, but it also applies to groups and relationships.

In domestic situations, 'controlling or coercive behaviour' can be a criminal offence in the UK, and some other countries. The UK Home Office says this is "a type of domestic abuse. The abuser uses violence, threats, puts them down or scares and frightens the victim. They do this so they can control the victim and make them do things they don't want to. This behaviour often happens with other abusive behaviours, including physical, sexual and financial abuse" (2022, p. 2). The Home Office list of controlling or coercive behaviours is included in Worksheet M3.3.

Evan Stark states that "Coercive control … is ongoing and its perpetrators use various means to hurt, humiliate, intimidate, exploit, isolate, and dominate their victims. Like hostages, victims of coercive control are frequently deprived of money, food, access to communication or transportation, and other survival resources even as they are cut off from family, friends, and other supports. … [It] undermines a victim's physical and psychological integrity. But the main means used to establish control is the microregulation of everyday behaviors" (2007, p. 5).

Coercive control also applies to those who have been in high demand and controlling abusive groups and relationships. I find former members often recognise its application to cultic and spiritually abusive experiences. At M10, we will explore how coercive control works with thought reform (or 'brainwashing').

Worksheet M3.3 provides an opportunity to chew over and apply relevant aspects to your setting. There are spaces for you to add any aspects that you feel help to define coercive control but are missing. Guidance on completing the Worksheet is above at the end of section M3.2.

I do not usually use the term 'victim', but as it is in the Home Office guidance, I have left it in. This Worksheet focusses on behaviours, rather than the underlying dynamics or psychological effects: these are explored throughout this Workbook.

Worksheet M3.3: Was your setting coercive control?

Date _____

	Coercive control includes... Note: Items 1–18 are from the Home Office guidance (2022, pp. 4–5). Items 19–21 are from Evan Stark (2007, p. 5).	Scale 1–10
1	Physical violence or threats of violence	
2	Sexual assault or abuse or threats	
3	Controlling the victim's daily activities and behaviour, for example controlling their time, what they wear, when they eat and sleep	
4	Financial abuse such as taking all the victim's money	
5	Controlling the victim using social media and phones	
6	Forcing the victim to do something that they don't want to do	
7	Threatening to give out information about the victim's sex life	
8	Telling lies to family members or the local community, including posting photos on social media	
9	Stopping the victim from making friends	
10	Using immigration status to threaten the victim	
11	Threats of being put into care (particularly for disabled or elderly victims)	
12	Separating the victim from family, friends and professionals who may be trying to support them	
13	Stopping the victim from communicating with others	
14	Stopping the victim from getting health or social care	
15	Stopping the victim from using birth control methods; or forcing them to get an abortion	
16	Using drugs or alcohol to control a victim	
17	Threatening to take the children away or harm them	
18	Harming or threatening to harm or give away pets	
19	Being deprived of money, food, access to communication or transportation	
20	Being cut off from family, friends and other supports	
21	Microregulation of everyday behaviours	
22		
23		
24		
25		

Having completed this Worksheet, are you able to draw any conclusions about the setting you were in, and whether it involved coercive control?

M3.6 Where did your cultic setting sit on the continuum?

It may help to revisit the continuum in Figure M3.1 and think about where your group or relationship sits, now you have had an opportunity to reflect on it from the three different perspectives. You could mark Figure M3.2 below to show this.

Date _____

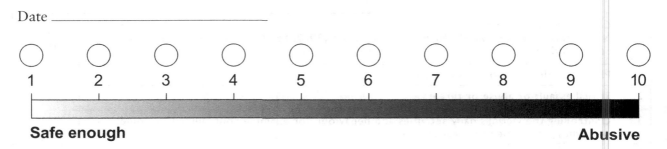

Safe enough   **Abusive**

Figure M3.2 Where did your cultic setting sit on the continuum?

Task: Compare your experience with another coercive, cultic and/or spiritually abusive setting

It can be helpful to hear life stories from former members of cultic settings different from our own. This helps us:

- realise we are not the only person who has experienced such things
- feel less alone
- highlight aspects of our experience that are not 'normal', but that we have accepted as such
- recognise what was wrong and abusive. It can be hard to see something as abuse when it is also a part of daily life – when, for example, spiritual abuse is "the air we breathed", as one former member described it to me.

So, you could choose a published former member's life story. This could be a book, podcast, film, TV programme or website. You could compare your different cultic cultures, and apply the diagnoses and definitions to their setting. This is not about whether others' experiences were better or worse than your own, as only you really know what it was like for you. But knowing about others can help us make sense of our own experience.

M3.7 What is the overall diagnosis of your group or relationship?

Now we have considered all three possible diagnoses, you have an opportunity, in Worksheet M3.4, to combine the coercive, cultic and spiritually abusive elements into an overall diagnosis of your own.
   To help you do this, you could consider:

1. What aspects from each were most significant in your situation? You could revisit each section and use coloured markers to highlight those most applicable.
2. Can you pull these together and summarise your experience for yourself?

   You could write your answer in the space allocated or in your journal.

Worksheet M3.4: Your diagnosis combining coercive, cultic and spiritually abusive elements

Date _____

_____

_____

_____

_____

_____

_____

_____

_____

_____

_____

_____

_____

_____

Now you have thought about the nature of your cultic setting, diagnosed it and understood it more clearly, your baggage will hopefully be a little lighter and you can continue your journey along the road to recovery and growth. The next Milestone 4 helps you to reflect on how merged or 'confluent' you were with your group and/or leader.

How confluent were you?

We have now reached Milestone 4 where we can sit and unpack the baggage related to confluence.

So, what is confluence, and how do we become confluent?

M4.1 What is confluence?

The term 'confluence' literally means 'flowing together' – where two rivers merge it is called 'the confluence'. I use it here to refer to a merged state, where our boundaries with others are blurry and indistinct, even non-existent, where we become enmeshed or entangled. When people are confluent, they merge and "behave as if they are one person ... without recognising the boundaries between them and the ways in which they are different". This merging can include "beliefs, attitudes or feelings" (Clarkson, 1999, p. 62). This often happens in coercive groups and relationships.

In a healthy free setting, some confluence can be life-enhancing, such as when we are sharing a creative experience. It may also be a natural by-product of being part of a relationship or group, for example, marriage, partnership, friendship or having a shared goal. Healthy confluence is limited and intentional, and it is possible to withdraw. It only becomes unhealthy when we do not or cannot withdraw from that merged or confluent state, which results in no boundaries, or weak boundaries (Clarkson, 1999).

DOI: 10.4324/9781003305798-10

We are more prone to confluence when we suffer abuse, which is "an assault on the boundaries – physical, emotional, personal" (Kepner, 2003, p. 65) and impacts our sense of identity. (We will consider the effects of trauma at M7.)

When we are confluent:

- We don't know where we end and the other begins.
- We are not autonomous individuals, that is, we are not independent, nor free to make our own decisions in our own best interests.
- We do not tolerate differences but expect likeness (Clarkson, 1999, p. 63). This is relevant in a cultic, thought reform, environment where we have to comply and be what we are expected to be – and perhaps we expect others to be a certain way as well.
- We don't allow ourselves to become aware of what we are unhappy about – we suppress our doubts (M2), awareness of concerns and critical thinking (M5.2).
- We are not in full contact with our authentic identity, the 'real me'. Instead, we are stuck in the pseudo-identity, serving the cultic setting.
- We are dependent – on the leader and the other members.
- We are not growing or developing as a person.
- Introjects flow in (see M5).
- Our locus of control is externalised (M1.7).
- We become separated from, and reject, whatever does not fit with our narrow view of life. This means our lives are reduced to just being focussed on the cultic setting and what is expected of us there, and may exclude virtually all other interests, people and things.

We could picture confluence as two shapes that are overlapping and partly, or completely, merged. In Figure M4.1, you can see the large circle indicating the cultic setting and leadership, overlapping the member, the smaller head shape. The dotted line indicates the member's broken boundaries.

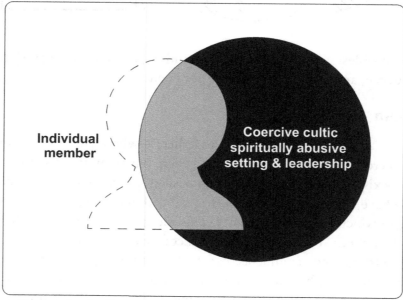

Figure M4.1 What confluence looks like

M4.2 The start of confluence – reciprocity and the favour

For those who join, confluence may begin early on in our contact with the abusive group or individual, especially if they do us a favour. This favour will likely hook into our natural need to 'reciprocate', which means to give something back in exchange. Cialdini (2001) refers to this as 'the rule of reciprocity'.

The favour can take many forms and may be small or large. A free book or meal, or a bed for the night, may mean we feel obliged to become more involved. At the other extreme, an offer of unconditional love, meaning in life, even eternal salvation, may mean that nothing less than a life commitment is called for. Abusive leaders often portray themselves as martyrs, giving their time and their lives for the sake of their followers. "How could anyone be so ungrateful as to walk away?" is what they might imply to the unsuspecting member, or potential member, who is manipulated into feeling that they owe them something in exchange for the favour (Martin, 1993). Thus powerful dynamics are created that draw in the new member and make leaving hard.

The principle of reciprocity also applies to those born and/or raised in the cultic setting. As they grow up, they are likely to be told often how fortunate or privileged they are to be there, and how much they owe to the leadership and other members. Any failure to obey and conform is, by implication, shocking and ungrateful.

Even when the reality of life as a member is very far from seeming like a 'favour', there is a perpetuation of the sense, or the illusion, that the member owes a huge debt. Just being allowed to be a member (belonging to these 'special' people), or being accepted back after leaving and returning, can be presented as a huge favour.

Figure M4.2 illustrates how we can become progressively more confluent.

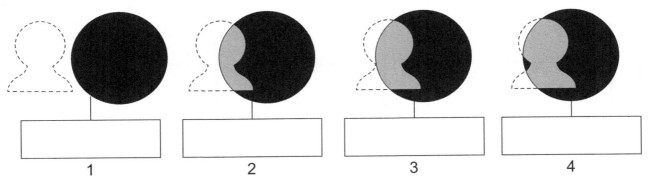

Figure M4.2 Becoming progressively more confluent

Before saying more about confluence, you might like to consider what favours were offered to you as you joined, or after you became a member; what impact this had on you; and what you feel about this now. Here is an example from my life, so you can see what I mean:

Favour	Impact	What do you feel about this now?
I was promised healing and eternal salvation and told that only they could provide it.	I was so grateful that they allowed me to join, and that I could be in a place which offered special privileges that could not be found anywhere else (even though daily life was miserable). It was impossible even to think about leaving.	I feel angry that I was tricked and lied to. I was cross with myself for a long time for being taken in, but as I have understood the dynamics, I have let myself off the hook. I now realise that they used the rule of reciprocity to hook me in, and promised me so much to ensure I became confluent, indoctrinated, socialised and psychologically entrapped.

You could add your examples to the Worksheet or in your journal.

Worksheet M4.1: What 'favours' caused you to feel you needed to reciprocate?

Date _____

Favour	Impact	What do you feel about this now?

M4.3 Living in confluence

Confluence occurs when we are in an environment where we have to submit, be obedient and conform, or we desperately want or need to be 'good' and compliant.

In a cultic setting, both our thoughts and our actions may become restricted, with fear of punishment for thinking or acting in ways that are not approved. We are unlikely to be able to think for ourselves because this may be regarded as being 'rebellious', 'from the ego', 'the flesh' or whatever loaded language was used to describe being independent and autonomous (for more about loaded language see M10.6). The 'wrong' actions may lead to severe, perhaps arbitrary, punishments.

We, therefore, become afraid of doing, or even thinking, the 'wrong' things, and it seems that the only safe course is to become confluent, to eliminate those parts of ourselves which might get us into trouble. For example, in the Community, I worked hard at doing the 'right' thing as much as possible to keep from being punished – told off or 'rebuked'. I was rebuked so often that I became timid and did whatever I could to ensure it didn't happen again. This resulted in me losing my autonomous authentic individual voice and confidence in my own mind. I was terrified much of the time and became almost completely confluent with the Community.

If you experienced something similar and could not withdraw from the confluence and enmeshment, you may have felt claustrophobic, stifled and like you were caught in a sticky spider's web. You may have tried to break free, only to have that freedom taken away from you again. I have told in my own story (P2.2) about the time I spent a few weeks visiting my father away from the Community, and wrote to the leader, Simon, asking to change community households. This indicated I was thinking for myself a little and expressing an independent desire – becoming slightly less confluent. Simon's severe and manipulative response caused me to panic, and quickly re-established my wavering confluence.

In terms of Figure M4.2, I had been almost totally overlapping with the Community before going away (4 on a scale of 1–4); when I was away with my father and connecting with my authentic identity, I began to move apart slightly (2 or 3), but after Simon's letter, I moved quickly back to almost fully overlapping (4). I ran back to doing what I was told, reconnecting with my pseudo-identity. In my fear, I also lost my voice and sadly did not tell my father, who might have challenged my confluence.

Those who are born and raised will most likely be highly, perhaps completely, confluent throughout their childhood and membership. In cultic settings, children are generally not helped to become the individuals they are or to develop critical thinking skills (M5.2). If they try to establish some autonomy, they may be punished, or be labelled a 'rebel', or something similar.

Some struggle against confluence. For example, Kevin told me that, on the one hand, he believed what he was taught in his religious group. He complied with the steps he was expected to take as he grew up, such as baptism. On the other hand, he longed to leave and didn't really believe what he was taught. He was split between his pseudo-identity, that confluent part of him which bought into the cultic beliefs, and his authentic identity which did not. He eventually left but was shunned by his family and the group. After leaving, both physically and psychologically, he stopped being confluent and he was no longer split; but he had to face the pain and loss he experienced on breaking free, losing his family and being labelled an 'apostate'. (Apostate simply means someone who has left a religion, but some groups and researchers use the term in a derogatory way.)

For most, there is an expectation that membership is a total commitment, and members cannot have divided loyalties (and they cannot, therefore, be anything but confluent). They give their time, resources and selves. There may be total confluence, with no doubts, little or no thought of leaving, and almost no internal criticism of the group or leader. When I was a member, at the most controlling time, I was totally confluent and do not remember having doubts. I did not think about leaving until the month before I left, when I started to think for myself a bit more.

For others, confluence may be partial, as they retain some sense of their authentic identity, which shows up in doubts, or inner dialogue that is critical of the setting (M2). Some are able to hold onto something of their authentic identity by making their own choices, however small. For example, Harriet hid a musical instrument, one small link to her life before and her authentic identity, although in all other aspects she was confluent.

The level of confluence can change over time. Some gradually become confluent as the expectation of total commitment evolves and is then enforced. They are like the frog being slowly heated in water: by the time it might realise it is in hot water, it is too late to jump out (Jenkinson, 2011). If it was thrown into boiling water, it would jump straight out! For others, the confluence breaks down and their authentic identity begins to re-emerge while still a member. For example, some begin to plan their exit before they leave physically (M1).

In Figure M4.3, I illustrate how it was for me at the worst time in the Community. There was very little of the 'real me'. I knew when I needed to go to the toilet, and sometimes when I was hungry, although meals were regimented. I couldn't choose what clothes to buy (and wore shared clothes) or when to see family. All my resources went into the cult. I hope this helps you to do the exercise for yourself.

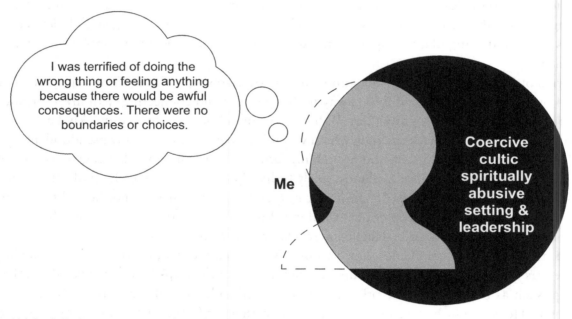

Figure M4.3 Gillie's experience of confluence

It is vital that we identify and challenge confluence, and move away from it to be our own person. In this section, you have the opportunity to think about how confluent you were, and how confluent your family were.

Can you identify with any of the situations and examples above, or was your experience different? In Worksheet M4.2, or in your journal, you can think about how confluent you were with the leader and other members by ticking a numbered box. Were you totally overlapping, or was there some space for your doubts, your independent and critical thinking, your authentic identity? If you were in more than one setting, or the level of confluence was different at different times, then you could tick several boxes and add dates to indicate when these happened; or photocopy the Worksheet; or replicate it in your journal and continue your reflection.

Worksheet M4.2: How confluent were you?

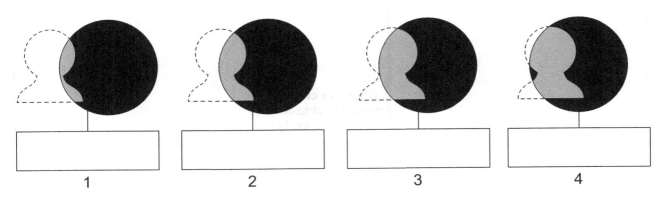

| 1 | 2 | 3 | 4 |

In this next Worksheet, you can reflect on how it was for you and your family members.

Worksheet M4.3: How confluent were members of your family?

If your family were also in the setting, you might like to think about how confluent each family member was, or still are if they remain members, and illustrate this in the diagram below.

The circle indicates the coercive, cultic and spiritually abusive setting. As an example, perhaps your parents and other family members were highly confluent and in the centre, and you sat partly outside or on the edge. You could depict each member of your family with circles or head shapes.

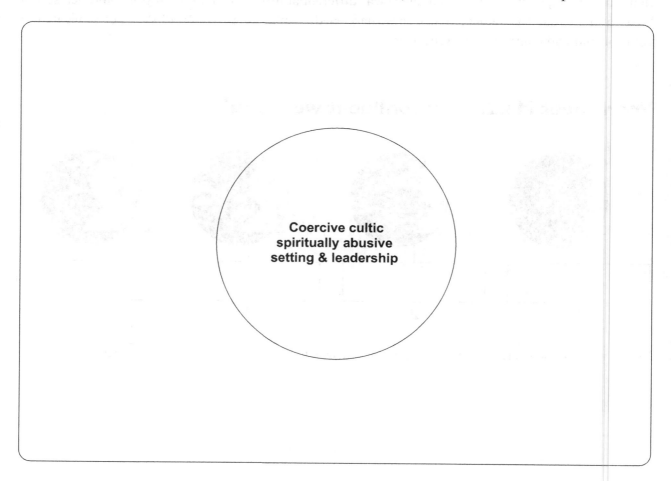

One of the purposes of the whole Walking Free journey is to undo unhealthy confluence and to become autonomous. Understanding how confluent you were is an important part of undoing its effects, and I suggest you continue to work on this as we journey on to the next Milestones.

Now you have explored this, your baggage will be a little lighter and you can continue your journey along the road to recovery and growth. The next Milestone 5 explores the idea of 'introjects', critical thinking and phobias, and gives you the opportunity to apply these to your experience.

Introjects, critical thinking and phobias

We are now at Milestone 5 and are making great progress! You could sit and unpack your baggage as I introduce you to an important issue – understanding introjects. I will explain what an introject is, so you can identify and challenge those that still affect you. To help with this, I also cover critical thinking skills, and handling those introjects that are scary and may have become phobias. This is an important Milestone, and it is one I encourage you to keep in mind and return to as often as you need to. You will notice I refer to introjects quite often throughout the Walking Free Workbook.

M5.1 What is an introject?

An introject is a belief or behaviour that we have taken into ourselves without consciously assessing it. It is 'swallowed whole' and remains sitting in our psychological system like a lump of unchewed and undigested food in our gut. The pressures put on us within the cultic setting make it almost impossible to 'chew over' what we are told, or what happens to us, and so these things may still remain within us and cause discomfort.

Introjects can cause us to view ourselves in negative ways and to act in negative ways towards ourselves. One way of telling if something is an introject is when you find yourself thinking that you

DOI: 10.4324/9781003305798-11

'must', 'should' or 'ought' – for example, you should be different or ought to have acted in a certain way. This is because introjects imply you are not okay as you are.

This is probably evidence that you have taken in a view of yourself that induces guilt and shame; and developed a cultic pseudo-identity. (I introduced the idea of pseudo-identity at P1.4 and will explain more at M6). For example, you may feel you 'should' be nice to everyone, and that you 'should not' stand up for yourself because it is rude or 'egotistical' – but this is likely to leave you open to exploitation and weakens your boundaries.

Realising that these introjected beliefs about ourselves are NOT the 'real me', not our authentic identity or feelings, but have become part of our cultic pseudo-identity, can bring HOPE. We are different from the person we were told we are and believed we are. This is important because introjects and false beliefs about ourselves can lead to despair and challenge our mental health.

Self-care is very important, and if you become overwhelmed you could remind yourself of Oasis Lake, and revisit your Safe Enough Space (P3.1.1) or the tips for grounding (P3.1.2). Or you might need to find another person, such as a trusted friend or therapist (P5), to talk this through with.

When we are confluent (M4) and our boundaries are weak or non-existent, and when we are suppressing our doubts (M2) and not using our critical thinking (M5.2), we lack a defence against introjects. Figure M5.1 illustrates this. Introjects flow in where the individual member is confluent with the cultic setting, indicated by the arrow.

Confluence makes it nearly impossible to stop the introjects flowing in, because we are frozen in a kind of trance, unable to think clearly for ourselves. I call this a 'confluential trance' (Jenkinson, 2019). This is a state in which we take in what we are told, but do not chew it over – we have no 'filter' or boundary.

I will now look at how the idea of introjects informs our understanding of our identity.

M5.1.1 Introjects and identity

When we introject something in a cultic setting, whatever is taken in sits in our psychological system undigested and adds layers to our identity. The introjects define us, they cause us to assume we are something we are not (more at M6).

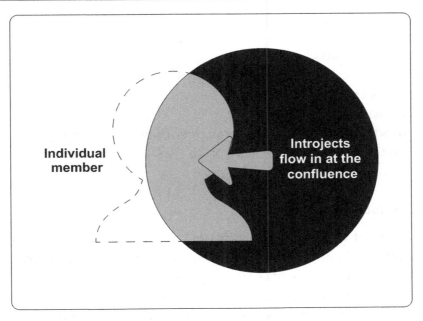

Figure M5.1 Introjects flow in when we are confluent

So, how do we recover from this? Well, it can be helpful to think of the process of introjection and recovery using the analogy of teeth, food and chewing, and how identity develops by stages in children.

As toothless babies, we all take in pre-digested food, but as we grow up, we develop teeth. We begin to chew over our food and, if we are free to, decide what we like and what we do not (Jenkinson, 2008; Perls et al., 1951).

When food is properly chewed and digested, it is absorbed and integrated by our body and it becomes part of us. It can be used by our body for nourishment, for us to grow and develop. When food sits unchewed and undigested in the stomach, it is usual to want to get it out of our system and 'throw it up'. For example, if we managed to swallow a carrot whole, it would sit in our stomach, undigested, causing pain and not nourishing us. We might not be able to vomit it up or poo it out. It would be introjected!

Ideally, as we grow, the process of chewing over and choosing what to swallow is encouraged by our caregivers.

This is similar to the process of building identity. Our identity develops as we encounter supportive caregivers and other people, and ideas and principles for living. Ideally, we take in, chew over and assimilate what is good for us (rejecting what is not), and this becomes restructured and used by our psychological system, building our authentic identity. Those lucky enough to grow up in a free setting usually, therefore, learn to work out what is good for them and make choices about what they like and believe, and how they want to behave – and they are able to reject the rest. That is, they can, to a large degree, chew over what they are experiencing or being told.

If we cannot chew over what is taken in (or forced in), we accept the introject as true. It is not digested or integrated and does not nourish us. It does not become part of our authentic identity, and we do not develop and grow. Instead, it becomes part of the cultic pseudo-identity. This applies both to those born and raised, and those who joined.

Reminder: Our pseudo-identity is the term I use to describe the person we have to be in the cultic setting, which forms in order for us to be a member. It overlays our authentic identity – the 'real me'.

Introjects can take many forms including:

- things we are told about ourselves
- how we see ourselves because of how we are treated by others
- behaviours that are expected of us
- a belief system or ideology we are taught
- things we take in without thinking them through or fully understanding them, simply because an authority figure is telling us what to believe or do
- 'loaded language': we will briefly cover this next.

M5.1.2 Introjects as 'loaded language'

Loaded language is one of the eight components of thought reform (M10) and is made up of the thought-stopping words and phrases which are used automatically, without critically thinking what they mean. This clichéd language prevents us from fully thinking and feeling. It is introjected and sits in our system undigested. We need to chew it over and challenge it, one loaded word or concept at a time.

Words and phrases from holy texts and cultic literature are often applied as loaded language. The individual has to introject the interpretation of the text as it is presented to them, and is not given space to think critically about what it means.

In the examples of introjects below, the term 'sinful' is loaded language. It uncritically assumes that an individual is a bad person, a 'sinner', who is disapproved of by 'God'. Feeling good about oneself may be negatively interpreted as 'sinful' or 'pride'.

There is an opportunity to think more about loaded language at M10.6.

It is vital to identify *and* challenge introjects, and we will explore this next.

M5.1.3 Identifying and challenging introjects

Identifying introjects is only half the story. We need to learn to put challenges into words so we process and get rid of them – and this helps to unlayer our pseudo-identity.

In order to challenge and get rid of introjects (and the pseudo-identity), we need to become *aware of what is not truly ours* – that is, we need to raise awareness of and identify what is ours (our authentic identity) and what belongs to the cultic setting (our pseudo-identity).

I know this can be hard, especially for those who are born and/or raised. This is because many deeply and totally believe all they were told. For many, the all-or-nothing, polarised thinking may be deeply entrenched. For example, if it is implied for many years that you are a bad person, you may have believed it and still believe it. Judgements about our character and our identity can go deep, making it hard to connect or reconnect with who we really are. Our authentic identity is layered over by these introjected beliefs.

One thing that can help is to acquire a selective and balanced attitude towards anything that is or was offered to you, using critical thinking (more at M5.2). We can develop the ability to examine critically (bite and chew over) what we are/were told, so as to decide whether to eliminate it (vomit or poo it out, metaphorically speaking!), or digest it and extract its healthy nourishment.

This is a balanced approach. Some things from the cultic setting may be worth holding onto, things that have truly been assimilated and become yours. For example, you may have made genuine friendships or learned things as a member that are useful to you on leaving. You can chew those things over and make a decision about what to hold onto and what to get rid of. Fred was in a cultic setting with a huge library that he could access whenever he wanted. He said of the things he learned there:

> It is still a wealth of knowledge that I carry with me, it's mine and I can use it in whatever way I see fit. It's all mine, it doesn't belong to anyone else.

You have an opportunity to reflect on what you learned at M14.

> Identifying introjects without challenging them may be counterproductive, because they will remain in our system causing harm, and we are in danger of simply reiterating them. It is best to chew them over, not just leave them.
>
> Debunking introjects is a vital part of unlayering the pseudo-identity and building an autonomous authentic identity after leaving, helping us to Walk Free and flourish!

Here are some examples of introjects to help you identify your own.

Examples of introjects are:

- "The only thing that matters is the mission or vision of the group."
- "I shouldn't think about myself, that is selfish."
- "Holidays are selfish and a waste of time."
- "I must never rest, but must burn out for God (and/or the leader and/or for 'freedom')."
- "Our group is the only one with the Truth."
- "I will cause serious negativity and harm in the universe if I eat anything but vegetarian/vegan/ approved food."
- "I will attract negative energy if I don't turn anticlockwise while preparing food."
- "There will be serious consequences to mankind and to the earth if I do not continue recruiting new members and/or meditating and/or attending church/temple, etc."
- "I am 'bourgeois', shallow and materialistic if I collect 'things' and live in a nice house."
- "I ought not to let people know I am good at something, that is pride."
- "If I don't do the therapy/spiritual practice/meditation techniques, exactly as I have been told, the world will come to an end."
- "World pandemics and disasters are signs of 'the end times', or a punishment for 'sin'."
- "If someone doesn't like me, it is my fault and there must be something wrong with me."
- "If the leader/ship says something about me, or about anything, it must be true."
- "Nothing anyone says is true, unless they are a member."
- "Only the leader/cultic setting can understand what I have been through."
- "I cannot tell anyone what has happened to me because that would be a betrayal of the other members and there will be terrible consequences."
- "I deserved to be punished because I am a bad person."

Some of these may sound strange, even ridiculous, to you, but someone else accepted them as facts. It may be interesting to consider whether some statements that you accept would sound strange and ridiculous to others!

You have an opportunity to highlight your own introjects in Worksheet M5.1, and to challenge them in Worksheets M5.2 and M5.3. For example, the challenge to "If I think about myself, I am selfish" could be, "It is essential that I think about myself, because as an adult I am free to be responsible for myself, and no one else can live my life for me".

If the introject is a religious belief, then it may be helpful (if this is not triggering for you) to challenge it using the Bible or other holy text. For example, the challenge could be, "The Bible says that I should love God and love my neighbour AS I love myself. It is therefore OK to love myself and the introject is a faulty interpretation, which enables the leadership to control and manipulate. I am allowed to think about myself and it is not selfish."

> **Reminder:** For some, it is especially difficult to challenge introjects because the introject is about *not* challenging! You are likely to have been taught that doubting or challenging the leader, the cultic setting or the beliefs is 'rebellious', 'from Satan' or 'the flesh' or 'negative energy', 'bourgeois mentality', etc. While this can be hard to do, it is really important to keep challenging and break through the hold of those introjects. If it is particularly scary, you can have a look at M5.3 about introjects that become phobias.

Before the Worksheets, let's look at how introjects sometimes come in cascades.

M5.1.4 Cascades of introjects

A waterfall or landslide can be a cascade – water, or rocks and soil, slipping in stages down a steep slope, building momentum all the way. Similarly, an introject often leads to another and another: they cascade down like a landslide.

Here are some examples of cascades of introjects, and how one leads to another and another:

The cult's (monstrous) version of 'god' is real
 I must do what this 'god' says
  If I disobey, I am doomed
   I will suffer terribly
    [And so I live in terror and remain confluent]

It is selfish and lazy to need a rest
 If I think about myself, I am selfish and lazy
  I must therefore suppress myself and keep working hard
   Tiredness is a sign of laziness and lack of commitment
    I must work harder
     [And so I exhaust myself and burn out]

Pride is a sin
 If I think I can do something well I am proud
  I need to suppress my pride
   I am a bad person because I was proud of what I did
    [And so I suppress myself and stop myself achieving or doing things I really want to do, that give me pleasure]

The leader knows best because they are the only one with the Truth and cannot be questioned or disobeyed
 If I say what I think I am disobedient
  Disobedience is serious because it can cause harm to the leader and the group (and even the whole world)
   I must therefore be obedient and do what I am told
    [And so I suppress myself and remain confluent]

If you are addressing a cascade of introjects, the challenges can follow a similar pattern. The first cascade of introjects above can be challenged thus:

The cult's monster 'god' is NOT real
> I don't have to do what this 'god' says
>> So, I am not disobedient and am not doomed
>>> I will not suffer
>>>> I am free!

M5.1.5 Worksheets

It helps to become practiced at highlighting, identifying and challenging our personal introjects, and determining what is right for us, as we find the freedom to make our own personal choices. You probably already identify with some of the introjects above, and you are likely to have many more of your own – you can add these to the Worksheets that follow.

> I encourage you to go on identifying and challenging introjects throughout your Walking Free journey. You don't have to identify them all in one go. I suggest you think of some now and capture them in the Worksheets or in your journal, but also keep noting them as you go through the Workbook. They are likely to arise in every Milestone.

These Worksheets are designed to help you identify and challenge introjects.

Worksheet M5.1 is to help you identify your own introjects in various categories. If you are struggling to identify these, it may help to consider the examples above. For each category, see if you can put one or two introjects into words in the table or your journal.

Worksheet M5.1: Identifying introjects

Date _____

Categories of Introjects	Can you put into words an introject from this category?	
Ideas		
Behaviours		
Rituals		
Beliefs about the world or society		
Beliefs about the status of the leader/ship		
Negative beliefs from what you were told about yourself		
Negative messages from the abusive behaviour towards you		
An exaggerated sense of importance		
An internalised harsh critic (where you speak or think harshly and critically to and about yourself)		
'Musts', 'shoulds' and 'oughts'		
Loaded language		
Anything else		

Worksheet M5.2 is to help you challenge the introjects you have identified, and others that you identify as you visit the other Milestones. It is important to put both the introject and the challenge into words, as part of the process of chewing over. If this is difficult, come back to this once you have looked at critical thinking (section M5.2). You could fill out the table or use your journal.

Worksheet M5.2: Challenging introjects

Date _____

Introject	Challenge

There is an opportunity in Worksheet M5.3 to identify and challenge a cascade of introjects. You may like to photocopy this or use your journal, so you can work on others.

Worksheet M5.3: Identify and challenge cascades of introjects

Date _____

Can you **identify** a cascade of introjects?

_____

_____

_____

_____

Can you **challenge** that cascade of introjects?

_____

_____

_____

_____

_____

We will now have a look at critical thinking.

M5.2 Critical thinking

The idea of 'chewing over' is a metaphor for using our critical thinking. We need this to keep us safe in life and to challenge introjects.

So what is critical thinking?

- It is the "ability to examine one's beliefs and consider the possibility of changing them" (Baker, 2012).
- It is carefully thinking through what is being said to us, so we have a basis for what we believe and act on.
- It allows us to consider whether we are adopting false ideas that need to be examined and possibly discarded (Baker, 2012). This is not just about ideological, political, religious or spiritual beliefs but also what we believe about ourselves.

It allows us to face our suppressed doubts and chew them over.

In a cultic setting, we have to do as we are told rather than using our critical thinking – which would be likely to lead to doubts and they don't want that (M2)!

This is what two people said about critical thinking:

> Critical thinking is processing how people get deceived, how they are gonna be able to see through the manipulations that people are putting on them. [Dillon]

> [Cultic behaviour] was completely out of balance with the more rational critical thinking, and 'can you have a basis for what you are saying?' - in other words, learning about how to be sceptical. [Marietta]

The idea of being 'sceptical' may have been seen as a negative thing in the cultic setting, and the word itself may be loaded language for you. But it is an important part of critical thinking. It means you allow yourself to face your doubts. If you are sceptical, you are not easily persuaded of things without a good argument and convincing evidence.

On leaving, it can be hugely challenging and painful to criticise an idea, or decide what we like, want to do and believe – and what we don't. But it is essential that we do so, in order to Walk Free. It is like exercising a muscle that has not been used: perhaps painfully and tentatively at first, but with growing confidence as it becomes stronger.

Gloria, a second generation former member, refers to the process of facing the reality of what happened to her, and the impact emotionally and practically. This included using her critical thinking, which she calls 'psychological chemotherapy'. She said it was worth going through even though it was extremely hard:

GLORIA: I didn't think it would take as long or be as hard. It was like psychological chemotherapy. And it is very, very painful to go back and pull it apart and realise that you can't trust everybody you used to love, and that you couldn't trust them then. And you then repeated the patterns with new people who were not trustworthy, and who were manipulative, because that is all you know, and that's what you defined as love. It's INCREDIBLY PAINFUL. It's psychological chemotherapy, you need to go through the chemotherapy to kill the cancer, it's REALLY ugly, it's REALLY painful, and it's the only way out.

GILLIE: So actually it does help but it really hurts?

GLORIA YES, and it was psychological chemotherapy and it was incredibly painful, but SO worth it.

For most of us, learning to think critically is an ongoing process, and it can take quite a lot of time, courage and practice.

> **Important:** Critical thinking is also necessary when working through this Walking Free Workbook. You are allowed to question (in fact it is vital that you do), think of alternative ideas, and note if you disagree or if something is not relevant to you. If you don't, you are in danger of just introjecting information again, or making me into a 'guru', or the Workbook into a 'holy text'!

In Worksheet M5.4, you have space to identify something you believe from the ideology of your cultic setting, or something you believe about yourself or the leadership. You can then consider the questions that a critically thinking person asks themselves, in order to challenge those beliefs.

I will illustrate the process of chewing over an introjected belief through Bem's story. When he was a member, Bem believed the world would come to an end on a particular date. Everyone in the group believed this, and he was told it numerous times by his leader and other members. After leaving, he still has some fear that they were right, especially when he watches the world news. This is his process as he critically debunks these ideas:

Bem's introjected belief
Global and catastrophic consequences would be the result of humanity not belonging to his cultic group; and of him (and the other members) not 'saving' them; and of him being disobedient, leaving and not keeping to the belief system.

Bem's critical thinking process:

1. He asked himself why he believed this (he is starting to chew over the information).
2. The answer was that he had been taught this from an early age, and he had never been presented with other views or perspectives.
3. He questioned what evidence there was for this belief and couldn't come up with any. In fact, he remembered that his parents had been told the world would end when they were teenagers growing up in the group, and that hadn't happened.
4. So, he decided that there was probably more evidence, arising from his parents' experience, that this predicted date would also come and go, and the world would not end!
5. Bem then thought about what other points of view there were, and he realised that most people in society did not think the world would end on that date – or ever!
6. All this evidence supported the view that the world seemed unlikely to be ending any time soon.
7. Bem then allowed himself to think about how this new view might be mistaken, misinformed or biased. He couldn't think of anything.
8. He did feel pressure, from his memories of what he was taught in the group, to continue believing the world would end, and he felt some guilt, especially about not being obedient to the beliefs, but he remembered he left because he did not believe these things!
9. The consequence of challenging and chewing over this belief, and critically appraising it, was that he began to feel free of the fear related to leaving the group and not believing anymore.
10. He came to see that there were no global or catastrophic consequences to his leaving (he wasn't that powerful!) and that there would not be any in the future, because he did not believe it was true anymore!

In Worksheet M5.4, you have an opportunity to use your critical thinking on introjected beliefs that may still be controlling you. This can be repeated as often as you need, to challenge any number of beliefs, so please photocopy it, or write the answers to the questions in your journal.

Worksheet M5.4: Questions to help with critical thinking

Date _____

1. What do you believe? (a specific belief that you wish to explore)

_____

_____

2. Why do you believe it?

_____

_____

3. What is the evidence?

_____

_____

4. Is there another point of view?

_____

_____

5. What is the evidence for that other point of view?

_____

_____

6. Could you be mistaken, misinformed or biased?

_____

_____

7. Do you feel pressure to maintain your position/belief and, if so, where does that pressure come from?

_____

_____

8. Are you free to change your mind?

_____

_____

9. What are the consequences of not believing this?

_____

_____

(These questions are adapted from Baker, 2012.)

Some introjects are so frightening they become phobias. If so, challenging them may result in a strong fearful reaction. In this next section, I apply the theory of phobias and discuss how to challenge the scarier introjects.

M5.3 When introjects become phobias

If you fear something and your reaction is overwhelming, consider whether it comes from an introject that has become a phobia installed by the cultic setting (Hassan, 2012).

Sometimes we suspect our reaction is 'over the top' and extreme, but we don't know what to do about it; or we are lost in the feelings of it, unable to see our way through or out. We will look at traumatic stress at M7, which may help to explain some of your reactions and symptoms, but here we look at phobic reactions. If you need help to feel safe enough then you could revisit looking after yourself (P3.1).

It may be difficult to recognise whether your reaction is out of proportion and if it is a phobia. One way is to check with others such as a safe former member, friend or therapist (P5). You could ask what they think about what you are struggling with, and whether they regard it as a rational and normal reaction or not.

For example, after I left the Community, I was terrified of not praying all the time. I had introjected the idea that I would be 'in sin' if I did not. I was frightened I would end up hurting someone without realising, or making a decision God would not approve of, and be punished again. I finally got up the courage and asked a (non-cult) Christian friend if she thought in the same way. She said she did not feel she had to pray all the time and was surprised I felt like this. This helped me to see how my behaviour was neither normal nor rational. I began to challenge the fear and this phobic introject, and change my behaviour even though it felt risky and scary at the time. The introject behind this phobia was, "I am a toxic dangerous person and I need to pray all the time or something terrible will happen". The challenge was, "I am not a toxic dangerous person, I am a good person with good intentions and I do not need to pray all the time to stop bad things from happening!"

M5.3.1 Understanding phobias

The UK National Health Service says: "A phobia is an overwhelming and debilitating fear of an object, place, situation, feeling or animal. Phobias are more pronounced than fears. They develop when a person has an exaggerated or unrealistic sense of danger about a situation or object. If a phobia becomes very severe, a person may organise their life around avoiding the thing that's causing them anxiety. As well as restricting their day-to-day life, it can also cause a lot of distress" (NHS, 2018).

This definition mentions "an exaggerated or unrealistic sense of danger about a situation or object". It is important to remember that phobias can be deliberately installed by the cultic setting, in order to control. This makes them rather different from most phobias, which develop from life experiences without anyone intending this.

Mary Grand, in her novel *Free to be Tegan*, tells the story of a woman called Tegan who was told, when she left her cult, that she would not be protected by God anymore, and this included protection from wild beasts. Only one day after leaving she saw red kites, large birds of prey, flying high in the sky. She assumed they were coming to attack her, in fact, she could imagine them grabbing her head, and she ducked down in terror even though they were far away (2015, p.35). This phobia was installed within her in the cult, to control her and stop her from leaving. She had introjected it and believed it was realistic and true. She did not consider that it was unlikely the birds would harm her because they would be afraid of her – all she could see was the 'wild beasts' she had been told about, coming to get her as a punishment for leaving.

Phobias about ill health and doom are often installed to stop people from leaving a cultic setting, and these may take various forms. For example, some believe they will get cancer and die if they leave. Others have been told they will be depressed or 'die spiritually'. Daphne was told she would become a 'spiritual vegetable' if she left. These introjects need to be challenged, once the phobia has been disarmed.

> **Reminder:** If the phobias are overwhelming, please seek support from a safe enough friend, therapist, General Practitioner doctor or local mental health provider. You could also remind yourself of your Safe Enough Space at P3.1.1.

M5.3.2 Strategies for dealing with phobias

It is important to identify introjected phobias, disarm and debunk them and these steps are designed to help:

1. **Learn what a phobia is** (definition above).
2. **Learn how other cultic settings deliberately install phobias to control** (Hassan, 2012). We can do this by reading or hearing other former members' stories. It can help to understand how phobias affect others, as this is likely to be less overwhelming than identifying our own. It can also help us to view our own phobic reactions more objectively.
3. **Explore well-known, common or usual phobias, and compare them to phobias installed in your cultic setting.** This is so you can normalise, challenge and debunk the phobia. Common phobias that have been identified are fears of confined or crowded places (claustrophobia), heights (acrophobia), flying (aerophobia), chickens (alektorophobia) and spiders (arachnophobia). There are many more that an internet search will identify.

   If you have any of these or similar phobias, consider whether they were installed in the cultic setting. If so, the underlying introjects need identifying and challenging (see below). There may be some that were not installed in that setting. For example, I always had a bit of a phobia of spiders, and this did not change either in my cultic setting or after leaving – I grew up in Africa where there are big spiders!
4. **Consider your phobias and related introjects in detail.** You could do this by unpacking, questioning and challenging your phobic beliefs using the steps set out for critical thinking above (see Worksheet M5.4).

   For example, Mary-Jane, like many from religious groups, believed she had a 'demon' living in her. After she left, she did not make eye contact because she was terrified others would see the 'demon' in her eyes. She tried to manage her high levels of anxiety by constantly cleaning (obsessive compulsive disorder or 'OCD'). It was only when she began to chew over this introjected belief and challenge it, that she realised it was absolutely not true. She understood that there was no demon and that she had been told this to terrify and control her. As a result, in time, she was liberated from this phobia and introject. She stopped compulsively cleaning and was able to look people in the eye, which was a happy day for her!
5. **Discuss introjects and phobias with other, safe enough, former members from your cultic setting, if you can.** It may help to ask them what their fears and phobias were – and this conversation sometimes leads eventually to having a good laugh about some of the ridiculous beliefs we can have. (Even if you can't meet with other former members, you might like to think whether you can identify any ridiculous beliefs from your experience!)
6. **Compare installed phobias with former members from other cultic settings.** This can be done through discussion if you can, or by hearing former members' stories. You may more easily identify their introjects and phobias that are 'over the top' and irrational, even though you have blind spots for your own. This exercise may help put both in perspective as being neither true nor real.

For example, as illustrated in the story of Bem (M5.2 above), the idea that the world is going to end on a certain date can be terrifying for someone who has grown up with that idea, and they may struggle to see through it. However, if your group had no doctrine about the world ending, this may be easy to challenge, since many dates have been given for the end of the world, from many different cultic settings, over the centuries, and those dates have come and gone, none were true, and the earth is still here! But you may have a different phobia which you struggle to see past.

7. **Determine what is genuinely dangerous and what is not.** It can be hard to ascertain what is actually dangerous and what is not after a cultic experience, especially if we have introjects about not being allowed to take care of ourselves. It is therefore important to recognise when we are responding to real danger, and when we have an exaggerated, phobic response.

   For example, if the leader or other members have a history of physical or verbal abuse towards former members, then some fear may be reasonable, and it is important that you take steps to protect yourself, while also challenging the introjects. If you have an introject that you deserve to be punished for leaving, it is important to challenge it as it is not true.

Reminder: *You deserve to be safe and to live your life free of abuse* and so protecting yourself may mean contacting the police. There are also many services that provide support for people in different circumstances, such as health services, and charities for mental health, domestic violence and survivors of abuse. An internet search can help you find your way to them. Remember to use your critical thinking when deciding whom to ask, and when you access help, so you can find support that is trustworthy and right for you.

If you find you are resistant to seeking help from the authorities or helping professionals because of what you have been told about them, then you could consider whether this is because of introjects which may need challenging. Many cultic settings install phobias about the police and other 'worldly' authorities including therapists and social workers – this is to stop their members from accessing the help they need, or reporting the leader's abuse!

---

8. **Imagine a future free of cultic control and abuse.** For example, after identifying the introjects and phobias, Mary-Jane (who had believed she had a demon living in her) could picture a future where she could begin to enjoy social contact and make friends. She also had the tools to deal with the phobia should anything remind her of it. She felt less lonely and more hopeful and had a great sense of relief as this heavy weight lifted from her.

9. **Challenge related introjects.** You could note and challenge any introjects related to your phobia in your journal, or return to the Worksheets on challenging introjects.

Worksheet M5.5 is designed to help you disarm and debunk introjected phobias.

Worksheet M5.5: Questions for disarming and debunking introjected phobias

You could reflect on these questions (drawn from the strategies above) here or in your journal:

Date _____

1. How do other coercive, cultic and spiritually abusive settings install phobias?

_____

_____

_____

2. How did your setting install phobias into other members?

_____

_____

_____

3. How did your setting install phobias into you?

_____

_____

_____

4. What are your introjected phobias or extremely fearful beliefs? Can you identify one or two?

_____

_____

_____

5. How can you challenge these?

_____

_____

_____

6. Were there any beliefs that became phobias, but which you now realise are ridiculous?

_____

_____

_____

7. Are they all introjects and phobias, or are there genuine dangers that need to be taken seriously?

_____

_____

_____

8. What can you do about any genuine dangers, and whom could you approach to help you?

_____

_____

_____

Your baggage will, I hope, be a little lighter now you have explored introjects, critical thinking and phobias. When you feel ready, you can continue your Walking Free journey along the road to recovery and growth.

At the next Milestone 6, we will explore how our identity can be impacted in a cultic setting, our pseudo-identity and our autonomous authentic identity.

Who are YOU?

We are making great progress! We are now at Milestone 6 where you can reflect on your identity: who you are now, who you were as a member, and if you joined, who you were before. At Milestone 5, we focussed on introjects and how to challenge them. Here we will look at how the cultic setting and its introjects work together to change who we are.

This is an important Milestone because everything in this Workbook is aimed at *understanding* what happened to you as a member, and how that *impacted your identity*.

We are all shaped in part by our social world and the people around us, but this process becomes super-charged in a coercive, cultic and/or spiritually abusive setting. When the cultic setting, its people and its purposes take over our lives, our identity is likely to change in fundamental ways, and we may develop an identity that enables us to fit in, but which is not authentically ours (which I refer to as our pseudo-identity).

Those who join normally have an idea of who they were before, and of their authentic identity, although this may have become deeply buried in the cultic setting. Those who are born and/or raised grow up confluent and enmeshed with the cultic setting, even if they don't buy into all the beliefs. As a result, their authentic identity can be hard to distinguish from their cultic identity, and they may only be able to recognise after leaving how tightly the cultic setting held them, preventing them from developing authentic aspects of their identity.

Whichever generation you belong to, Milestone 6 can help with the challenge of unpicking the difference between your cultic pseudo-identity and your authentic identity.

DOI: 10.4324/9781003305798-12

I will refer to the 'real you/me', and 'authentic identity' interchangeably – they mean the same thing here.

When I refer to the 'pseudo-identity', I mean our identity formed as a member – our cultic identity. Even though I use the term 'pseudo', which means 'not the real thing' or 'not genuine', I am not saying that this isn't a genuine change in us. We really do change as people. But we are not changing in the way we would if we were able to live our lives freely and authentically. In the cultic setting, we are put under great pressure to become the person they want us to be, to fit in and do what is expected of us – or we would be harmed (rejected, shunned, rebuked, given the silent treatment, physically punished, etc.).

If you were born and/or raised from an early age, I am not suggesting that there was nothing authentic about the person you were, even if the cultic setting was your entire reality. But former members have told me that, as adults after leaving, they have recognised that much of their identity was imposed from outside, and many aspects did not feel like part of who they really were.

The pseudo-identity can, therefore, be damaging and uncomfortable, but we need it to survive in that setting because we cannot (easily) leave. After leaving, even though it is no longer needed, it does not simply disappear. It takes work to discover and establish, or re-establish, our authentic identity.

> There is nothing wrong with YOU being YOU – in fact, it is essential!
>
> It is important to recognise that we all have an authentic identity and that this part of us has always been there, however small a seed it is. With the right information, help and patience, it can be revived, nurtured and enabled to grow, though it will take time to discover as you slowly but surely Walk Free.

Did you know: There are lots of different theories and philosophies about 'identity', 'self', 'ego' and 'personality'. Your cultic setting probably had specific ideas about these, and some of these words are probably, therefore, 'loaded language' for you. (This is the clichéd language adopted in the cultic setting, see M5.1.2 and M10.6.) It is important to chew over these ideas and think about them for yourself because, when I use the word 'identity', I probably don't mean the same thing as the cultic setting did!

When we get in touch with our authentic identity, we are also likely to get in touch with difficult memories and feelings. If this is happening then you could revisit P3.1.1 and remind yourself of the Safe Enough Space exercise. At M7, we will look at understanding traumatic stress, and at M13, you will have an opportunity to process your emotions/feelings a bit more. If you need support, please consider finding a therapist (P5).

Before introducing you to the Worksheets and giving you an opportunity to reflect on your personal experience, I will say some more about:

1. The pseudo-identity
2. The 'masks' we build when interacting with outsiders after leaving
3. Building an authentic identity
4. How the issue of identity differs between those who are born or raised and those who joined the cultic setting

M6.1 Revisiting the pseudo-identity

In this section, I will build on the concept of the 'pseudo-identity' introduced in P1.4 and M5.1.

When we are confluent (M4) and introjecting (M5), we do not have strong boundaries and are ruled by 'musts', 'shoulds' and 'oughts' – we are not being who we really are, our 'real me'. Instead, we are likely to be who we are expected to be. As members, we may *act, think and feel as the coercive, cultic and spiritually abusive group or relationship expects us to act, think and feel* and this changes or forms us – this is what I refer to as our pseudo-identity. As I reflected in P1.4, I see this as a hopeful concept which can free us from identifying with the cultic setting, and help us identify with our authentic identity!

I see the pseudo-identity as formed of the introjects. As we saw at M5, if we introject something, we take it in whole without chewing it over – like a lump of indigestible food sitting in our gut. We can't digest it or get rid of it. It remains in us but does not become truly a part of us.

I envisage the cultic setting as a "relentless machine, like a steamroller on hot tarmac with hooked spikes in it" (Jenkinson, 2008, p. 215), layering down this pseudo-identity like tarmac or asphalt over us. This layering is established through a two-way process, involving both us and the cultic setting: the machine bears down on us, as we introject what it is pressing onto us. So we lose touch with our 'real me', which becomes buried underneath. What is layered down includes all that we believe and do in the cultic setting, under pressure from the other members and the leadership.

The member (be they adult or child), or potential member, does not realise what they are getting into, or what is behind what seems like 'love' or 'Truth' or the answer to the world's problems. And so, they may welcome the ideas and comply, becoming confluent (M4), buried under the tarmac without realising the threat to their identity. Some who are born and/or raised may not welcome the ideas but have little choice but to comply.

In order for the pseudo-identity to form and layer over us, the cultic setting anchors itself (Hassan, 2012), like the hooked spikes on the machine, to parts of the member's authentic identity, including the past experiences of those who joined. This is a complex process, and as there is a power imbalance, we may not recognise the pressures on us to conform. Margaret Singer, a psychologist who worked with numerous former members, states that "the key to successful thought reform is to keep the subjects unaware that they are being manipulated and controlled" (2003, p. 52). When it is happening we are not aware of it, and after we leave there are likely to be numerous blind spots.

Oversharing ensures that the other members and the leader know more about us than we may realise. It gives them ammunition to control and manipulate by playing on our personal vulnerabilities, which we have already told them about. This is 'confession', one of the eight components of thought reform, when members let down their barriers and openly discuss their innermost thoughts and feelings (more at M10.4).

Margaret Singer reflects on how the identity of those who joined is *re-formed* as the pseudo-identity layers over their authentic identity: "As part of the intense influence and change process in many cults, people take on *a new social identity*, which may or may not be obvious to an outsider. When groups refer to this *new identity*, they speak of members who are transformed, reborn, enlightened, empowered, rebirthed, or cleared [my additions: saved, surrendered]. The group-approved behavior is reinforced and reinterpreted as demonstrating the emergence of 'the *new person*'. Members are expected to display this new social identity" (2003, pp. 77–78, italics mine). The member is thus encouraged to welcome the pseudo-identity as a great benefit of membership and to see it as more valid than their previous identity. After leaving, they are likely to experience confusion and conflict between aspects of their identity before joining, and their pseudo-identity.

For those who are born and/or raised, I suggest that there is normally a similar process, but it starts from an early age because they have little or no choice. Their identity is being formed under the pressures of the 'relentless machine' of the cultic setting. They 'take on' (introject) the 'social identity', the pseudo-identity, which overlays and entangles with their authentic identity.

Many have told me that they are left feeling they have nothing other than a cultic pseudo-identity, and they do not know who their 'real me' is. Their authentic identity is deeply buried, and the process of reconstructing it can be especially challenging. It means disentangling authentic and cultic elements, discerning which is which and deciding who they want to be – perhaps, after chewing over, keeping aspects of both in the process! This is because sometimes there are aspects of what we have learned and become in a cultic setting that we want to hold onto – we will explore this in more depth at M14.

If this is you, please be patient with yourself, and take the time to chew over who you are and who you want to be! I have worked with those who are second and multi-generation who have successfully reconstructed their identity, and live a fulfilling life after leaving.

For all former members, it is important to recognise that much of what you were told about yourself was probably incorrect. If you were told that you were not good enough, imperfect, sinful, wrong, evil and even toxic, you are likely to have a skewed idea of yourself. Or you may have been told in the cultic setting that you had a particular gift or 'calling', but after leaving you question whether that is true.

As I said in P1.4, the process of understanding our authentic identity is like completing a jigsaw puzzle with the wrong picture on the box. For example, Jenny loved creativity and art, but it was seen as a waste of time in the cultic setting where she grew up. As a result, she suppressed this part of herself assuming it was 'bad', and instead studied subjects approved by her cultic group that she was not interested in. When she left, her authentic identity began to emerge and she went to art classes and eventually studied art at University (her authentic identity).

Jerry was sporty and loved football, but it was frowned on as 'worldly' when he was a member, and so, from an early age, he had to suppress this part of himself and spend his time doing 'mission work' instead. When he left, he joined a local football club and enjoyed it immensely! These activities helped Jenny and Jerry to build parts of their authentic identity. More about this is in M6.3.

Summary: The pseudo-identity is an identity that is not truly ours or part of us – it is built up of introjects in psychological layers. Each layer overlays the authentic identity like tarmac or asphalt overlaying the buried seed, squeezing, constricting and stifling it.

As we look at each psychoeducational area (the Milestones in this Workbook), and as *understanding* increases, the pseudo-identity is unlayered and we free our authentic autonomous identity, the seed. As we are exposed to the light, we can begin to grow, flourish, blossom, thrive – and Walk Free!

Some former members 'mask' themselves after leaving, we will look at this next.

M6.2 Developing a 'mask' after leaving

Some develop a 'mask' after leaving, hiding both their former membership and their authentic identity. This can happen for various reasons, including:

- shame at having been a member
- shame at having been abused
- to hide who they were
- to hide what happened as a member
- feeling unable to fit into society outside
- thinking people will not understand why they are like they are
- fearing people won't understand their cultic history
- fearing people won't accept them as they are
- struggling to find the words to explain the weird world they have come from
- not wanting to admit they were in a 'cult' or cultic setting

They invent a version of themselves that will hide their history, including all they have been through. Unfortunately, when we avoid telling people about our experiences, there will be huge gaps in their knowledge about us. They will not be able to know us for who we really are – and both parties miss out!

Some former members have told me they felt they had to lie to their friends in order to keep their history hidden, and then struggled because they couldn't keep up with the different lies told to different people. This can be exhausting and stressful, and often goes against their ethics, but as they can't find another way forward, they feel trapped. Whilst this is understandable, the danger is that we are masking our authentic identity and so we are not fully free of the effects of the cultic setting.

You have an opportunity to reflect on aspects of your 'mask', if you relate to this, in Worksheet M6.3.

As you Walk Free, I hope you will feel freer to tell others where you are from, and to let them see who you are. This does not mean telling people everything about ourselves, especially those that we do not know well and trust. As we will address at M10.4, cultic settings want us to 'confess' our thoughts and failings to control us. Letting go of our masks is different. It does not mean 'full disclosure' to everyone. It means we are able to choose to be authentic when, and with whom, we choose. This must happen in your own time, and only with safe enough others who are open, accepting and prepared to learn about you and understand your experiences.

Next, let's think a bit more about what is our authentic identity and how to build the 'real you' after leaving.

M6.3 Building our authentic identity

Being authentic means you are not a copy of someone else, you are autonomous and true to yourself, in touch with your body and your feelings, the 'real you'.

Stephen Joseph says:

> Authentic people know what they like and what they dislike, what they are good at and what they are less good at, what they are prepared to do and what they aren't prepared to do. They are able to be present in the moment, aware of what is going on inside them emotionally and of what is happening around them, and they are able to take in what is happening for what it is. They are able to notice without labelling or judging.

(2016, p. 20)

What Joseph says is so important, but it can be challenging to achieve, and it takes time, self-compassion and patience to get there!

One way of thinking about the healthy authentic identity is that it can remain in contact with, and be responsive to, ourselves, the world around us, and others. A useful term for this, from Gestalt psychotherapy, is 'creative adjustment' (Clarkson and Mackewn, 1993, p. 55). This is how we grow and change. When we are free and psychologically healthy, we can meet situations creatively, willing and able to respond, adapt, grow and learn. This contrasts with the pseudo-identity which is *twisted against ourselves* in the service of the cultic setting.

Let's look at some ideas about how to build an authentic identity.

> **Reminder:** As you Walk Free, everything we are doing is working towards *chewing over and unlayering the pseudo-identity* and *building or rebuilding the authentic autonomous identity*. Finding the 'real you' is a key part of this Workbook adventure, and will help you Walk Free from coercive, cultic and spiritual abuse.
>
> It helps to see this as an investigative journey on yourself – like a detective. This is not selfish or egotistical! **I suggest you have a creative and fun time working out who you are, now you are out!**

So, how do you build your authentic identity and learn to live in an authentic, fluid and flexible way after leaving, especially if you begin with little or no idea who you are?

One way is to learn to recognise, identify – and do – what you like to do (like Jerry and Jenny, M6.1 above). It helps, therefore, to seek out and experiment with different activities, finding out which you like, or love. This helps to create structure from the outside, in order to build an authentic identity on the inside. It is like scaffolding, a temporary structure used by workers in order that they can safely repair or clean a building. Emma says:

> …with transgenerational cult survivors [born and/or raised] … a lot of recovery has to begin on the outside, which is why the term 'scaffolding' is apt.

After leaving, it is important to turn your attention to yourself and allow yourself to engage with new projects. Daphne put it like this:

> Maybe you don't know what you like; so go to a bookstore and look at magazines or books and become interested and develop a social interest. You know, learn, and figure out what you might like to do. It could be a career, it could be hobbies, it could be relationships, healthy relationships, because that is what life is about. Life is about relationships, it's not about unhealthy relationships that are coercive and exploitative.

As we work out what we like after leaving, we may find clues from what we liked, or were good at, as members, whether or not that was approved of in the cultic setting. Some people are good at sports (like Jerry above), some at drawing and painting (like Jenny), some are studious, some love writing, music, dance, working with children and developing IT and computer technology – there are numerous examples! In Worksheet M6.4, you have an opportunity to think about the things you liked to do (and some you were maybe good at!) – because it is an important way of getting in touch with the "flashes of the real me" (as one client put it) or your authentic identity.

As well as what we liked to do, there may be aspects of our identity that showed through despite the setting. Lavinia put it like this:

Even amidst all of this chaos and confusion and role confusion and boundarylessness, in the cult, there seems to always be some sort of kernel [or seed] of, 'I was able to stand up for myself, or stand up for my sister, or I was the only one who could draw that thing just the right way'. Whatever it is, look for those kernels, yeah, look for those kernels, those are positive identifications.

I know it can be baffling to work out how we know what we like. For example, why do we like, say, a Labrador dog more than a poodle? How do we know we prefer pink or green to blue? We just seem to! Wherever these preferences come from, they are important in working out who we are. **It can be helpful therefore to simply notice what we like.**

This is what Jane had to say about this adventure. (I have put the word 'second' in brackets because those born and/or raised have probably never had a 'first' chance to decide who they really are or want to be.)

> One good thing is that actually you are getting a (second) chance to really decide who you wanna be and what you are going to do. I know it's a bit of a consolation prize but actually that's really quite exciting, you know, you can start again.

Harriet notes how the experience is, therefore, one that can lead some people

> …to completely invent themselves or reinvent themselves and do so much self-examination.

Another way to work out who we are is to ask someone we trust what positive things they see in us. Putting positive aspects into words can be affirming, and builds a sense of authentic identity. A kind friend or therapist (P5) can do this for us.

We also need to know which things about ourselves it might be good to change. Being realistic, there probably is something! But it is important that we don't focus on them to the detriment of the 'positive' things (the things we like about ourselves), especially as we may be more inclined to see the 'negative' things (the things we don't like about ourselves) because of our cultic history and the introjects. It has been said that, if you are going to criticise someone, tell them ten positive things and then tell them what they may need to change – and we need to do the same for ourselves! This process can act like a mirror, to help us see ourselves in new ways, rather than as we used to see ourselves in the cultic setting (remember the jigsaw puzzle and the box at P1.4).

Those who are neurodivergent, for example autistic, Asperger's, attention deficit hyperactivity disorder (ADHD) and others, may have this aspect of their authentic identity deeply buried and overlayered in the cultic setting. Neurodivergent people face challenges being accepted in society generally, but they may find it especially hard to meet the expectations in a cultic setting, and perhaps to hide their differences.

For example, Jackie didn't find it easy to chat with people. She felt shy, awkward and anxious in the (numerous) meetings, and found social interactions, which were expected of her every day, exhausting. This was interpreted by her cultic setting as a lack of commitment, and she had to work doubly hard to hide her differences and show how committed she was. Because she introjected their views, she became highly critical of herself, guilty and ashamed. Her authentic neurodivergent identity was suppressed in the effort to be a 'good' member.

There is also the problem that neurodivergence is poorly understood in society generally, and is often wrongly labelled as a disorder. For example, Luke Beardon rejects the idea that "being autistic means that there is something 'wrong' with you, and that there are 'impairments' that need 'fixing'" (2017, p. 17). Whilst neurodivergent people face additional challenges, it is who you are, and that can be celebrated. When you are ready, take the time to explore these aspects of your 'real you'. You can use Worksheet M6.4 on your authentic identity to reflect on this.

Reminder: We build our authentic identity at the same time as we get rid of the pseudo-identity. We do this by:

- challenging the introjects
- chewing over what we were told and believed
- *understanding* the coercive, cultic and spiritually abusive dynamics
- studying the psychological layers one step at a time
- identifying our own personal authentic identity and who we are
- challenging confluence and building autonomy

Before we visit the Worksheets, let's look a bit further at how finding our authentic identity differs between the generations.

M6.4 Identity and the generations

Previously, we explored 'Which generation are you?' (P3.2.1), and this is important to keep in mind because of the impact on your identity.

Those who joined as adults have an identity from before to return to, but those born or raised from an early age do not. The sections below discuss some specific points about these generations when it comes to connecting with authentic identity. Those who joined as children after the age of around five may find both sections relevant to some extent. They usually have some memories of life before, which may help them in their recovery process. However, they were not old enough to have a fully developed identity, which usually settles around our late teens to early 20s.

M6.4.1 Identity if you were born or raised in the cultic setting

Ideally, children within a healthy free family naturally develop their authentic individual identity as they grow up, one developmental stage at a time. They are ultimately not expected to be confluent and fit in, but to explore and find out what they like and what is right for them.

If you grow up in a cultic setting then confluence and fitting in are expected. Showing your authentic identity, or 'flashes of the real me' may be regarded as 'rebellion'. This is likely to be crushed or punished, harming you psychologically (and sometimes physically) and resulting in self-suppression. The authentic and pseudo-identities become confused, and they need to be disentangled after leaving.

For example, Carina was clever as a child and loved to study (her 'real me'), but the cultic setting only valued knowledge about its own worldview and teachings, so her authentic intelligence and enjoyment of learning were layered over and unable to grow. After leaving, she was able to uncover this part of her, to go to university and train professionally.

Growing up, Lambert had some doubts (his 'real me') about the religion in which he was brought up but did not feel he could say so. Over years of hearing the cultic doctrine, he felt like he both believed and doubted it at the same time. After he left, he gradually sifted through what he really believed and was able to discard what he didn't.

Even though neither Carina nor Lambert had an identity from before to return to, they were able to find elements of their authentic identities in what they loved to do, and what they truly believed. I imagine you can relate to this one way or another – and there is an opportunity to reflect on aspects of your identity at different stages in the Worksheets at M6.5.

If you were born, or raised from an early age, you did not have a life experience before the cultic setting, from which you can now draw information about your identity. *This does not mean you do not have the seeds of an authentic identity.* Your pseudo-identity and authentic identity are likely to be intertwined, so it can be useful to think about the 'seeds' of yourself that made you stand out from others when you were a member, for example:

- What did you like to do that was different from what others liked to do?
- What were you good at that was different from what others were good at?

M6.4.2 Identity if you joined

It is a myth that all those who join as adults have emotional issues that lead to joining. As we will explore later (M10 and M11), cultic settings create powerful dynamics to draw people in and hold them there. But it is not uncommon for those joining to have emotional issues from their life before (see M13). For those who joined because they wanted to resolve childhood trauma and abuse or other difficult experiences, getting in touch with their authentic identity can be challenging and problematic (Jenkinson, 2016). Their earlier problems may not have been healed and resolved as members and they have, in addition, the abuse from the cultic setting to recover from. Marietta says:

> When they pushed me out the door, all of my baggage that I had brought with me when I had entered the group was still sitting on the front step of the building and they pushed me out the door and there was all my stuff, and it was like, OH!

It is nevertheless important that those who joined get in touch with how they were before joining, as this can help them identify their authentic identity, and the aspects that thread throughout their life from before, through membership to life after. There is an opportunity to reflect on and address pre-membership emotional healing issues at M13.

Let's look at the Worksheets.

M6.5 Working through identity

The Worksheets in this section are designed to help you start to recognise your identity from before you joined; your pseudo-identity; and your 'mask' since leaving; and to build your post-membership authentic autonomous identity. This will be an ongoing process while you continue on the Walking Free journey through the rest of the Workbook – and throughout your whole life probably!

The four Worksheets represent the different stages of your life and identity under these headings:

Worksheet M6.1: Your identity before joining (joined after the age of 4 or 5)
Worksheet M6.2: Your pseudo-identity (all generations)
Worksheet M6.3: Your 'mask' after leaving (all generations)
Worksheet M6.4: Your authentic identity and the seeds of the 'real me' (all generations)

You will see that each Worksheet includes the outline of a person representing you. There is space around the person where you can fill out aspects of your identity at each stage. For example, if you were creative, sporty, kind, friendly, unfriendly, etc., you could add those by the figure.

Please be as creative as you want to be! You could draw on the figure, colour it in, draw the shape of your hair, add clothes, cut out pictures from a magazine and stick them on, whatever you find helps you represent the different aspects of your identity at different stages. Or you could use photos of yourself to indicate different times in your life, if it is not too triggering. You might prefer to use a large sheet of paper or your journal.

If you don't like the way this is set out and have a better way to do it, please do it your way. Whatever suits you! The important thing is that you help yourself identify these various aspects and stages of your identity.

If you are struggling to identify much or anything, I have also included some questions in each Worksheet, to help you to reflect on different aspects. You can take things you learn from answering the questions and add them to the picture, or answer the questions in your journal and see if that helps.

Reminder: It takes time and patience to identify some of these aspects!

I suggest you keep these Worksheets in mind as you work through the rest of the Walking Free Workbook, and return to them whenever you notice something that is part of your identity – which may happen quite often.

M6.5.1 Your identity before joining

If you joined either as an adult, or as a child after an age where you can remember something of life before, you can use Worksheet M6.1 to think about and create a profile of who you were before life in the cultic setting.

This can be applicable, to a degree, even if you were very young. You might remember certain toys you loved. For example, one former member told me they had a beautiful doll, but they had to give it away to 'the poor children' when they joined at age 5. They were heartbroken at the time, but it was important to remember that doll and what it meant to them when thinking about who they were and what they liked before.

Worksheet M6.1: Your identity before joining (joined after age of 4 or 5)

Date _____

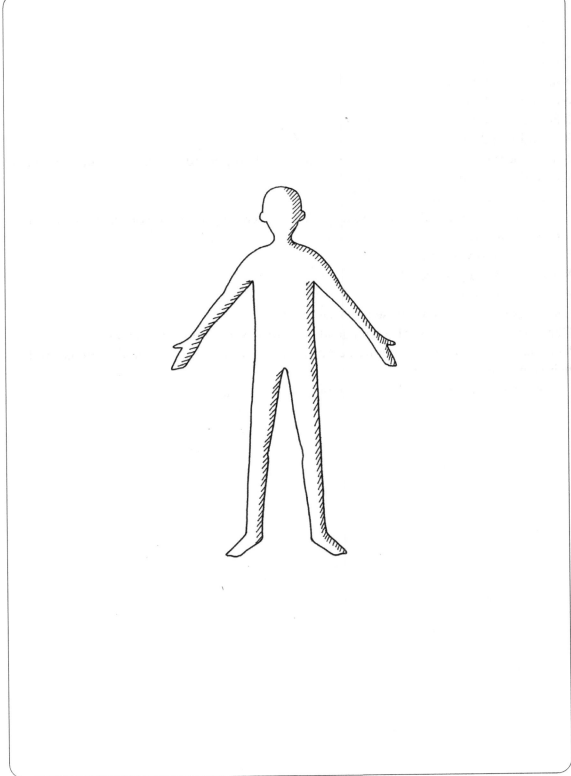

You could consider the following questions to help you build a picture of your identity before joining. You could list words or simple statements on the Worksheet in response to these questions and/or say more in your journal.

1. What sort of person were you (e.g. quiet, gentle, loud, energetic, argumentative, compliant, etc.)?
2. What did you like (e.g. painting, colour, studying, time alone, reading, acting, music, activities, etc.)?
3. What were you good at?
4. What were you less good at?
5. What filled your time?
6. What gave you pleasure?
7. Who did you love?
8. Who did you like?
9. Who did you dislike?
10. What education did you have (e.g. mainstream school, boarding school, home school, etc.), and what did you think about studying?
11. What toys did you love?
12. What aspects of your cultural and racial identity were important to you (such as ethnicity, nationality, religion, etc.)?
13. What music did you listen to?
14. What clothes did you wear?
15. What food did you eat?
16. What was your experience of sex and sexuality?
17. What aspects of your sexuality and gender identity were important to you?
18. What names, nicknames or 'pet names' did people use for you? Which did you like and what was their significance for you?
19. Any other aspects of your identity you want to mention.

M6.5.2 *Your pseudo-identity*

Whether you joined or were born and/or raised, you can use Worksheet M6.2 to think about who you were as a member. If you were a member of more than one coercive, cultic and/or spiritually abusive group or relationship, you could copy it, or split it into sections to indicate who you became in each.

If you were a member for a long time, or were born and/or raised, you might want to represent different ages and developmental stages of your life as a member, for example pre-school, 5–8, 9–12, young teen, older teen, young adult, etc. (whichever stages stand out for you). If this is the case, you could copy several Worksheets. This exercise may be aided by revisiting P3.2.

It is helpful to include details of how your pseudo-identity looks, sounds, acts and relates. For example, some who are born and/or raised have a particular accent because they were moved between various different countries and cultures. I have known former members who have worked hard to change their accent to fit in with the country they finally settle in, so others would not know they were brought up internationally – all this has an effect on their identity.

In my pseudo-identity, I used to feel the pull to be 'nice' (agreeable and pleasant, no matter what the situation) and compliant and confluent. I lacked confidence, became fearful and was unsure whom to trust. However, in my authentic identity, I am mostly confident, feel clear that I know what I am talking about, within the limits of my knowledge, and am usually able to test people out and decide whether or not to trust them.

Names are also important and have an impact on our identity and how we see ourselves. Some have had to change their name from their birth name to a 'special' name they received from the cultic setting, and it is important to decide which name you want to use. I like my name 'Gillie', which is short for Gillian. If I'm called 'Gillian', it feels unfamiliar – it isn't who I am. If my name is spelled wrong, it is not my name, and so, I often spell it out for people! My name is important to me because it identifies me as me. Maybe your name is important to you too. You could add your cultic setting name to Worksheet M6.2, and your preferred name to Worksheet M6.4.

Worksheet M6.2: Your pseudo-identity (all generations)

Date _____

You could consider the following questions to help you build a picture of your pseudo-identity, by reflecting on your life in the cultic setting. You could list words or simple statements on the Worksheet in response to these questions and/or say more in your journal.

1. How did you change on joining, if you joined as an adult or child (e.g. became quiet when you were noisy before, or became fearful when you were confident before, etc.)?
2. Did you have a new name assigned to you whilst a member? If so, what was it, and what was its significance?
3. What clothes did you wear?
4. What food did you eat?
5. What filled your time?
6. Did you do what you were good at? If so, could you say what and why (e.g. were your abilities exploited)?
7. Were you able to say 'no' to doing things you were not good at or didn't like doing? Were you compliant and confluent?
8. What activities/sports did you do?
9. Who did you love?
10. Who did you like?
11. Who did you dislike?
12. Who brought you up?
13. What education did you have, for example, mainstream school, cultic school, boarding school or home school, and what did you think about studying?
14. What countries did you live in?
15. What aspects of your cultural and racial identity were important to you (such as ethnicity, nationality, religion, etc.)?
16. What music did you listen to?
17. What changed in terms of sex and sexuality? (If this is too upsetting, please feel free to move on to another question.)
18. What aspects of your sexuality and gender identity were changed? Did you have any choices about this?
19. What role/s did you fulfil as a member?
20. Any other aspects of your identity you want to mention.

M6.5.3 Your 'mask' after leaving

Worksheet M6.3 is to help you think about those times after leaving when you have hidden or 'masked' your past membership and the person you are or were, resulting in you still hiding the real you.

For example, even though I left the Community, I did not understand what being in a cult actually meant, and I continued to be full of shame and fear. I was unable to show my authentic identity to others or to get rid of my pseudo-identity, so a lot of emotional energy went into masking who I really was. This included the pain I felt, so I was not able to ask for the professional help I needed.

The purpose of this Worksheet is not to make you feel bad or ashamed about masking! We all mask to some extent, and it is not healthy to feel we must always be telling others all about ourselves. But it is helpful if we can **notice** for ourselves when and how we are masking. We can then use our critical thinking and decide whether, and when, we will let aspects of the mask go, and let our authentic identity show through.

Worksheet M6.3: Your 'mask' after leaving (all generations)

Date _____

You could consider the following questions to help you highlight your 'mask' developed after leaving. Think about what you show of yourself to others, and list words or simple statements on the Worksheet and/or say more in your journal. The following questions may help you:

1. How do you feel about your previous membership, with those who were never members?
2. Do you disclose you were a member of a cultic setting? If so, to whom?
3. Do you live in fear of others finding out?
4. Do you feel shame about having been a member, and don't want to let others know?
5. Have you invented a different life history to tell others?
6. How does your 'mask after leaving' differ from your pseudo-identity? (You can refer to the Worksheets above.)
7. Do you make choices to fit in, or do you choose what you prefer, for example, clothes, food and drink, music and pastimes?
8. Do you put up with exploitation after leaving (perhaps because you think that is what you have to do, or you still believe certain introjects about yourself)?
9. What name do you use and what is the significance of that name?
10. How do you act when wearing your mask after leaving, that is different from your real you?
11. Any other points you want to make.

M6.5.4 Your authentic identity

You can use this Worksheet to identify aspects of your authentic identity – who you really are without your pseudo-identity and without having to mask. Some aspects may be clear from your identity before joining, or from what you have learned about yourself since leaving. Others may be the seeds or 'flashes of the real me' which showed themselves during your membership.

It is important to think about and identify those aspects that have always been there that feel like the real you – those things that thread through each stage, age and identity.

It is also important to think about who you **aspire to be** now. This is a vital part of the process because as you highlight the person you want to become, including your values, hopes and ambitions, you can gain insight into your authentic identity. (If you don't yet have clear ideas about who you aspire to be, that is OK! As you walk towards recovery and growth, these ideas can emerge in their own time.)

Worksheet M6.4: Your authentic identity (all generations)

Date _____

You could consider the following questions to help you build a picture of your authentic identity. You could list words or simple statements on the Worksheet in response to these questions and/or say more in your journal.

For some points, you may realise that you want to make new choices or move forward from where you are now. It may be helpful to take note of these things, as they point to aspects of your authentic identity.

1. What 'flashes of the real me' or aspects of your authentic identity showed themselves when you were a member?
2. What aspects of your authentic identity showed themselves even though you masked after leaving?
3. How have you changed since leaving?
4. What is your preferred name, and what is its significance to you now?
5. What clothes do you choose to wear?
6. What food do you choose to eat?
7. Who do you choose to love?
8. What things do you like (e.g. what kind of pets, colours and flowers)?
9. How do you know what you like?
10. Who do you like?
11. Who do you dislike?
12. What are you good at?
13. What do you like to do, even if you are not that good at it?
14. What music do you choose to listen to?
15. What fills your time?
16. What gives you pleasure?
17. Who do you admire, and why?
18. What are your values (principles for living that you feel are important)?
19. What aspects of your cultural and racial identity are important to you (such as ethnicity, nationality, religion, etc.)?
20. What do you choose to do with your sex life?
21. What aspects of your sexuality and gender identity are important to you?
22. What have you learned about yourself?
23. How have you changed as a result of that learning about yourself?
24. What sort of person do you want to be?
25. What new things would you like to do, or try out?
26. Any other aspects of your identity you want to mention.

M6.5.5 Summing up identity

Now that you have completed the Worksheets, it may be helpful to go through them and highlight what has consistently remained with you of YOU; what you have begun to let go of that is NOT YOU; and perhaps things, such as new skills, which have become part of you and you want to keep (I say more about this at M14). You could use coloured highlighters, or write a comparison in your journal. This can help you to find the threads of your authentic identity throughout all your different life experiences.

> If you want to go on exploring how your identity has changed, and the differences at different stages of your life, you could imagine a discussion between you as you were in the cultic setting, and you now. What would you agree on and what might you argue about? What might come as a surprise? What would you say to one another?

At the end of each Milestone, from now on, you might like to reflect on what you have learned about yourself at that Milestone. You can return to these Worksheets whenever you realise something new about yourself, and this will help you build a clearer and more accurate picture.

Now you have thought about your identity, your baggage will be a little bit lighter and you can continue your journey along the road to recovery and growth. The next Milestone 7 is the one that will help you understand traumatic stress and how it affects your body.

Understanding traumatic stress

We have now reached the Milestone where we will sit down and unpack the baggage related to the traumas you may have experienced in your life, especially as a member and since leaving. At this Milestone, I have broken down the complex subject of trauma theory, and whilst this might seem like a challenging topic, I hope you will find that understanding it is helpful.

The word trauma is from the Greek for 'wound', and it can be applied to "*physical injury* caused by some direct external force or *psychological injury* caused by some extreme emotional assault" (Reber and Reber, 2001, p. 764, italics mine). We are dealing here with psychological injuries, but they often have physical effects.

Being a member of a coercive, cultic and/or spiritually abusive group or relationship has an impact on our mental well-being, feelings and stress levels. Painful and difficult incidents and situations often occur in quick succession, bringing with them intensity, stress and fear responses.

Living in a setting where one is so often assumed to be 'getting it wrong', and is punished or threatened with punishment for small so-called transgressions, wrongdoings, misbehaviours or rebellions, is in itself highly stressful. As is believing one is being watched all the time by an authority figure such as a leader or their representatives, or a 'god' or higher being; and having to account for every detail of life to that powerful figure. We are likely to be marinated in the beliefs, practices and controlling culture and so usually assume that we are the problem and not the cultic and abusive setting.

DOI: 10.4324/9781003305798-13

In addition, what we are taught about our feelings or emotions can have a huge impact. We may be taught to suppress our feelings and that they are 'selfish', a distraction from focussing on 'God's work', 'from the devil' and 'sinful', 'unenlightened' or 'morally deviant', or a sign of mental illness (the language will vary depending on the setting). Therefore, we mistakenly assume that *not having feelings* is 'good', 'from God', evidence of enlightenment, etc. Alternatively, in some settings, we may live our life *flooded with feelings*, overwhelmed and taught that this intensity is 'good', 'enlightened', from a 'god', etc.

Whatever the situation or language used, our feelings are vital if we are to discover who we are (our authentic identity) and complete our journey to recovery and growth. We need to be able to feel our feelings, but also to regulate them for ourselves, so we remain grounded in our authentic identity (see M13 for more on feelings).

As we have seen previously at M1, leaving is also often difficult, involving overwhelming reactions and painful feelings (towards an alien world outside and towards the cultic setting we have left behind), even if we are not fully in touch with them. All these factors leave an imprint on our body, memory and mind.

For example, Jane describes, in the quote below, her stress levels and state of mind after leaving, and the stages she went through. I know others feel equally destabilised and traumatised. Just making a choice to leave deeply impacts them (this may be the first genuine choice they have ever made), even though they know it is good they have left. I have retained Jane's hesitancy in the quote (where she says 'um' and repeats words), as it shows how hard it was telling me about the fallout from leaving:

> Well, its um, it's taken on, I mean it, it has just been, been mad, absolutely mad, just the most tumultuous - is that a word? - just crazy year, the most up and down year of my life really – and I have had a pretty crazy life! You know, so this year really takes the biscuit and um, er it started off um with shock, I think, you know, um, and then a kind of period of numbness, while, while the shock was sort of going in and then when the shock hit I would say there was about three months of just really um, violent emotions, I don't mean violent as in I was violent but just as they hit me they felt violent, um, and, um just not even knowing who I was, my sense of identity just evaporated, all my coping mechanisms that I had built up over the years just vanished. I felt like the rug had been completely pulled out from underneath me and um, ah, you know, I just didn't know whether I was coming or going.

This was a 'traumatic' experience for Jane, impacting her body, memory and mind and her stress levels – which I will also refer to as levels of 'arousal'. The rollercoaster of intense feelings Jane is experiencing all indicate symptoms of post-traumatic stress (PTS) (more below).

After we have been exposed to a series of dangers or threats that pile one on top of another, resulting in strong emotional reactions and traumatic stress, we can remain affected by the stressful impact and memories, perhaps long after the threats have passed. This can result in us struggling to recover and live a satisfying life. This struggle can show itself in various symptoms and reactions (more below in M7.4).

The responses we have to trauma may be challenging, but they are *normal*. "We human beings are *designed for trauma*" (Biddulph, 2021, p. 81), and our bodies are wired to ensure our best chances of survival and to keep us alive, whether we realise it or not.

This Milestone is designed to give you information about the potential effects of stress levels or arousal on your body, memory and mind from the perspective of trauma theory. It is important to *understand* and make sense of what is happening in your body, the biological processes all humans go through, but also to be able to apply this directly to your personal experience.

Understanding our physical and emotional responses *in the present* is a vital part of the recovery process and *is more important than identifying every traumatic event and memory.* It can be overwhelming to keep going over your story or to try to remember every single incident that happened. This is likely to be re-traumatising and is not necessary for recovery.

It is much more important to concentrate on:

- *understanding* the principles of what is happening in your body *now*
- identifying the after-effects of trauma – the signs and symptoms in your body, and their source
- learning to manage those symptoms and stress levels
- giving your body cues (messages) that the stressful event is over, so you can complete your 'stress cycle'
- learning to focus your attention where it is needed, on your recovery rather than on past events
- learning to support and reassure yourself in the present.

To help you heal, recover and move forward in your life, I am going to unpack aspects of trauma theory throughout this Milestone. This is an important area, worth exploring in some detail. I will draw from my personal and clinical experience, and from some of the extensive literature and research on trauma. The aim is to help you:

- identify how you are affected
- understand and make sense of your stress or arousal levels in your body, feelings and mind
- learn to feel 'safe enough' in your body
- manage the physical and emotional reactions and responses to triggers (reminders of the past), and traumatic memories that may arise while you are working through this Workbook – and in your life in general
- recover from your traumatic stress

Self-care is very important, and if you become overwhelmed you could remind yourself of Oasis Lake, and revisit your Safe Enough Space (P3.1.1) or the tips for grounding (P3.1.2). Or you might need to find another person, such as a trusted friend or therapist (P5), to talk this through with.

Until I understood this theory, I felt overwhelmed and lost in a soup of painful emotions and memories. It was a relief to be able to make sense of what was happening in my emotions, body and mind from the perspective of trauma theory – although it took time and patience to learn and process.

I suggest you take your time chewing over and 'digesting' this information as it is a hearty meal! I have placed Worksheets at the end of relevant sections to help with the chewing-over process. You could approach this Milestone either by reading all the explanations and then returning to each section and completing the Worksheets, or by completing them as you go along – whichever suits you best.

Let's look at managing realistic expectations for recovery, before addressing trauma theory.

M7.1 Managing expectations

Before we proceed, I want to say another word about healing and recovery, and expectations of what that might look like. Recovery is never 100% because we have memories. What has happened to us has happened, we remember, and those memories are likely to 'trigger' sometimes. Triggers or reminders often show themselves when we have strong reactions (emotional or physical) that do not seem connected to what is happening in the present. For example, you might suddenly feel uncomfortable and realise your heart is racing, as if you need to run, but not be able to identify exactly what caused this. If you have checked and are safe, then on reflection you may realise that there is something in the environment that reminds you of someone or something from your past, 'triggering' that response.

Triggers often happen unexpectedly, and they cause us to feel, react or behave in the same way we did during or just after the original traumatic event. This is because, in the moment, our body and brain associate what is happening now with what happened then. This has often happened to me, and I have now settled in myself that sometimes I get triggered, and feel those feelings or have those reactions (again). I have learned to accept myself with them (most of the time!), and even welcome them as they often give me new information about myself. It is uncomfortable, but not something I am afraid or ashamed of anymore.

As we Walk Free, we are also *purposefully remembering,* and this is similarly likely to cause you to experience certain feelings and physical reactions, and it may sometimes feel the same as it felt back then. This Milestone is here to help you process and *understand* what is happening to you.

You might also like to revisit what recovery looks like (P1.16).

Let's look at how we respond when faced with a potentially traumatic incident.

M7.2 Responses to trauma – fight, flight, freeze and submit

When we are in danger, our body selects the best strategy to stay safe. If our body senses we are in danger, we may want to **flee** (get away), or **fight back**, or **freeze** ('play dead') and **submit**. In a cultic setting, we are unlikely to be able to flee or fight back, so we may live in freeze/submit for much of the time.

Freeze is a sign of feeling in extreme danger. Our authentic identity becomes immobilised, squashed and squeezed. In a cultic setting, this allows the pseudo-identity (M6) and introjects (M5) to take over. We often freeze and submit in order to survive as members – but this is stifling, constraining and traumatic as we mutate ourselves to 'obey' in response to the coercion and pressure. This may happen when living with threats such as physical punishment or public shaming. For example, we may be in a setting where group confession or rebuking sessions take place, and we are terrified of being shamed and humiliated. There are numerous other possible examples; for some more, see 'small t' traumas below.

The term '**submit**' is used here, as applied in trauma literature, to mean that in order to survive, we unconsciously judge it to be safer to give in and 'submit' than to fight or flee. I am not using it, as some cultic settings do, to mean you have to submit to the will of the leadership and do as you are told, or face serious consequences. That is an example of 'loaded language', the clichéd language adopted in cultic settings (M10.6).

In an abusive cultic setting, it is generally not safe, or possible, to **flee** or **fight**, so we remain unprotected and unable to protect ourselves. We cannot **flee** (get away) because we are psychologically, and sometimes physically, trapped. The psychological trap often comes from the beliefs we have introjected, such as the need to remain a member for our eternal salvation, or to put the aims or 'mission' before everything else, including our well-being.

We cannot **fight** because the setting gives us little control, and the leadership has almost all the power. When I talk about fighting back in this context, this does not normally mean using physical force, but rather simply standing up for ourselves, and challenging what is being said and done. We are likely to be in trouble and danger and might be punished, shunned or rejected, if we did. We may have previously experienced this, or seen it happening to others who tried.

The decision to **fight, flee** or **freeze**, in a dangerous, potentially harmful and traumatic situation, is an **unconscious decision**. Although we are not consciously aware of it, our brains are "continuously evaluating risk in the environment, making judgments, and setting priorities for behaviors that are adaptive" (Porges, 2017, pp. 55–56) and useful for our survival. Being adaptive means responding to the environment as needed, including unconsciously (more in M7.6 below).

I will illustrate fight and flight, and freeze and submit, by telling the stories of the lion and the antelope, and the cat and the mouse! I will refer to 'unconscious awareness', which may seem like a contradiction in terms, but refers to situations where our unconscious becomes aware of things before our conscious mind does, and our body responds. The technical term for this is 'neuroception', which "is the process through which the nervous system evaluates risk without requiring [conscious] awareness. This automatic process involves brain areas that evaluate cues of safety, danger, and life threat. Once these are detected via neuroception, [our] physiological state *automatically shifts* to *optimize survival*" (Porges, 2017, p. 19, italics and additions in square brackets mine). That is, we unconsciously act to ensure the best strategies for our survival. Our response is outside of conscious awareness – this is what I mean by 'unconscious awareness'.

M7.2.1 The lion and the antelope and the cat and the mouse

Two illustrations may help to understand what happens in our body when we are in danger.

First, we will look at fight and flight.

On the plains of Africa, when the antelope gets wind of danger in the form of a lion which wants to eat it, its **unconscious awareness** knows it is in danger, the hormone **adrenaline** is released and it goes into heightened arousal and hyper-alert (hyperarousal) in order to **mobilise** it for action – fight or flight. Its body says, "Don't just sit there – do something!" (Fisher, 2021, p. 33). If the lion approaches, the antelope will flee. If the lion gets close, the antelope might fight by kicking back at it, and then flee if it is able.

When the antelope escapes, or the lion loses interest and moves away, the hormone **cortisol** is released to calm the body (Rothschild, 2000). The physiological effect is that the antelope is likely to shake, as its body calms and returns to a resting place of safety: it completes its 'stress cycle' (Nagoski and Nagoski, 2019). This place is referred to as the 'window of tolerance' (more below).

While the lion is close, and the antelope is in survival mode, it will not be thinking about anything other than survival, and it cannot be socially engaged with others. This also happens to us humans.

However, the memory of the dangerous and traumatic incident is also likely to stay with us and may cause problems later (Fry, 2019).

We will now look at freeze and submit.

When a cat catches a mouse, the mouse will often automatically assess the need to **freeze** or 'play dead' and **submit**, which "is similar to a human passing out in fear" (Porges, 2017, p. 55) and indicates immobility and dissociation. Its body is saying, "Don't move – it's not safe" (Fisher, 2021, p. 33). Dissociation helps us to survive and is when we "'tune out' threatening experiences. [It is a]…division between the part of you involved in keeping up with daily tasks of living and the part of you that is holding emotions of fear, shame, or anger" (Schwartz, 2016, p. 30).

When it freezes, the mouse is less interesting to the cat, because many predators ignore an apparently dead animal. This strategy is low arousal (hypoarousal) and **immobilisation**. Once the cat loses interest and drops the mouse, adrenaline kicks in and the mouse may try to flee.

Freeze happens, in a terrifying situation, when our unconscious awareness judges that it is too dangerous to fight back or try to escape. This is common in an abusive cultic setting – we freeze and submit (examples below). Our body makes a decision that it is safer to 'play dead' (do as we are told and comply) than to fight or flee (disagree, stand up for ourselves or leave).

Another trauma reaction we are likely to see in a cultic setting is the compulsion to **appease**. This is a mixture of flight/fight and freeze/submit, where we actively try to please others in order to reduce harm or potential harm. For example, if the leader is in a rage we may try to calm them down, if we possibly can, by our appeasing behaviour (e.g. flattering and conforming), rather than confronting them (using assertive anger – see M8) for their inhuman and abusive behaviour. This is a protective response that we also see, for example, in dogs when they bow their head to other dogs, or roll over onto their back, in order to avoid attack (Parker Hall, 2009).

I organise these survival responses into 'zones' in M7.5, but before that let's look at types of traumas and the resulting symptoms.

M7.3 'Big T' traumas and 'small t' traumas

Former members Winnie and Maribel had this to say about their cultic experiences:

> It was a traumatic experience, it impacted us deeply. [Winnie]

> Being in a cult is traumatising, whether you have what I would call PTSD or not, it's traumatising and there are traumatic events. [Maribel]

Members are likely to suffer as a result of many traumas of various kinds, and I have found that it is helpful to look at these in two categories: 'big T' traumas and 'small t' traumas (Shapiro and Silk Forrest, 2004). Maribel had this to say about it:

> A 'big T' trauma is seeing someone die, or, you know whatever your traumatic event is. And sometimes it's not big trauma, it's 'small t' trauma, you know, being humiliated in the group; being afraid of what the guru thinks of you; you know, letting people down. Those are the 'smaller t' traumas that are very important because when you leave a cult, even if you weren't raped or didn't see anyone die, you still have a series of smaller traumas that are stuck.

'Big T' traumas may be easier to identify than 'small t' traumas because they are more obvious, and easily recognised by psychologists and society.

M7.3.1 'Big T' traumas

'Big T' traumas include witnessing death or serious injury; sexual abuse and assault; physical assault or punishment; life-threatening experiences or illness; and culture shock due to moving from one culture to another, including leaving a cultic setting.

'Big T' traumas also include experiencing natural disasters, such as a major fire or flood, pandemic, tsunami, volcanic eruption or life-threatening earthquake. The sense of threat may be increased if you believe that such an event is sent from a 'god', higher being, or your leader or guru, as a form of punishment; or you believe that a disaster is about to occur (such as Armageddon, the Rapture or the end of the world).

Other 'big T' traumas are related to attachment. Attachment traumas arise when the natural attachments to caregivers, and others we are close to, are broken or abused. This includes not being protected by our caregivers or parents; being brought up by someone other than our parents; having parents who are more focussed on the cultic group or relationship than their children; abusive or changeable caregivers or parents; abusive or changeable peers and friends; and being shunned on leaving by family and friends who remain members.

All these 'big T' traumas are generally recognised to be possible causes of Complex Post-Traumatic Stress Disorder (C-PTSD) (Herman, 2015) (more in M7.4 below).

Worksheet M7.1 gives you an opportunity to briefly reflect on your memories of 'big T' traumas. The symptoms of these traumas, and how we recover, are covered later in this Milestone, but for now, it may be helpful just to identify some.

> **Reminder:** Although you are likely to be able to identify numerous examples, you do not need to go through and find every single one. You can simply identify enough to illustrate the point and to help you understand how the theory applies to you.
>
> I suggest that you do not spend too long on this Worksheet. If it is too difficult to do now, you could return to it later. It is vital that you take care of yourself before anything else.

Worksheet M7.1: 'Big T' traumas – reflection

In the space below or in your journal, you could identify some 'big T' traumas, and reflect briefly on your memories.

Date _____

_____

_____

_____

_____

_____

_____

Let's look at 'small t' traumas next.

M7.3.2 'Small t' traumas

When considering trauma, it is important that we do not overlook 'small t' traumas. These occur in common, apparently trivial, but actually upsetting and harmful everyday incidents (Shapiro and Silk Forrest, 2004). For members, these can include, for example, public humiliations in group meetings; confidences being broken; being ignored by the leader; being punished for minor so-called 'sins' or 'rebellions'; being told we "do not have enough faith"; gaslighting (M11.3); and being subjected to any aspect of 'brainwashing' or thought reform (M10). There will probably be many others that you can think of.

For me in the Community, 'small t' traumas occurred every day in the ongoing spiritual and religious abuse including: 'discipline'; rebuking; constant fear of punishment; fear of disobeying God/the leader; fear of thinking certain thoughts; confusion due to arbitrary and frequently changing rules; oppression; self-suppression; not being able to make my own choices about what to eat or wear, or who to socialise with; loss of family and pre-membership friends. The list goes on with small but terrifying things happening every day over years.

'Small t' traumas also occur after we have left, for example: fear due to wondering, "What if they were right after all?" (M1); not understanding society; shame about being a former member; hiding our history; knowing we are different to those who have not been members; feeling we are 'weird'; and there will be many others.

These can have far-reaching consequences, as they result in some of the same feelings as 'big T' traumas, but their significance may not be recognised. And so, if we suffer C-PTSD (M7.4) as a result of these 'small t' traumas, it may go unnoticed, and our trauma may be unacknowledged or minimised. These 'small t' traumas, which occur as members and after we leave, can result in "an accumulation of emotional shocks that creates substantial and lasting psychological damage; something that severely jars the mind or emotions" (Shapiro and Silk Forrest, 2004, p. 15).

Since 'small t' traumas are subtler, former members may need a safe person to help them raise awareness of the impact they have had.

You could reflect on your 'small t' traumas in the next two Worksheets. The purpose here is to identify the sorts of traumas you experienced, not to try and think of each one. You can come back to these Worksheets at any time to add more that have occurred to you. The symptoms, and recovery, will be discussed later.

If this is too difficult to do now, you could return to it later. Remember to take care of yourself as you work through this.

One way of illustrating the effects of the 'small t' traumas is to consider each one to be like a rock or stone that piles on top of you, one stone at a time, slowly but surely, so you don't notice it is happening until you are buried underneath. Using the illustration of a pile of stones in Worksheet M7.2, you could reflect on this in relation to your experience. I suggest you label each stone with a 'small t' trauma you have identified from your experience, either as a member or after you left or both. If you have more to say or need more room you could use your journal.

To consider:
Once you have identified these 'small t' traumas and labelled the stones, you could imagine each stone being removed, one at a time, as you unlayer the effects of these traumas. You might like to reflect on this in your journal.

Worksheet M7.2: 'Small t' traumas – the pile of stones

Date _____

Worksheet M7.3: Add to your personal timeline

You might find it helpful to track some of the 'big T' and 'small t' traumas on your timeline. It can be hard to remember what happened when. This was certainly the case for me as I began to try to make sense of my life story, but putting events in order was helpful. You can use the timeline below or your journal, or add to the timeline you started in P3.2.4.

Date _____

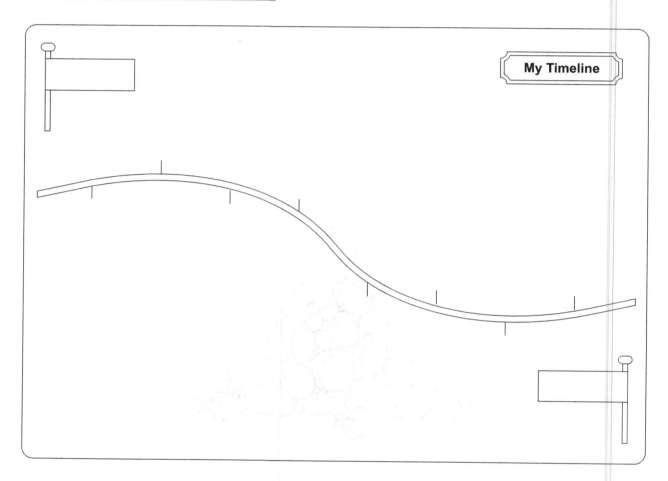

I will now explore some of the symptoms that result from these 'big T' and 'small t' traumas.

M7.4 Symptoms of trauma

Former members often experience trauma as a *psychological injury* that shows itself in PTS symptoms. These result from the survival responses and stress reactions to what has happened (fight, flight, freeze and submit), and may be short-lived. Many suffer a longer term (or 'chronic') form of PTS, that is, C-PTSD. C-PTSD develops in response to trauma when a person's normal ability to cope has been completely overwhelmed by a terrible event or events (Herman, 2015).

We all have an 'autonomic nervous system', which is an essential part of our body and brain that ensures that our bodies function as they should. It "regulates the internal organs in the body without conscious awareness"; and, as the name implies, this "occurs in an 'automatic' manner" (Porges, 2017, p. 4). Deb Dana states that "the job of the autonomic nervous system is to ensure we survive in moments of danger and thrive in times of safety" (2018, p. 17). However, with C-PTSD, traumatic stress overwhelms this system. It changes the way we react to and remember things that happened, so we cannot make sense of them. We will look at this in more detail at M7.7.

You have an opportunity to explore some of the common symptoms or signs of trauma, and whether you recognise them in yourself, in Worksheet M7.4. It is important to note that not everyone who has these symptoms has C-PTSD. With C-PTSD, there are likely to be various symptoms clustered together, rather than just one or two. If you can relate to a number of these, and think you would benefit from a formal diagnosis, then you could investigate this – there are different routes to diagnosis and it takes a trained professional, such as a psychologist or a psychiatrist, to formally diagnose C-PTSD.

A **symptom** is an indicator of something that can't itself be seen. For example, coughing and a temperature are symptoms of flu, an illness that we can't see directly. Trauma symptoms can be especially difficult to manage if they are related to experiences and memories from a cultic setting – and their presence may be a sign that we (still) feel unsafe or in danger in our life to some degree.

Symptoms that former members may find hard to identify, understand and control include: intrusive, unwelcome and disruptive thoughts; overwhelming emotions (feelings); strong physical reactions, such as stomach pain, heart palpitations or sudden loss of energy; no or little emotion; exhaustion; depression; anxiety; loss of hope; helplessness; sadness; feeling trapped; and physical illness caused by stress in the body, such as chronic (long term) unexplained physical symptoms (Fisher 2021). Remember, this is not a way to diagnose C-PTSD, but simply a list of some symptoms that you may experience. More symptoms are set out in M7.5 and in Worksheet M7.4.

In the introduction to this Milestone, I quoted Jane. Her symptoms included: feeling 'up and down'; shock; numbness; powerful emotions; sudden loss of sense of identity (her pseudo-identity, without having had time to build an authentic identity); sudden loss of her coping mechanisms; feeling unstable and disorientated; and not knowing what to do with herself.

It may help to think of your symptoms as speaking from the hurt part of you, to help you heal. However terrible you feel, don't forget that you survived the awfulness so far, which means it is very likely you can survive and get through what you are remembering now. If it is overwhelming, you could ground yourself by revisiting P3.1 or seek support from a trusted friend or therapist (P5).

You could reflect on your symptoms in the following Worksheets.

Worksheet M7.4: Identifying your symptoms

I have created a word circle with many symptoms that can result from trauma. (The list of symptoms is adapted from Fisher (2021) and Singer (2003, pp. 295–333).) You could highlight the symptoms you identify with by using a different colour, or by circling or ticking them. It may be that you are aware of these symptoms occasionally; that you experience them at a specific time such as after a trigger; or that you live with them much of the time.

   You will have an opportunity to say more, and to connect symptoms to memories, in Worksheet M7.9.

Date _____

Figure M7.1 Trauma symptoms word circle

Worksheet M7.5: How did your symptoms help you survive?

Janina Fisher, in her Workbook *Transforming the Living Legacy of Trauma*, asks the question, "How did your symptoms help you survive?" (2021, p. 19). This is a great question! If our body and mind are wired to keep us safe, then our symptoms are part of this process.

In this Worksheet, you have an opportunity to consider some of the symptoms above and ask yourself, "How did this help me survive?". For example, my fear alerted me to the danger of rebukes and physical abuse, so I would try and hide in order to survive. You will see I have created space for three symptoms, and you could reflect on this by answering the questions here or in your journal.

Date _____

1. Symptom

   _____

   How did this symptom help you survive?

   _____

   _____

2. Symptom

   _____

   How did this symptom help you survive?

   _____

   _____

3. Symptom

   _____

   How did this symptom help you survive?

   _____

   _____

Certain symptoms tend to belong in certain 'states' or 'zones', and I will explore this next.

M7.5 Responses – the zones explained

To help clarify what might be happening in your body, I am now going to build on the discussions above and explore our survival responses by looking at three different states or 'zones':

- window of tolerance
- fight or flight
- freeze and submit

I will explain how our autonomic nervous system shifts us between zones with unconscious awareness, to keep us safe, in M7.6.

Before explaining the zones, let's have a look at Figure M7.2 which summarises what occurs in each zone. I suggest you have a good look at this figure, and take in the different functions of each zone before we look at the different symptoms that belong to them.

Window of Tolerance
– can think and feel at the same time
- optimal arousal zone
- safe enough
- grounded
- can process feelings, information, memories
- introjects chewed over and challenged

Fight or flight
– "don't just sit there do something"
- hyperarousal zone
- sense danger
- mobilise and respond
- overwhelmed by feelings and sensations
- introjects unnoticed and unchallenged

Freeze and submit
– "don't move it's not safe"
- hypoarousal zone
- sense extreme danger
- immobilise and collapse
- shut down feelings and sensations
- introjects active and unchallenged

Figure M7.2 The three zones

M7.5.1 Window of tolerance – safe enough

The window of tolerance or 'optimal arousal zone' (Ogden et al., 2006) is at the top of the figure because it is the newest brain pathway in evolutionary terms (Dana, 2018). This is where our stress levels can be managed and tolerated and we can *think and feel at the same time* – we feel *safe enough*. 'Tolerated' means we can manage something, and stay in the present with our thoughts and feelings.

Have you ever noticed that, when you feel traumatised and overwhelmed, you can't think straight? Well, one way of knowing you are in the window of tolerance is that you *can* think straight!

Life can be stressful, but in this place, we cope with the stress (arousal) and still function, because the stress levels are manageable. We can act and consciously mobilise for safety if we need to, but we are not overwhelmed. We can also process feelings, information and memories; express our assertive anger; protect our boundaries and stand up for ourselves (M8). We are also more likely to love ourselves and have confidence (M9).

In a healthy setting, we can be attached to other people who can soothe us and help us to feel safe. It is important for our development, and even survival, to be attached to others – and safety in numbers. If the people around us are unsafe, such as in coercive, cultic and spiritual abuse, then we will *feel* unsafe and in danger, and may live our lives predominantly in the other two zones.

> We can identify, chew over and challenge **introjects** in this zone.

M7.5.2 Fight or flight – mobilisation in danger

The second oldest pathway in evolutionary terms is 'fight or flight'. This activates when we are in danger. We are able to mobilise for action and respond, but we are no longer in the 'safe enough' zone, and are outside the window of tolerance. We are in a state of heightened arousal and stress (hyperarousal), overwhelmed, and cannot tolerate our feelings enough to think and feel at the same time – like the antelope with the lion (M7.2.1).

Fisher (2021) and others list signs and symptoms of chronic (long-term) hyperarousal, including: irritability, defensiveness, emotional overwhelm, confusion, panic and panic attacks, impulsivity, risk-taking and self-destructive behaviour, hypervigilance, defensiveness, feeling unsafe, reactive and racing thoughts, decreased concentration, insomnia, nightmares, intrusive memories, flashbacks, mistrust, generalised anxiety, feeling trapped, confusion, substance abuse, eating disorders and all or nothing thinking; and hot rage, which turns against others and is an attempt to defend ourselves against the impact of the trauma (Parker Hall, 2009) (M8).

> We are too stressed to notice or identify **introjects,** so these go unchallenged in this zone.

M7.5.3 Freeze and submit – immobilisation in danger

The oldest pathway in evolutionary terms is freeze, and this activates when we are in extreme danger and terror. It is a protective state of collapse – we 'play dead' and freeze or submit (hypoarousal) – like the mouse with the cat (M7.2.1).

Fisher (2021) and others list symptoms and signs of chronic (long-term) hypoarousal, including: depression, dissociation, numbness, loss of interest, few or no memories, passivity, no feelings, no energy, can't think, disconnected, shut down, 'not there', feeling detached, ashamed, can't say no, decreased concentration, insomnia, loss of a sense of the future, helplessness, hopelessness, shame, worthlessness, mistrust, fear, terror, wanting to die, feeling unreal or out of body, loss of sense of 'who I am', sense of unreality, indecision, low self-esteem, dread, chronic pain, headaches, unexplained physical symptoms (such as myalgic encephalomyelitis/chronic fatigue syndrome (ME/CFS) and fibromyalgia), substance abuse, eating disorders, self-destructive behaviour, all or nothing thinking, conformity, compliance and obedience; and cold rage, which turns against ourselves and is an attempt to defend ourselves against the impact of the trauma (Parker Hall, 2009) (M8).

We are too low to notice, identify or challenge **introjects** in this zone.

Worksheet M7.6: Link your symptoms to the zone

In Worksheet M7.4, there was a word circle with symptoms of trauma listed, and I suggested that you might identify some that affect you. In this Worksheet, you have an opportunity to reflect on those symptoms, and whether the ones you chose were from fight or flight, or freeze and submit, by completing the table. For example, if your symptom is 'can't say no', the zone is likely to be 'freeze and submit'. (You may have noticed that a few symptoms were mentioned above for both zones. If you are uncertain which zone applies, it may help to reflect on whether they were linked, for you, with other symptoms which give a clue as to which zone you were in.)

Date _____

Symptom	Which zone does your symptom belong to?

Let's now look at how we shift between zones and the role of our unconscious awareness.

M7.6 Responses – zone shifts and unconscious awareness

We *naturally, unconsciously and involuntarily move from one state or zone to another.* Why and how will depend on what is happening in our lives. Our body decides for us. To illustrate this, it may help to look at a non-trauma-related example – Fraser's Monday morning! You can track his movement through the zones by following the arrow.

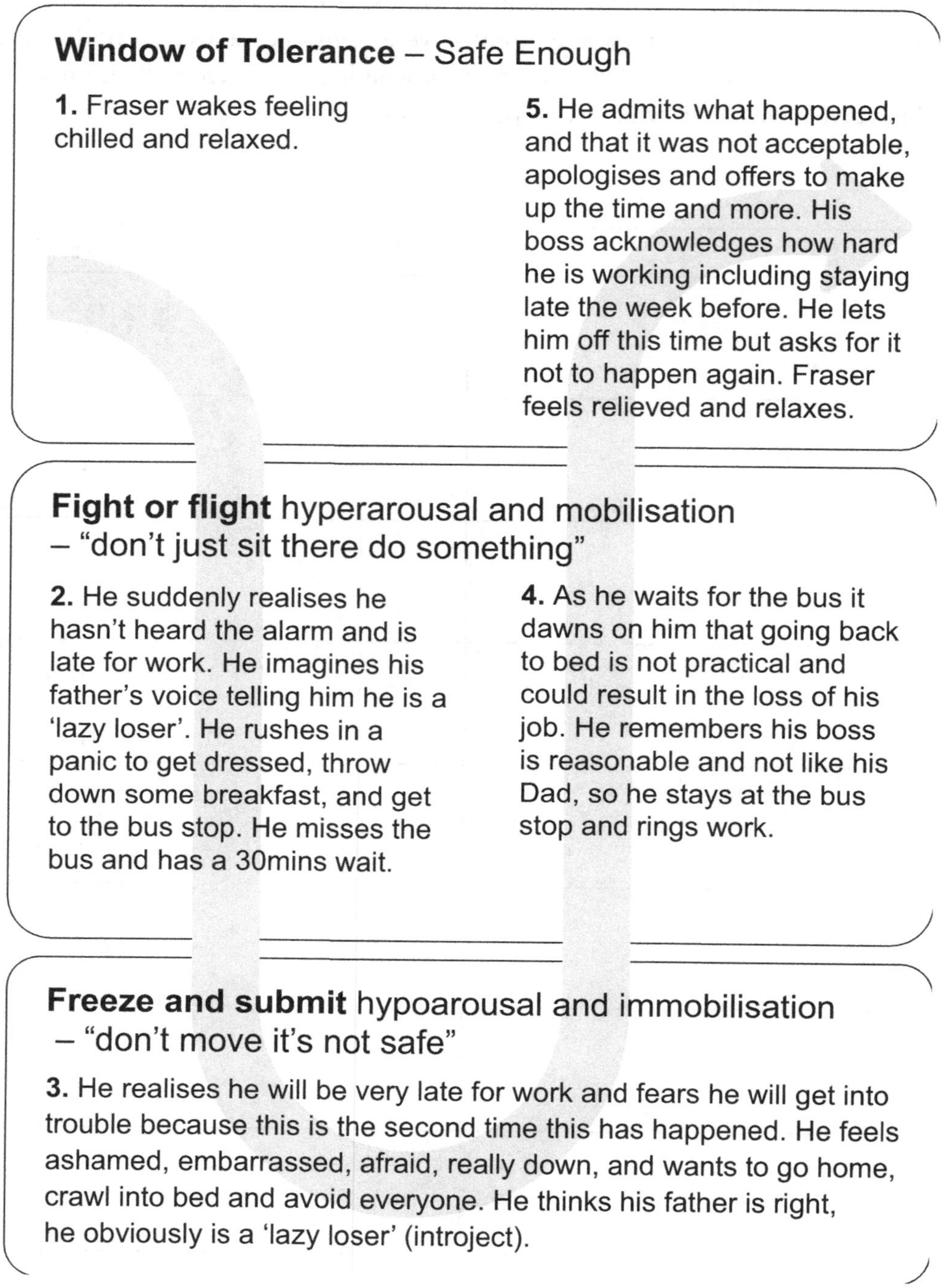

Window of Tolerance – Safe Enough

1. Fraser wakes feeling chilled and relaxed.

5. He admits what happened, and that it was not acceptable, apologises and offers to make up the time and more. His boss acknowledges how hard he is working including staying late the week before. He lets him off this time but asks for it not to happen again. Fraser feels relieved and relaxes.

Fight or flight hyperarousal and mobilisation – "don't just sit there do something"

2. He suddenly realises he hasn't heard the alarm and is late for work. He imagines his father's voice telling him he is a 'lazy loser'. He rushes in a panic to get dressed, throw down some breakfast, and get to the bus stop. He misses the bus and has a 30mins wait.

4. As he waits for the bus it dawns on him that going back to bed is not practical and could result in the loss of his job. He remembers his boss is reasonable and not like his Dad, so he stays at the bus stop and rings work.

Freeze and submit hypoarousal and immobilisation – "don't move it's not safe"

3. He realises he will be very late for work and fears he will get into trouble because this is the second time this has happened. He feels ashamed, embarrassed, afraid, really down, and wants to go home, crawl into bed and avoid everyone. He thinks his father is right, he obviously is a 'lazy loser' (introject).

Figure M7.3 Tracking Fraser's zone shifts

Similar processes operate in more traumatic situations, although the effects on us are likely to be more marked, and more challenging to resolve. These unconscious zone shifts enable us to survive, whatever is happening in our lives. Each time we move from one zone to another, it has a "profound impact" on our behaviour (Porges, 2017, p. 65), and on the different symptoms we experience, but it helps to remember this is an unconscious process.

These zone shifts and our reactions in response to traumatic events are not intentional. It used to be assumed that we were making conscious decisions to flee, fight or freeze, and as a result, our motivation would be questioned, or we would question ourselves and the resulting outcome. Put simply, as survivors, we were blamed for our reactions ('blame the victim' mentality), or we blamed, shamed and judged ourselves.

It is therefore vitally important that we do not criticise or judge ourselves for acting on unconscious decisions. Our body makes a judgement in a split second, in hugely challenging, dangerous and difficult circumstances. In a cultic and abusive setting, we are likely to be experiencing or sensing danger at almost every turn, as we encounter both the 'big T' and 'small t' traumas.

I worked for many years in an assault crisis centre, and heard many survivors say, "Why didn't I just fight back or run away?". This unconscious decision to 'play dead' and freeze to *survive* is why.

It is vital to remember that humans *evaluate risk automatically without conscious awareness* and that *we automatically shift zones to give us the best chance of survival*. Although this is 'unconscious awareness', it is signalling to us through "the gut feelings, the heart-informed feelings, the implicit feelings that move us along the continuum between safety and survival response" (Dana, 2018, p. 35) (fight or flight, or freeze and submit). When we perceive we are safe enough again, our body "triggers physiological [physical] states that support trust, social engagement behaviors, and the building of strong relationships" (Porges, 2017, pp. 19–20) as we come back into the window of tolerance and 'safe enough' zone.

In a cultic setting, we were probably told that we cannot trust our judgement, intuition or 'gut feelings'; and that we need the leader or a higher power, who has the answer to all issues and problems. One way of learning to trust ourselves again, and helping ourselves to process the thoughts, emotions, physical reactions and symptoms, is to track which zone we are currently in (as we did with Fraser).

The next Worksheet can help you track your zone shifts. Doing this can help you see where you are in terms of hyperarousal (fight or flight), hypoarousal (freeze and submit) or the window of tolerance. Tracking your zones in this way may help your 'noticing brain' (more below) to observe with curiosity what is going on, and help you ground yourself and return to the window of tolerance, as Fraser did in Figure M7.3.

To show how you can track your zone shifts, there is an example in Figure M7.4. The arrow indicates how someone is moving between the zones.

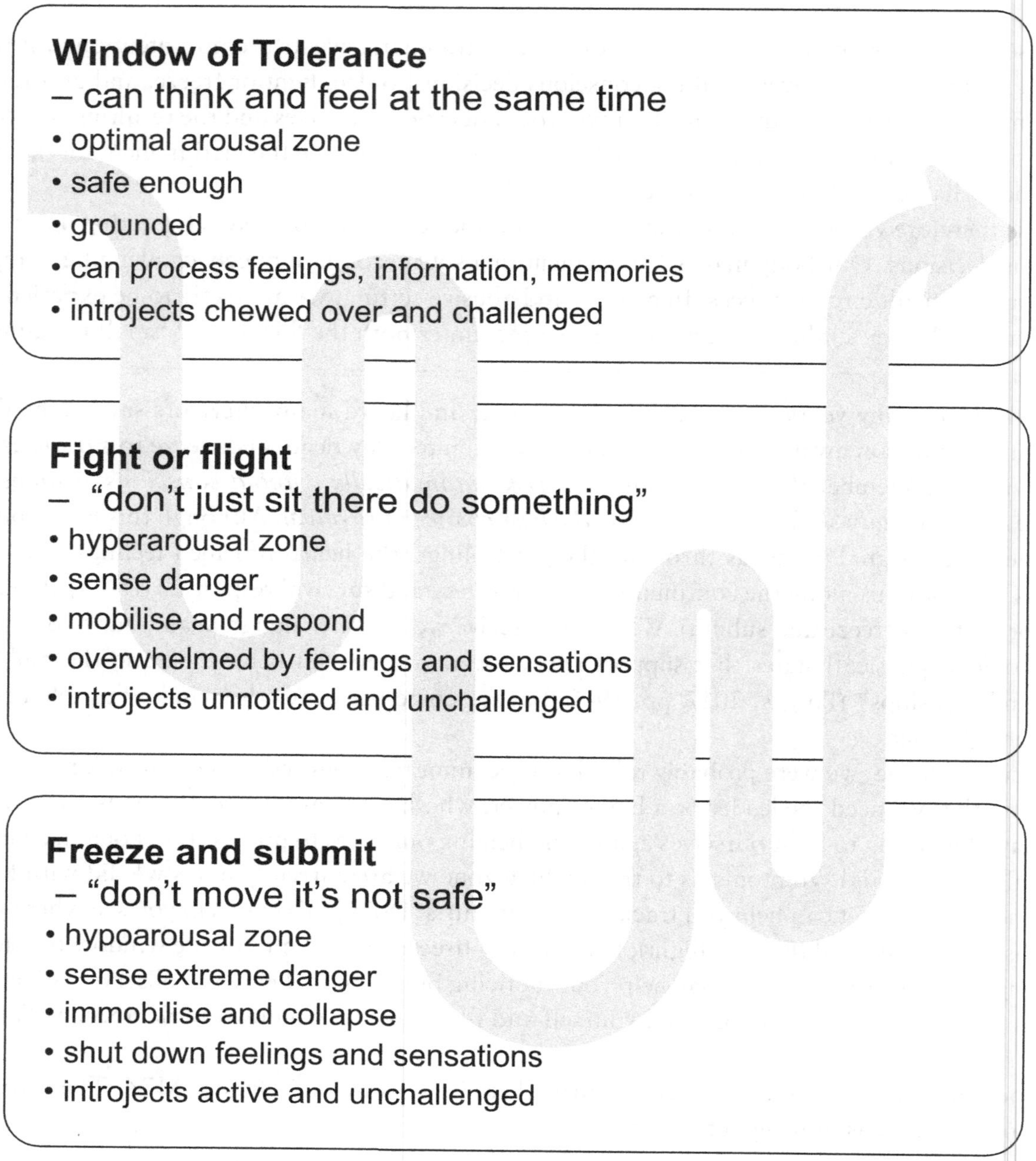

Window of Tolerance
– can think and feel at the same time
• optimal arousal zone
• safe enough
• grounded
• can process feelings, information, memories
• introjects chewed over and challenged

Fight or flight
– "don't just sit there do something"
• hyperarousal zone
• sense danger
• mobilise and respond
• overwhelmed by feelings and sensations
• introjects unnoticed and unchallenged

Freeze and submit
– "don't move it's not safe"
• hypoarousal zone
• sense extreme danger
• immobilise and collapse
• shut down feelings and sensations
• introjects active and unchallenged

Figure M7.4 Example of how to track your zones

In Worksheet M7.7, you have an opportunity to record the zone shifts that occur for you in life, especially when you trigger. You might like to photocopy the page or replicate it in your journal. You could decide whether you are going to look at a short or longer period – a matter of minutes or hours, or perhaps a day. There is space to write on the Worksheet if you wish.

If you are struggling to identify this process for yourself, it may help to start with a non-trauma-related everyday example (similar to Fraser's above) before moving on to zone shifts that seem related to trauma from your cultic setting.

Reminder: It will help if you approach this exercise with *curiosity and compassion towards yourself, not judgement.*

Worksheet M7.7: Tracking your zone shifts over time

Date _____

Window of Tolerance

Fight or flight

Freeze and submit

In Worksheets M7.10 and M7.11, you can reflect on situations where you have and have not listened to your unconscious awareness.

We will look next at how trauma affects the way memories are laid down and the idea of 'pattern matches'.

M7.7 Memories, symptoms and pattern matches

If we have suffered a number of 'big T' or 'small t' traumas, we may continue, long after the traumatic incidents, to feel we are still in danger when we are not. Some of us, therefore, live mainly outside the window of tolerance, and rarely feel safe enough – our bodies remain prepared for danger, even when there is none. *It is important, therefore, to be able to tell the difference between actual danger, and a trigger or 'pattern match'.* This is related to how our memories are stored.

Our memories are laid down in a different way when we have suffered a trauma. It is a bit like scattering papers in fragmented pieces on the floor, instead of filing them in the correct section of a filing cabinet. We then cannot find them, or we find fragments which are not with other papers belonging to the same file.

Similarly, traumatic memories can be fragmentary, separated from their context, and in the 'wrong place'. This has huge implications in terms of remembering what happened to us; finding and accessing those memories; identifying the memories our symptoms are connected to; and understanding how and why they are affecting us. Former members often tell me they remember bits of their time as members, but it is often not a coherent narrative, especially for those born and/or raised. Trauma is likely to be a principal reason for this. This is one reason why it may be helpful to create a personal timeline (P3.2.4 and Worksheet M7.3).

I find this quote intriguing and interesting:

Trauma survivors have symptoms instead of memories (Harvey, 1990, cited in Fisher, 2009).

Say you suffer various symptoms, maybe anxiety, or depression, but you don't know why. You may even say to yourself, "It is illogical, my life is fine now, it used to be awful, but I am happy now". Well, perhaps what you are experiencing is a symptom of a memory of a traumatic incident, or perhaps of many incidents (both 'big T' and 'small t' traumas), rather than something that is happening in the present. Perhaps the memory (which is 'filed' in the wrong place, so you cannot find it or recall it clearly) is causing you pain and distress but you struggle to identify why.

Sometimes a fragment of memory triggers and links to something in the present (M7.1), leading to symptoms now. This is a '**pattern match**': when the present seems the same, or very similar, to the past. Something feels, sounds, tastes, smells or looks like something we experienced then – and we feel in danger again. This may result in strong feelings and a compulsion to either fight, flee, freeze or submit.

For example, for a couple of years, I had to do all the cooking in the Community and was often harshly criticised and mocked for my attempts. Now, when I cook, I sometimes feel overwhelmed and suddenly feel that I hate doing it – I want to flee! This is a pattern match as it looks like my previous experience (the action of cooking), although my situation is entirely different.

Jem told me that just going to a place where there are lots of people already gathered (e.g. the dining hall at his university) causes him extreme anxiety and a panic reaction (symptoms), and he wants to run away and hide. He realised this was a pattern match from attending meetings in the cultic setting. The present group of people looked like those who gathered for meetings, and this reminded Jem of the associated expectations of him. This resulted in fear and a desire to flee.

Janice is triggered with heightened anxiety when she sees older men in dark suits. This is a pattern match with the suits the leaders wore in her group. Pat realised that he finds public speaking so difficult because it reminds him of the expectantly silent crowd in the cultic setting, all with their eyes towards him, the speaker, and he freezes.

The sense of danger may also arise from introjects, which act as reminders and traumatic triggers. Introjects indicate that we still believe, deep down, what we were told about ourselves, and that we still identify with the cultic setting and our pseudo-identity. It is, therefore, important that we continue to notice and challenge introjects (M5).

Another source of traumatic triggers is language. If we hear similar, or 'loaded' language – clichéd words and phrases that were used and introjected in the cultic setting (M10.6) – this can act as a pattern match and trigger. For example, the language can be triggering when former members from a religious setting go to a church or other place of worship, and hear texts such as the Bible again (see my example below). Similar triggers may arise when those from an abusive political setting re-engage in politics; when those who were in abusive therapy return to therapy, etc.

In the Figure M7.5, there are two shapes, one marked 'then' and one marked 'now'. They are not exactly the same, but similar enough to be a pattern match and cause the present to seem like the past. This results in a trigger, leading to trauma symptoms.

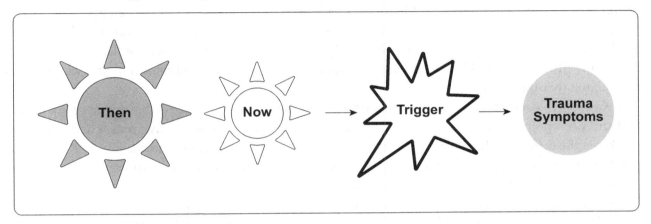

Figure M7.5 Pattern match, trigger and trauma symptoms

I don't think of these triggers and pattern matches as 'negative': challenging, yes, but not negative. It is worth holding in mind that they can be clues! They are helping us to do the detective work, to find the root causes of our reactions.

These are memories that we need to process, acknowledge, feel, heal and recover from. The symptoms, triggers and pattern matches can help us to make these connections.

Important: *If we are actually in danger in the present, we need to get away.* If we are not in actual danger, and we are struggling to understand our symptoms, then we may need help from a safe friend or a therapist (P5), who can help us reflect on what is happening, raise awareness and make those connections.

To clarify these ideas, I will illustrate this theory with two examples: one relating to a former member client; and one from my life that occurred just after I finally left abusive churches behind.

Frances came to my consulting room. She smiled and seemed to settle in, and then suddenly froze. I saw her go very still and her eyes looked blank – a symptom. I suspected that something in the room was a pattern match and triggering her. I asked and this mobilised her slightly as she answered my question – she had unfrozen somewhat. She found her voice and was able to tell me that some cushions with tassels reminded her of the colourful and highly decorated meeting room in her abusive cult, which had numerous scatter cushions, many with tassels. I offered to remove them from the room. She said yes, breathed a sigh of relief, and returned to her smiling self. She was back in the window of tolerance, and we were able to proceed with the counselling. If I had not noticed her freeze response, or had left the cushions, we might have wasted much counselling time because she wouldn't have been able to think and feel at the same time and process what we were doing together.

In my own case, I left an abusive church three months before my beloved parents-in-law had a 50th wedding anniversary service in their non-cultic and benign Anglican (Episcopalian) Church. I was vaguely aware of not really wanting to go to church, but did not realise the impact attending would have on me!

I was asked to sit in the middle of a long wooden pew in the musty old English church, with people sitting on either side of me, and far from the door. As the service began, I started to feel tearful. As I tried to suppress my tears, I began to sweat, and I wanted more than anything to run out. I was triggered and experiencing hyperarousal and an adrenaline rush.

Although I wanted to, I couldn't run (flee), because it would draw too much attention to me. I had some capacity to think, because, if I hadn't, I would have run out regardless of the impact on others; but I could not stop crying. Everything in me was telling me I was in danger (I was not), but I didn't feel I could leave because I would upset the family, so I felt trapped. As I could not flee, I had to sweat it out, literally. It was terrible. As I couldn't escape, I froze, shut down, submitted to the situation and dissociated (blanked off).

It was some years later, when I understood trauma theory, that I realised that my nervous system had still been prepared for danger in that setting, and that my unconscious awareness had been unable to see the difference between my past experience (of abusive churches) and the present. There was a pattern match leading to a trigger, and an inaccurate assessment of the level of danger.

I also realised that the sense of danger was particularly strong for me because I was hearing the Bible again, and this was setting off numerous traumatic triggers as I was remembering incidents from the Community; but I did not realise I was just remembering. I had the symptoms but did not connect them to the memories. My unconscious awareness was warning me, but I wasn't actually in any danger. Now I understand this, it can help to let myself know it is **"just a memory"** (Fisher, 2009).

My experience in the church was therefore a pattern match with past experiences. There were too many similarities, and they overwhelmed my feelings, body and mind, as well as my coping strategies, and took me way out of the window of tolerance.

I wonder if you can relate to these examples? You might like an opportunity to chew these ideas over for yourself in Worksheet M7.8.

Worksheet M7.8: Identifying your pattern matches

Figure M7.5 illustrates a pattern match, resulting in a trigger and in trauma symptoms. You might like to reflect on how pattern matches occur in your life by answering the questions below. If you are finding it hard to make the connections, the examples above may help. You could use this Worksheet or answer in your journal.

Date _____

1. Where were you when you triggered off, and what was happening 'now'?

_____

_____

_____

2. What felt, sounded, tasted, smelled or looked like something from the past? If you can identify the memories that you are connecting with, can you say something about them?

_____

_____

_____

3. Can you see how what you are experiencing 'now' is different from what you experienced 'then'? If so, note down some differences.

_____

_____

_____

4. How do you feel after making these connections?

_____

_____

_____

This next Worksheet gives you an opportunity to make connections between symptoms and zones, and the memories they are connected to.

Worksheet M7.9: Connecting symptoms to memories and zones

In M7.4, we considered a word circle of trauma symptoms (Figure M7.1 and Worksheet M7.4). In this Worksheet, I am asking you to choose a symptom you relate to, and to use the questions below to help you connect this to a particular memory and zone.

If you cannot work out what belongs where, it may help to return to M7.5 to refresh your memory as to which symptoms belong to which zone.

This can be repeated for other symptoms, and you may wish to photocopy the Worksheet or use your journal.

Date _____

1. Which symptom have you chosen?

   _____

   _____

2. When, why and how do you experience this symptom – could you say more?

   _____

   _____

3. Do you experience this symptom occasionally, daily or all the time?

   _____

   _____

4. Can you connect this symptom to a memory or several memories?

   _____

   _____

5. Can you identify which zone your symptom belongs to (fight or flight/freeze and submit)?

   _____

   _____

In the next section, I will explain how using our perception and the 'noticing brain' can help us recover.

M7.8 Recovery: using perception – the 'noticing brain'

Conscious awareness or **perception** is vitally important in our recovery. It means engaging what Janina Fisher refers to as our "**noticing brain**". In order to support ourselves to return to the window of tolerance and the safe enough zone, we need to **notice** what is going on in our thinking, emotions and bodies, so we make those connections, identify the symptoms, and bring what is happening into awareness (Fisher, 2021, p. 59).

It is possible to learn to stand back, engage our 'noticing brain', and 'witness' what is happening to us and "observe while safely allowing adrenaline to pump, the heart to race, and muscles to tremble" (Thompson, 2018, p. 142).

Once we can notice that we are not actually in danger, and that what we are experiencing is "**just a memory**" – a symptom caused by a pattern match and not a real threat in the present – we begin to soothe, calm and **ground** ourselves (Fisher, 2021). When we are grounded, we can more easily return to the window of tolerance, as the levels of stress and arousal become manageable. We are in touch with our 'gut feelings' and our assertive anger (M8). There are strategies for grounding in P3.1.2.

Our perception also helps us to be aware of our environment and any threats in the present, so we can consciously act to keep safe now if necessary.

> If we can approach what is happening with mindful **curiosity**, with a **non-judgemental, observing** and **compassionate** stance towards our own feelings and sensations, then we can more easily, and in our own time, return to the window of tolerance.

It would have made things a lot easier for me if I had known and understood this when I went to my in-laws' 50th anniversary service. When I started to experience trauma symptoms, I could have stood back (within myself), used my noticing brain, and recognised them for what they were: pattern matches linked to fragments of old memories, not current reality. I might have been able to soothe and ground myself and return to the window of tolerance.

If I had known more about trauma theory generally, I might also have **anticipated** the pattern match: that is, I would have expected it, and accepted that it was likely to happen – but not feared it! I find it saves a lot of stress and reduces shame if we let ourselves know in advance that there is likely to be a pattern match and resulting triggers!

In the next two Worksheets, you have an opportunity to think about occasions when your unconscious awareness warned you, and you either allowed those 'gut feelings' to become conscious (perception and noticing brain) and listened to them, or ignored them (flight or freeze). Raising awareness of this can help you to trust your unconscious awareness, gut feelings and judgement in future.

This is an example from my life of a situation when I listened to my unconscious awareness. I met someone who came over as 'nice', but I had a feeling that something wasn't right and that all wasn't perhaps as it seemed. I had no evidence of them being untrustworthy, but I decided to listen to my 'gut' feeling and chose not to see them again. I later heard from someone I trusted that they were highly narcissistic and could be really mean, and I was so relieved I had listened to myself.

As an example of not listening to unconscious awareness, Stephanie told me that her first impression of the leader was one of suspicion and concern, but he was so charming he 'groomed' and 'love bombed' her, and she gave in, not listening to her 'gut feeling'. She was also persuaded because others around this leader said he was wonderful. She regretted this for many years to come.

Worksheet M7.10: Examples of when your unconscious awareness warned you and you listened

Date _____

Can you think of some examples of times when your unconscious awareness tried to keep you safe and warn you and *you did listen to it* and trusted yourself?

Worksheet M7.11: Examples of when your unconscious awareness warned you and you didn't listen

Date _____

Can you think of some examples of times when your unconscious awareness tried to keep you safe and *you didn't listen* to your doubts and concerns?

Now that we have discussed some cognitive strategies for resolving trauma responses, it is important to understand physical strategies that help us to resolve the heightened adrenaline and cortisol (M7.2.1) in our body, to let our body know we are now safe, so we can calm, soothe, regulate and ground ourselves. This is the next section.

M7.9 Recovery: letting your body know you are now safe

Whilst noticing cognitively with curiosity is vitally important, it is not enough to dispel the physical response to danger and complete the stress cycle. We also need to let our body know that we are safe by giving ourselves 'cues'.

In the story of the antelope and the lion, the antelope shakes, and this signals to its body that the danger is now past and it is safe. We need to do something like this, or else we'll stay in that state, "with neurochemicals and hormones degrading but never shifting into relaxation" (Nagoski and Nagoski, 2019, p. 7). We, therefore, need to find the things that help us personally.

Exercise and activity (mobilisation) can help with this. Nagoski and Nagoski say that "*physical activity is the single most efficient strategy for completing the stress response cycle*" (2019, p. 15).

You may find, therefore, that walking, running, cycling and other simple but effective activities can help. You could also try Pilates (a physical fitness system), which can be helpful in working through tension in the body, building core strength and balance, and raising heart rate in a controlled manner.

Others prefer yoga, which has been shown to be helpful in recovering from trauma (van der Kolk et al., 2014). If you have been exposed to yoga or similar practices in your cultic setting you may, however, struggle with this. Yoga, therefore, needs to come with a warning, because some cultic settings deceptively market themselves through yoga classes, and you should proceed with a level of caution.

If you notice symptoms that may be indicative of a triggered memory, for example, you're becoming anxious (fight or flight), feeling down or going into a dissociated state (freeze or submit), grounding techniques can be helpful tools. They can bring your attention to the present moment, and take you back into the Safe Enough Space and window of tolerance. You can then think and feel at the same time, and this will help you to connect with the here and now, your noticing brain and perception, and to process your trauma. You could revisit the grounding tips (P3.1.2).

We have now completed Milestone 7!

Now that you have thought about trauma theory and ways to recover, I hope your baggage will be a bit lighter, and you can continue your journey along the road to recovery and growth. You can, of course, return to this Milestone whenever you feel the need to.

The next Milestone 8 is to help you understand how to set boundaries, using your 'assertive anger'.

Milestone 8

Boundary-setting assertive anger – and rage

We have now reached the Milestone where you can sit and reflect on the relationships between:

- your boundaries, or lack of them
- your healthy 'assertive anger'
- the difference between anger and rage

Some of these ideas may be new to you because I am applying the terms 'anger' and 'rage' in slightly different ways than usual – so please bear with me as I explain! Before we get to that, I will explain what boundaries are.

M8.1 Boundaries

Establishing or re-establishing personal boundaries after a coercive, cultic and spiritually abusive experience is vital if we are to live healthily, but it can be challenging. How do we have connection and relationships with others, and also independence and autonomy? How do we stop becoming confluent and enmeshed (again)?

Well, we need good strong boundaries – so what does that mean?

DOI: 10.4324/9781003305798-14

Boundaries are:

- lines between us and others, indicating where we begin, and the other person ends
- like our skin, the element that defines and separates us, protecting us from becoming confluent and losing our authentic identity
- in geography, markers of someone's land, a country or a state; but in relationships, invisible markers that protect our personal space and our minds, emotions, bodies and souls (Parker Hall, 2009)
- the means of showing that we are separate individuals, helping us move forward with our own best interests at heart.

Boundaries help us become autonomous and our own person. They help us listen to our 'gut' feelings and intuition. They help us chew over what others are saying to us. We don't just introject everything when we have good boundaries. We are neither too open to others, nor too closed off. Sometimes, when we leave a cultic setting, we can swing one way or the other – being too open and trusting everyone, or too closed and trusting no one.

A lack of boundaries results in confluence, which is, in a cultic setting, expected and enforced (M4). There is little or no boundary between us and others. If our boundaries are ineffective, we cannot stand up for ourselves and we may be abused, and 'taken for a ride' (deceived or cheated), again and again.

Figure M8.1 illustrates how, when there is a weak boundary (indicated by a dotted line around the individual member), and when we are not free to use our healthy assertive anger to hold our personal boundaries, the leadership or abusive others can merge with us (confluence). This undermines our ability to stand up for ourselves and to maintain a strong boundary and our autonomous authentic identity. Also, *when we are confluent, negative introjects flow in* (M5).

Worksheet M8.1 provides an opportunity to consider where your boundaries may be weak or non-existent.

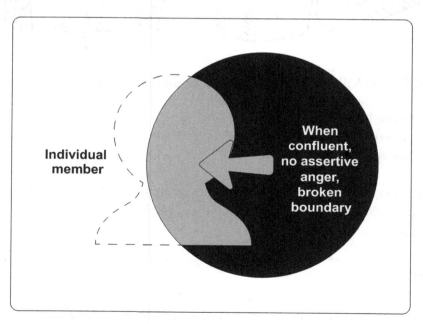

Figure M8.1 Confluence and lack of assertive anger

Worksheet M8.1: Checking your boundaries

After life in a cultic setting, we may have a distorted understanding of what is normal and appropriate. We may have become used to broken boundaries and to complying with others. This Worksheet will help to raise awareness of areas where your boundaries may be broken or ineffective. There is space for you to add more areas if you can identify them.

As you go through the Worksheet, you could ask yourself whether these signs applied to your own experience and whether you knew that they were unhealthy. You may be able to think of examples. You could write your answers in the spaces provided or in your journal. Some of these points are adapted from *Take Back Your Life: Recovering from Cults and Abusive Relationships* by Lalich and Tobias (2006, p. 171).

Date: _____

Evidence of broken boundaries	Your experience
Being too open about yourself, for example, telling people a lot about yourself before you have got to know them	
Feeling it is necessary to agree with or go along with others, even when this means overriding what is important to you	
Not realising until it is too late that someone is involved with, and controlling, aspects of your life	
Feeling unable to say no to unwanted gifts or attention	
Feeling unable to say no to others' requests and demands	
Believing what others say about you, even where this contradicts what you believe about yourself	
Letting others override your sexual preferences, such as when you are ready to have sexual contact and your sexual orientation	
Exhausting yourself trying to meet others' needs	

The way to build good boundaries is to develop our healthy assertive anger. Karla McLaren says

> Channel the fiery intensity of anger into your boundary instead of repressing it or exploding with it – then speak your truth or make your correcting actions. This will reset your boundaries in healthy ways, which will protect you and your relationships …and restore your sense of self (2010, pp. 167–168).

M8.2 Healthy boundary-setting assertive anger

In order to establish and maintain healthy boundaries, it is important to be able to develop our healthy assertive anger, which is a protective *boundary-setting emotion*, a guard at our door both physically and psychologically. It helps us differentiate ourselves from others and undo confluence. We need the energy of healthy assertive anger available to us, to protect ourselves and set our boundaries. It is a force that helps us push away what we need to push away – including people and ideas – and it counteracts fear.

Although anger is often understood in a negative way, as I will discuss in the next section, it is important to see healthy assertive anger as a positive emotion if we are to keep safe. This is because it has many functions, including helping us to navigate our lives, respect others and ensure our boundaries are strong but flexible – we are able to protect ourselves, but also let others in when appropriate. Healthy assertive anger is, therefore, a subtle and benign energy that ensures our safety and protection (McLaren, 2010; Parker Hall, 2009).

I love this quote from Sue Parker Hall. See what you think about it. (I have added 'healthy' in case the words 'pure' and 'sacred' are loaded language from your cultic setting.)

> Anger is a pure [healthy] emotion, a vital piece of intelligence about the immediate environment we are in, and it provides the energy and motivation for the sacred [healthy] task of self-care…. It operates as an emotional infrared sensor in relationships, making it possible for a person to navigate the delicate and tenuous, even treacherous at times, human and relational path between dependence and independence, 'self-assertion and mutual respect'…, or 'autonomy and belonging' … *It is entirely constructive in nature and we ignore it at our physical, emotional and social peril* (Parker Hall, 2009, pp. 1–2, italics and words in brackets mine).

An infrared sensor is an electronic instrument that senses what is happening in its surroundings. It is often connected to a house alarm set up to catch intruders. Assertive anger can be like this, warning us when our personal boundaries are being challenged.

When we have healthy assertive anger, we can judge whom to trust and whom not to trust. We do not swing like a pendulum too far one way, then the other. In order to heal, we need to carefully develop healthy relationships, and let safe enough others in. So we need to *both* protect and allow in. I have come to see healthy anger like a ring of fire around us. When we want someone close, it warms them, but when we want them to stay away, it burns them. (We will come back to this idea in M8.6.)

Assertive anger can be fiery and hot, it can be loud, but the key is, it is purposeful and we are always in control of it. It is never harmful to other people, things, nature or animals – and it respects both our own personal boundaries and others' boundaries.

It helps us to understand ourselves and our own needs, to overcome fear and depression, to access physical and emotional energy, to think clearly, to make decisions and act on them, to express ourselves, to process grief and loss, to keep healthy, to make positive changes in our lives, to be authentic and have genuine relationships (Parker Hall, 2009).

Do you find it surprising that assertive anger can have such positive outcomes? You may like to reflect on this in your journal.

There are some Worksheets to help you think about healthy assertive anger at the end of this Milestone, but next, I will explore the negative connotations, loaded language and introjects about anger.

M8.3 Anger – negative connotations, loaded language and introjects

In a cultic setting, personal assertive anger is likely to be prohibited and prevented through oppression, loaded language, introjection and self-suppression. So, unfortunately, for many former members, the term 'anger' has negative connotations from the cultic setting. Also, in wider society, the emotion of anger is often viewed as a problem, so former members are likely to have negative views of 'anger' coming from both directions.

Cultic settings usually give specific meanings to the concept of 'anger'. They 'load the language', implying or stating that 'anger' is out of bounds, harmful, unhelpful or negative; and perhaps going to cause the world to implode or you to explode, if you get 'angry'! It is likely to be labelled as 'sin', 'rebellious', 'unenlightened' or 'selfish' (whatever the language used) and outlawed or punished. In Samantha's group, members were told that, if they showed any sort of 'anger', they were releasing 'negative destructive energy' into the universe, causing untold harm, and so she had to suppress her feelings of anger. Members are, therefore, likely to be disarmed, and unable to stand up for themselves or set healthy boundaries.

Some cultic settings may regard 'anger' as wrong or 'sinful' if it is directed towards the leader or other members, but acceptable or even encouraged if directed towards the 'world' or people (including family) outside. This can lock members in more tightly, as they are unable to have healthy boundaries within the setting, but their separation from the outside is deepened.

Those from religious or therapeutic settings will most likely have been told they need to 'turn the other cheek' and 'forgive'. Although this may sound positive, it can be loaded language, with an underlying message that anger must be suppressed, and that it is wrong to maintain good boundaries.

It is important to highlight the loaded language, beliefs about 'anger' and associated introjects, as these need chewing over and challenging if we are to walk free (M5 and Worksheet M8.2).

Lawrence told me that his group only allowed what they called 'righteous anger' (which is also loaded language) from either the 'elders' or 'God'. This actually meant the leaders could 'rebuke' or discipline members whenever they wanted, for whatever they judged was wrong. They would unpredictably tell off members, and sometimes shout and be rageful, which was terrifying. He also told me that he was taught that "God was angry" a lot of the time, and that this was frightening to him growing up. The group produced magazines with drawings and scary graphic images depicting war and destruction – apparently the consequences of displeasing this 'God' and making him 'angry'.

Healthy assertive anger that sets boundaries helps us to separate ideas (beliefs) from facts. Lawrence concluded that the ideas about the end of the world, depicted in the magazines as a consequence of 'God's anger', were in fact lies to control rather than truths to be afraid of – but it took him time, using his healthy assertive anger, to chew these over and realise that they were not true. You may recall we looked at challenging these sorts of introjects and using your critical thinking skills, at M5.

As we see in Lawrence's experience, for some, the idea of 'anger' is terrifying because they were told that 'God's anger' was violent and destructive, and perhaps they have experienced the so-called 'righteous anger' of the leadership. I would describe these concepts as 'narcissistic rage' (M8.5). I am using 'anger' in a different way.

If the term 'anger' remains problematic for you, it may be easier to think of 'assertiveness' instead. If 'assertiveness' is also loaded for you, then feel free to think of your own words to make it easier for yourself. What is important is to identify and chew over the related introjects and challenge them, so you are able to protect your boundaries with this healthy emotion and appropriate force.

These negative introjects about anger can also result in a fear that 'being angry' means you are weak, a bully or like your leadership or abuser. This can be difficult and challenging when learning to stand up for yourself, as it can be hard to tell the difference. This is a reason to distinguish it from rage, as we will explore in the next section. We will look in more detail at how this relates to the leadership or abuser at M12.

Because of abuse and the introjects about anger, it is often a great challenge to assert oneself after a cultic experience. Sometimes, we think we are being angry when we are in rage, and sometimes, we think we are in rage when we are merely asserting ourselves. But healthy assertive anger is essential, so it is important to understand the difference and keep it in mind.

So that we can activate our assertive anger and establish our boundaries, we need to identify and chew over what we were told about 'anger' in the cultic setting – the introjects we are left with. You can use Worksheet M8.2 for this.

Worksheet M8.2: Exploring 'anger' introjects and loaded language

In this Worksheet, you have an opportunity to explore what you believe about anger. You could think about the loaded language and negative introjects you still hold in relation to anger, with a view to challenging and undoing them. You could answer the questions here or in your journal.

Date: _____

1. What did your cultic setting teach you about anger?

   _____

   _____

2. What 'loaded language' was used to describe anger?

   _____

   _____

3. What introjects and beliefs do you still hold relating to anger? (Give as many examples as you can.)

   _____

   _____

4. Can you chew over these introjects by writing down some statements that challenge them, and help build your boundary-setting assertive anger? (For example, "I have a right to protect my boundaries and stop people abusing me" or "I have a right to say no if I don't like what is being asked of me".)

   _____

   _____

5. Anything else you want to say about this?

   _____

   _____

M8.4 Rage

It can be helpful to think about rage as a different psychological process from anger, and not just as a different way of expressing it, or a more intense version. I am using 'rage', in Sue Parker Hall's words, as "not an emotion at all", but as a response to trauma, an unconscious "defence mechanism evoked when a person is overwhelmed by their experience and cannot integrate it". It is a trauma symptom when we struggle to process what we have experienced. It is "damaging to relationships, estranges us from ourselves and others and is only ever a destructive experience" (2009, p. 2).

Rage can be 'hot' or 'cold'. As rage is related to trauma, it may be helpful to recall the responses to trauma, and the three zones: window of tolerance; fight or flight; and freeze and submit (M7.5) – see Figure M8.2.

Hot rage is the exploding form of rage, often mistaken for anger. It is usually linked with 'fight or flight' (hyperarousal). Hot rage is highly charged, agitated, anxious, can be critical of others, complaining, sarcastic and dominating. Someone in hot rage is likely to try to coerce others to help, instead of being assertive and simply asking. Hot rage may be verbally and physically abusive or intimidating. It may also be linked with risk-taking behaviour (Parker Hall, 2009, p. 95). Cultic settings often stir up members' feelings against the outside world or those who oppose them, but this is likely to be hot rage rather than assertive anger.

Cold rage is less well recognised but is usually linked with 'freeze and submit' (hypoarousal). Cold rage is turned against the self, for example, in self-harm, wanting to die, suicidal thoughts and putting oneself down. It is low in energy, with little feeling, depressed, self-critical, perhaps trying to please others. Someone in cold rage may be silent or have a flat uninterested voice. They may be cynical and assume others will not or cannot help, so are unlikely to ask. They may avoid confrontation, be indifferent to others and be detached (Parker Hall, 2009, p. 95).

A common feature of hot and cold rage is that the underlying trauma is not being processed – in fact, the rage adds to the trauma for the individual. It may also traumatise others involved – in hot rage because of the explosive energy directed at them; in cold rage because of the sense of being shut out.

In contrast to rage, when we express assertive anger, we are in the window of tolerance and can think and feel at the same time. We can remain healthily connected to others, and the underlying trauma can be processed. Figure M8.2 is an updated version of the three zones diagram from M7.5. You will see that I have added 'assertive anger', 'hot rage' and 'cold rage' to show where each is located.

Window of Tolerance

– can think and feel at the same time

- optimal arousal zone
- safe enough
- grounded
- can process feelings, information, memories
- **assertive anger**
- introjects chewed over and challenged

Fight or flight

– "don't just sit there do something"

- hyperarousal zone
- sense danger
- mobilise and respond
- overwhelmed by feelings and sensations
- **hot rage**
- introjects unnoticed and unchallenge

Freeze and submit

– "don't move it's not safe"

- hypoarousal zone
- sense extreme danger
- immobilise and collapse
- shut down feelings and sensations
- **cold rage**
- introjects active and unchallenged

Figure M8.2 The three zones showing assertive anger, hot rage and cold rage

When we lack assertive anger, we still need to try and protect ourselves, but we struggle to defend our boundaries. Because we may feel overwhelmed and traumatised, we are likely to resort to rage, but this is counter-productive. Figure M8.3 illustrates the effects of hot and cold rage. Hot rage breaks through our weakened boundaries and explodes out towards others, whilst cold rage twists back against ourselves.

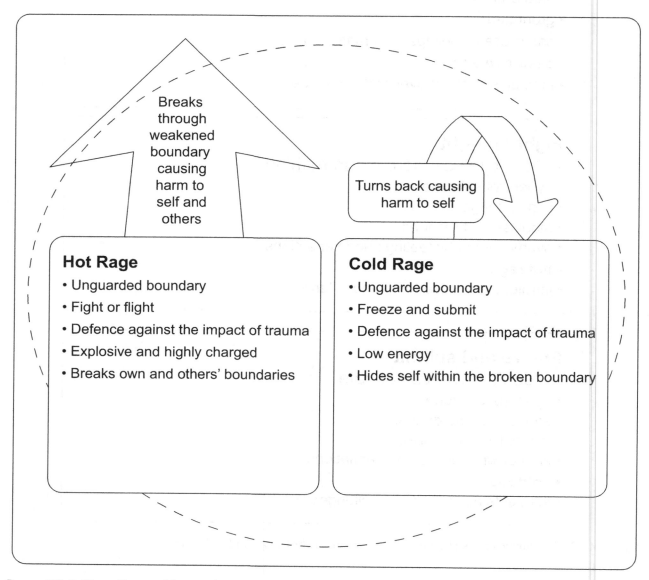

Figure M8.3 The effects of hot and cold rage

It helps to view healthy assertive anger as a purely positive emotion, and our 'rage' as a response to our trauma, requiring support and compassion so that it can be processed. We can then begin to take steps to increase our self-acceptance and self-love, and protect ourselves in healthy ways.

Worksheet M8.3 gives you an opportunity to explore and identify your hot and cold rage reactions, and to distinguish rage from assertive anger.

Worksheet M8.3: Identify your hot and cold rage and assertive anger

In this Worksheet, you could think about times you express, or have expressed, rage or anger and identify whether this was hot rage, cold rage or assertive anger. For example:

Example	Is this hot or cold rage, or assertive anger?
I shout and block other people from speaking because I am terrified about what they will say and don't want to hear their opinion.	Hot rage
I sometimes have no energy and lie in bed all day feeling very upset with myself.	Cold rage
I am no longer prepared to go along with people who are trying to manipulate and shame me into doing things that are against my values.	Assertive anger

You could note down your own experiences below or in your journal.

Date: _____

Example	Is this hot or cold rage, or assertive anger?

One problem with rage is that it is often directed at the wrong people – including, in the case of cold rage, ourselves. The thing that triggers our rage is probably different from whatever caused the underlying trauma. It, therefore, helps if we can work out what triggered our response, and why. It may be a pattern match linked to past traumas (M7.7). The next Worksheet is an opportunity to look at this. If we can identify the underlying trauma, we can then take care of ourselves and start to process it and recover (M7.8 and M7.9).

Worksheet M8.4: What caused your hot and/or cold rage responses?

You could reflect on what caused you to have the hot and cold rage responses that you entered into Worksheet M8.3, by asking yourself these questions and writing answers here or in your journal.

Date _____

1. What happened in the present that was a pattern match (M7.7) for a past experience, and triggered your hot or cold rage? (For example, I walked into a room full of people and found myself shouting/going silent.)

    _____

    _____

2. What was that past experience? (For example, meetings in the cultic setting.)

    _____

    _____

3. How could you challenge this pattern match? (For example, you could consider ways in which the present is different from the past, and how you can handle similar pattern matches in future. Remember that this is a symptom of a memory.)

    _____

    _____

> **Reminder:** Rage, like other trauma symptoms, provides clues for understanding ourselves and what we have been through. I suggest you be curious, patient and compassionate with yourself, find your way back to the window of tolerance and continue to support yourself.

M8.5 Narcissistic rage

We have discussed how rage, both hot and cold, is a defensive response when we are struggling with trauma. I think we all experience rage from time to time. But there is another type of rage – narcissistic rage – which happens when a narcissist (someone with an over-inflated view of themselves, such as a cultic leader) is hindered or thwarted and does not get their own way. This can result in them blaming and attacking the members, those who have left, and outsiders. This is the kind of rage you may have experienced from a leader who seemed out of control, and punitive or indifferent towards you.

It may be frightening to be the object of or to witness narcissistic rage. It may also result in a fear that 'being angry' means you are weak, a bully or like your narcissistic leader. For now, it is important to note that narcissistic rage is qualitatively different because it arises from the narcissism of the leader. We will revisit issues arising from the leader at M12, and narcissism at M9.

M8.6 The ring of fire

Now that we have considered how anger is often (wrongly) viewed negatively, and how it is different from rage, this Milestone ends with three Worksheets to help you set boundaries and exercise your healthy assertive anger.

I suggest you imagine a ring of fire around you – warming those you want close, but burning or warning off those you do not. It is normal to have 'layers' of people in our lives: some we trust more and let close; some, perhaps work colleagues, who are a step away but we trust to a degree; and those we do not and should not trust at all.

For example, Jonah came to see me for counselling. He told me he never got angry and had weak personal boundaries. In his cultic setting, he was highly confluent, which resulted in him often being exploited. After we had worked on his introjects about assertive anger and boundaries, I suggested he imagine a ring of fire around him to protect himself.

He arrived at the next session and reported an incident at work where someone was asking him to do something he was unhappy with: "I didn't like what they were asking, and I felt my assertive anger and my ring of fire flare up and I said no!" I loved that – his ring of fire flared up and protected him, which surprised and delighted him (and me)! He had made a big step towards setting up healthy boundaries and using his assertive anger to protect himself.

Worksheet M8.5: Ring of fire – who to trust and who to hold at bay

This Worksheet contains an image of a ring of fire protecting 'you' inside. There is space to write down who/what you want close, and who/what you want to keep away using your assertive anger.

Date: _____

Who do you want to come close?

Who do you want to be kept away?

You

Worksheet M8.6: Questions about your ring of fire

You could see if you can use this idea of a ring of fire as a picture of assertive anger, to help you rebuild your boundaries, by asking yourself these questions. You could write here or in your journal.

Date: _____

1. Do you feel you have a right to have a ring of fire around you?

   _____

   _____

2. If not, can you reflect on why not – what introjects stop you from protecting yourself?

   _____

   _____

3. What must be protected?

   _____

   _____

4. What boundaries need to be restored?

   _____

   _____

Worksheet M8.7: Boundary-setting physical exercise

One way of visualising asserting your boundaries is to represent this with your own body like this:

- stand or sit, well balanced with feet rooted on the ground
- raise your arms straight ahead
- turn your hands up, palms facing forwards, so they create a boundary around you
- push your hands away from you as illustrated below.

As you do this, you could say 'no', or 'back off', as loudly as you want to or write on the Worksheet what you might say to whoever does not respect your boundaries. Think about who or what you are speaking to. I suggest you have fun with it as it can be surprisingly empowering!

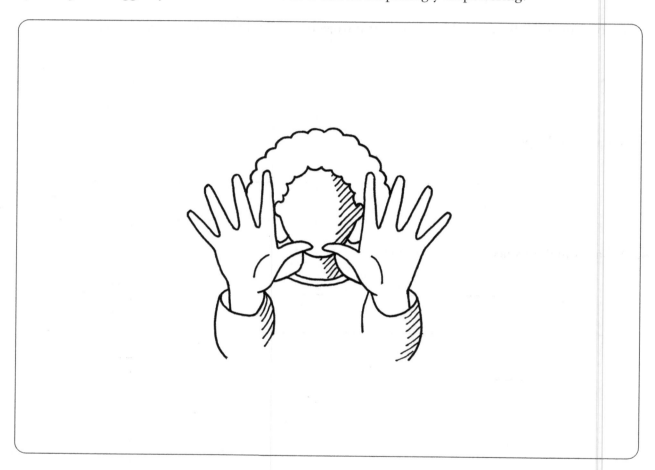

We have now completed this Milestone and can proceed on our Walking Free journey to Milestone 9 and look at healthy self-love.

Healthy self-love

We have arrived at Milestone 9 where you have the opportunity to sit and unpack your baggage in relation to loving yourself – which I will call 'self-love'.

Self-love is a good thing! How do you react when I say that?

If we love ourselves, we know we can take care of ourselves and our needs; protect ourselves with our assertive anger; have an authentic voice to speak our 'truth'; and grow in confidence as we learn to appreciate our own abilities and qualities.

This idea is likely to go against the grain for most former members, because in a coercive, cultic and spiritually abusive setting, we may introject the belief that appreciating our own abilities and qualities is 'selfish', 'egotistical', 'bourgeois' or 'proud' (or whatever language was used). As a result, we may equate self-love and confidence with pride or selfishness. To recover and grow, we need to chew over and challenge these introjects, but after leaving a cultic setting, we may have (very) mixed feelings about ourselves, and struggle to love ourselves.

The psychological term for excessive self-love is **'narcissism'**. To give some context and explain the ideas around narcissism and self-love, I am first going to tell you a story – the myth of Narcissus and Echo.

DOI: 10.4324/9781003305798-15

M9.1 The myth of Narcissus and Echo

The term 'narcissism' comes from the ancient Greek myth of Narcissus. A myth is a story passed down over generations, which illustrates and gives meaning to aspects of human life and relationships. There are numerous versions of the myth of Narcissus – this is my summary.

First, I will introduce you to the cast of characters:

- **Narcissus** was a hunter, beautiful but arrogant and aloof. Men and women fell in love with him, but he did not think any of them worthy and treated them with contempt and disdain.
- **Echo** was a beautiful nymph, a spirit of nature living in the woods and rivers.
- **Juno** was a powerful goddess, who had punished Echo for talking too much by stopping her from communicating freely – she could only repeat words spoken by others.
- **Nemesis** was the goddess of revenge.

The story goes that, while Narcissus was arrogantly thinking he was better than his friends and admirers, Echo saw him and fell in love with him. She became obsessed, longing for his attention. When he became separated from his companions and shouted, "Is anyone there?", she had her opportunity, but could only repeat back his words. He was not impressed, and spurned her, saying he would never love her. She ran off feeling rejected and shamed, but despite this, her love for Narcissus grew.

Nemesis put a spell on Narcissus to punish him for his arrogance, telling him he would only live to a ripe old age if he never looked at himself. But Narcissus looked into a still pool of water, saw his reflection and was captivated by his own beauty – he thought he had finally found someone worthy of his love! Narcissus dived in to try to embrace this beautiful person, and drowned! (He was then turned into a flower!)

Echo continued to be obsessed with him and wasted away until only her echoing voice was left.

Not a happy ending, but a story that says a lot, as I will unpack next!

M9.2 The continuum of self-love

'Narcissism' has come to mean unhealthy and excessive self-love, as we can see in the mythical Narcissus. In psychology, it is seen as part of a continuum, including both healthy and excessive self-love; and Craig Malkin (2015) adds the interesting idea of 'echoism', from Echo in the myth.

In the sections below, I will look at how too much self-love (narcissism), and too little (echoism), are both unhealthy. I will also explain how, in cultic settings, there can be a harmful mixture of both extremes. I will then look at healthy self-love.

We can think of these on a continuum (adapted from Malkin, 2015), as illustrated in Figure M9.1.

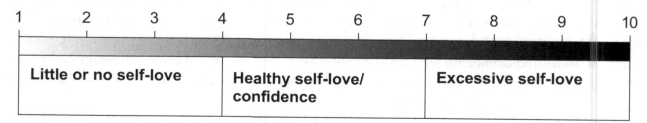

Figure M9.1 Continuum of self-love

The Worksheets in this Milestone are all in the final section.

M9.3 Unhealthy excess of self-love – narcissism

Those who have excessive self-love, interest in or admiration of themselves like Narcissus, are referred to as 'narcissists'. They sit at the right side of the continuum, and on the whole only care for or are interested in themselves.

You are likely to encounter such people in a cultic setting in the top layer of leadership, but also, to some degree, in other layers including personal monitors, 'caring brothers or sisters', 'shepherds' or 'disciplers' (or whatever term is used). We will return to the subject of leaders, and their narcissism, at M12.

Unfortunately, narcissists also crop up outside cultic settings and so, to keep safe, it is important to know about them and to be wary – although they can be hard to identify.

M9.4 Unhealthy lack of self-love – echoism

Malkin (2015) calls those with little or no self-love 'echoists'. They sit at the left side of the continuum. In a cultic setting, they are likely to feel they have no intrinsic value, other than being an 'echo' of the leader, other members and the introjected beliefs.

When I first visited Wellspring, a facility for counselling former members, as an intern in 1999, the clients completed psychological tests on arrival, which were then 'read' through a computer programme at the local University. Among other things, this measured their levels of narcissism. Invariably, their scores were extremely low – they were echoists on Malkin's scale. Many clients had virtually no self-love, as they had not been allowed to think about themselves or consider their own needs in the cultic setting. They had learned to suppress many thoughts and feelings about themselves, including positive thoughts about their own value and abilities, and the need to take care of, or make decisions for, themselves.

The Wellspring clients went through the two-week 'Thought Reform Programme', talking to a specialist therapist and attending psychoeducational sessions to gain a psychological understanding of what happened in their cultic setting. At the end, they repeated the psychological tests. The results showed that their narcissism levels had in most cases risen – they had moved closer to the middle of the continuum. This was regarded as a good thing. These clients had more of a sense of themselves and more self-love. They had chewed over and processed some of the introjects that said they were not allowed to love or value themselves, take care of themselves or have assertive anger and set personal boundaries.

I was surprised at first that more narcissism was regarded as good because I had always assumed it was a bad thing. However, for an echoist, it is healthy to move up to the middle of the continuum – in a sense becoming a 'bit more narcissistic' – and to love and value themself more.

I will come back to healthy self-love, but first I want to address a mixed version of narcissism and echoism that can occur in cultic settings.

M9.5 Echoing the cultic setting's narcissism

As we have seen in previous Milestones, as confluent members of a cultic setting, we introject the beliefs and behaviours of the leaders and the setting. These become part of our pseudo-identity. We are echoists, without our own voice but repeating what we are told. But ironically, this includes narcissistic ideas about the setting and its importance. We are 'echoing' the narcissism of the leadership and the beliefs.

Cultic settings commonly believe they are the *only* ones with the 'Truth', that they are special or chosen, and members are taught to reject outsiders. This can lead to a high level of self-importance and 'grandiosity' (feeling superior to others). This is part of our cultic pseudo-identity, not our authentic identity. It is not healthy self-love, but is an unhealthy narcissism, introjected from the group.

Members are likely to believe the 'mission' is of the utmost importance: for example, they are saving the world or bringing the universe into balance; or their political views will revolutionise society. There are many other variations depending on the setting. Some participants in my Doctoral research had beliefs about their group's mission which resulted in a sense of great purpose, grandiose importance and feeling unique and special. Sean believed that his getting closer to his guru would have a global impact and contribute to:

> ...the glory of the guru and God and everybody else, and the whole wide world.

That is, his leader, his cult and the mission were all extremely special – and because he was part of that, so was he!

When I was a member of the Community, I felt important by association, superior to all those 'unsaved' people who needed to become part of our group in order to be 'saved' – even those in other churches.

And so, we may be an echoist and voiceless, with a suppressed authentic identity, but also exhibit a level of grandiosity and narcissism within our pseudo-identity. Paradoxically, the introjects tell us we are a 'bad' person, but also a member of a 'perfect' group with a 'perfect' leader.

In some groups, certain children are given special status, so that they introject a narcissistic narrative in a very personal way. Some who are born and/or raised have been told they are a 'blessed' or 'golden' child, 'Prince' or 'Princess', specially chosen for one purpose which is to serve the leader, and that the hope and future of mankind rest on them. In Gloria's group, the children were there:

> ...just to serve this role, to serve the leader and the scripture or the directives, the higher purpose, the meditation and chanting.

They are doubly special, first as a member and second because of their special purpose. This can result in a grandiose sense of identity and status while in the setting. However, when they leave, they may have little or no sense of self or purpose. Their primary sense of identity has been lost, and they are left bereft (Jenkinson, 2016). This can leave them feeling fragile and insecure, and they may oscillate between feeling ordinary and special. They may experience much emotional pain because they don't know who they are, or who to be, in an alien world outside the cultic setting.

If our introjected grandiose attitudes are not challenged, we may annoy and alienate others, because they are unlikely to understand why we think these things, or how our cultic experiences and pseudo-identity have affected us. We may then be ostracised further, and fear we are 'weird' and unlovable.

It is vital therefore that, after leaving, we address both the introjects that told us we had little value and those that told us we were special and superior. As we chew over these introjected ideas and attitudes, and challenge them, we can build a realistic, grounded authentic identity outside the cultic setting. The Worksheets are designed to help with this.

The antidote to both echoism and narcissism is to develop a realistic, nuanced and balanced view of ourselves, building up our healthy self-love around the centre of the continuum. This is a key part of the Walking Free journey!

We may have no one who sees us as special – a normal need that a healthy family can meet. This may be especially relevant if our family members remain in the setting, or if we were in a cultic *and* abusive family, and we know no one, or only a few people, outside. If we have been rejected and 'shunned', perhaps leaving family behind, this can only make the pain and trauma of leaving worse.

If this is the case for you, I encourage you to keep going with the Walking Free journey, but also to seek support. We are only human, and it is normal to have needs and to get help. You could revisit the sections on looking after yourself (P3.1) and understanding trauma (M7), or consider seeking therapy (P5).

M9.6 Healthy self-love

Healthy self-love sits around the centre of the echoism/narcissism continuum. It is a balanced place and is necessary for us to live a fulfilling life. (Some people call it 'healthy narcissism', but I am using 'healthy self-love', to make clear that it avoids the harmful aspects of narcissism.)

Healthy self-love means we can feel special sometimes without becoming obsessed with our specialness. We can move "seamlessly between self-absorption and caring attentiveness – visiting Narcissus's shimmering pool, but never diving to the bottom in pursuit of our own reflection" (Malkin, 2015, p. 32). We can also be realistic that we will not necessarily change the world, but that we have something unique to contribute, "a voice, a presence of our own, to make an impact on the world and people around us or else, like Echo, we eventually become nothing at all" (Malkin, 2015, p. 14).

Healthy assertive anger (M8) and healthy self-love combine to give us an authentic voice, stopping us being an 'echoist' and moving us to the centre of the continuum.

For years, I thought I needed others to give me permission to do things I wanted to do. I was so used to looking to God, or the leaders, or others to tell me what I could do, and what I was good at, because I was an echoist. I didn't believe in myself or trust my own abilities. It took a long time, but I gradually realised that I didn't need others' permission or validation. I could recognise my own strengths and make my own decisions about my life. I still listen to others and often take their advice, but ultimately I can make up my own mind.

A misunderstanding some make about healthy self-love is that it is fixed, and that we can't or shouldn't change our degree of narcissism. In fact, it is healthy for our level of narcissism to vary (within limits!). There are times when we need more help and attention from others, such as when we are ill or seeking promotion at work; and times when we need less, such as when we are caring for a child or supporting a partner. We may, therefore, move up or down the scale but, to stay healthy, only for a time, returning to the centre (Malkin, 2015). In contrast, an unhealthy echoist or narcissist is largely stuck at one extreme of the continuum, unable to be flexible.

It is important to remember that it is not 'selfish' or 'self-centred' to love ourselves, or to consider and promote ourselves. The idea that healthy self-love is a negative thing, whatever language or terms are used, indicates introjects.

Each of us needs validating as a unique individual who is both special (you and your life matter) and ordinary (it is not on you to save the world, or to be the best of the best – you can just be you!). You are allowed to, and it is essential to, receive affirmation and encouragement that you are both special and ordinary, and this is something a trusted friend or therapist can do.

Remember to take care of yourself and take your time, as these can be difficult and painful issues to look at. The good news is that our levels of self-love are flexible and movable, and we can develop a healthy authentic identity, a sense of self-love and a voice – and recover!

All these aspects of self-love are brought together in Figure M9.2.

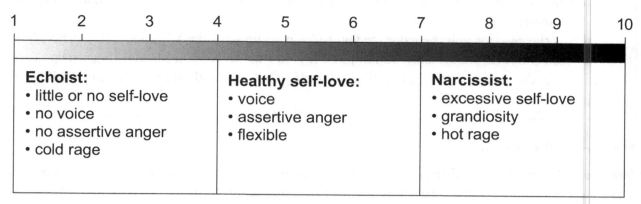

Figure M9.2 Summary of the self-love continuum

These Worksheets will help you reflect on these issues.

M9.7 Worksheets

In the following Worksheets, you can reflect on your levels of self-love and narcissism when you were a member, and now.

Worksheet M9.1: Reflection on self-love and levels of narcissism

In this Worksheet, you could reflect on aspects of self-love and narcissism that may apply to you, both as a member and since leaving. If the wording does not quite describe your situation, then feel free to change it.

    If there are other stages of your life you want to think about (for example, before joining, or if you were in more than one cultic setting or abusive relationship) then you could copy the Worksheet or recreate it in your journal. You can mark how much each applied to your situation on a scale of 0–10 (0 not applicable and 10 very applicable). If you have more to say, you could reflect in your journal.

Date _____

When you were a member/since leaving, how much have you...	As a member	Since leaving
Lacked self-love and felt that you are not personally important or special?		
Been an echoist – an echo of the leader and others?		
Felt superior to and more special than others (grandiose), especially non-members or those below you in the structure of the cultic setting?		
Felt the loss of status after being a 'special' person on a 'special' mission?		
Felt you are 'weird', not 'normal', compared to others in your life?		
Struggled to find a voice and exert your boundaries, for example, not thinking you are allowed to say 'no'?		
Struggled to find your voice and say how you see things?		
Struggled to find your voice and tell a (safe) other what has happened to you?		
Found it hard to view yourself in a positive light?		
Found it hard to respect others' views?		

Worksheet M9.2: Introjects about loving yourself

This Worksheet provides an opportunity to identify and challenge introjects specifically related to the idea of loving yourself. For example:

Identify introjects related to 'self-love'	Challenge to introject
Self-love is 'egotistical', 'sinful', 'selfish' and must be suppressed.	Self-love is essential if I am to stop being an echoist and move up the scale towards healthy self-love. It will also help me feel more confident and better about myself, develop a voice and assert my boundaries.
If I have confidence, it shows I am 'proud'.	The word 'proud' is loaded language and was used to suppress me. I redefine 'pride' or 'proud' to mean I can be pleased with myself and happy with my achievements! And so having pride and confidence in myself is a good thing.

You could add your examples in the table below or in your journal.

Date _____

Identify introjects related to 'self-love'	Challenge to introject

Worksheet M9.3: Have you introjected grandiosity?

This Worksheet is to help you raise awareness of whether you introjected grandiosity or narcissistic thinking. You can write comments or examples in the spaces or in your journal.

Date _____

1. Were members generally considered special, and if so, how?

   _____

   _____

   _____

2. Were you regarded as special within the setting, for example, as a 'prince', 'princess', 'blessed child' or another term?

   _____

   _____

   _____

3. Did you feel a split in your identity – that you were 'special', but also of little value?

   _____

   _____

   _____

4. How do you see yourself now, for example, special, ordinary or both?

   _____

   _____

   _____

Worksheet M9.4: Reflection on leaving and self-love

This Worksheet is an opportunity to reflect on how leaving has affected your self-love, and what support you may need. You can write comments or examples in the spaces or in your journal.

Date _____

1. What was it like when you lost your 'special' member status and identity?

    _____

    _____

2. Since leaving, how has your self-love grown and developed?

    _____

    _____

3. Who/what has helped you?

    _____

    _____

4. Who do you trust to support you?

    _____

    _____

5. Are you able to ask for help?

    _____

    _____

6. What do you need as you continue on your Walking Free journey, and how can you access it?

    _____

    _____

Worksheet M9.5: Where were you on the narcissism scale as a member?

This Worksheet gives you an opportunity to reflect on *where you were* on the narcissism scale when you were a member. Did you have too little self-love (1–4), too much (7–10) or a healthy level (4–7)? If you were in more than one setting, or the answer varied over different stages, you can note this below, copy the Worksheet or replicate it in your journal.

Date _____

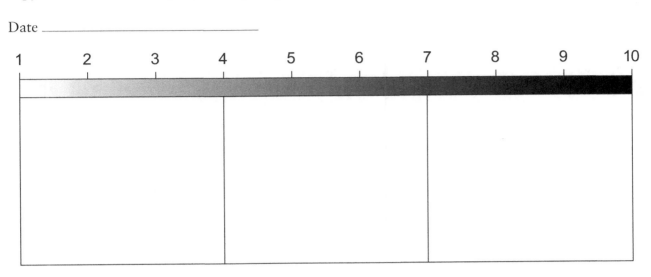

Worksheet M9.6: Where are you now on the narcissism scale?

This Worksheet gives you an opportunity to reflect on *where you are now* on the narcissism scale, post-membership, in the same way as Worksheet M9.5.

Date _____

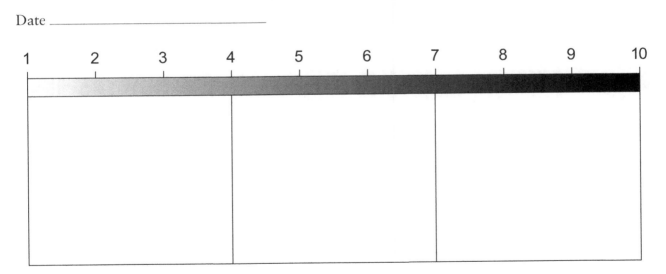

We are now coming to the heart of our journey and this Workbook – understanding cult dynamics and the cult mindset, including thought reform. We will look at this next in Milestone 10.

Thought reform

M10.0 Introduction

We are making great progress! We have now arrived at the heart of our journey – the area on the Roadmap illustrated by eight hills – the thought reform range. These provide us with a clear overview of the eight components of thought reform and the controlling coercive cultic dynamics: a view that is hidden from us when we are in the midst of them.

At the top of each hill, there is a bench, a place to sit and unpack the baggage related to your experience. As you understand each component, grasp the dynamics of thought reform and apply these dynamics to your own story, you will continue to Walk Free.

Hill walking may take more effort, but the view is better, we can see further, and everything is clearer from the top. Similarly, this Milestone includes a lot to consider but provides a different and revealing perspective on all that has gone before and all that is to come.

The term 'thought reform' describes the system and dynamics of control in a coercive, cultic and spiritually abusive group or relationship. It has eight components which we will work through in turn.

The purpose of going through this in detail is to help you *find words* for the systemic abuse in your group or relationship and *understand more clearly* how you may have been unduly influenced – and how you are still affected. The aim is to tell and make sense of your story, recognise blind spots and free your authentic identity, one step at a time. Thought reform works through deception, and its

DOI: 10.4324/9781003305798-16

methods are hidden in a cultic setting. Simply understanding this system and its components, and how they operated in your case, is key to moving forward.

I find it remarkable how accurately thought reform describes the experience of all the former members I have counselled, even though they have come from so many different types of cultic settings. Former members 'get it', relate to it and tell me they find it hugely helpful. I hope you find it as liberating as I and others have.

Before proceeding, I will briefly tell you where the theory of thought reform came from, and what it is.

M10.0.1 History and terminology of thought reform theory

The theory of thought reform emerged from research conducted in the 1950s by Robert Jay Lifton with former Chinese and Western prisoners of war who were 'converted' and 'brainwashed' by the Chinese Communist regime. If, after working through this Milestone, you would like to look further into this, Lifton's book, *Thought Reform and the Psychology of Totalism: A Study of 'Brainwashing' in China* (1989) is worth reading, especially Chapter 22, which describes the eight components. (This chapter was republished in *Losing Reality: On Cults, Cultism, and the Mindset of Political and Religious Zealotry* (2019).)

Thought reform theory provides powerful insights into the cultic mindset and setting, and has been found to apply to former members of many kinds of coercive, cultic and spiritually abusive groups and relationships (Lifton, 1999, 2019; Martin, 1993; Lalich and Tobias, 2006). It has helped many former members to make sense of their experience and Walk Free.

I have developed and applied Lifton's thought reform theory, with the benefit of others' research, and use it as a springboard for understanding the cultic experience in Post-Cult Counselling. I adopted it as a theoretical framework for analysing the data in my research. In this Milestone, the explanations, descriptions and applications of each component, therefore, draw from Lifton (1989 and 2019), my Doctoral research (Jenkinson, 2016) and my clinical and life experience. I have used anonymised examples from my research participants and counselling clients, with their permission.

Although I use Lifton's term 'thought reform', if you were born and/or raised in a cultic setting, the term 'thought forming' is more accurate. This is because your thoughts and emotions (and identity) have been formed there, rather than re-formed (as is the case with those who joined). For simplicity, I will use 'thought reform' to imply both forming and re-forming and will highlight any differences when applicable.

M10.0.2 The eight components of thought reform

Lifton's eight components of thought reform, with my brief comments, are:

1. Milieu control – control of the environment and communication
2. Mystical manipulation – stage-managed phenomena to elevate the leader
3. Demand for purity – 'purity' as they define it
4. Confession – over-share so you feel better, but give them ammunition
5. Sacred science – they have 'THE Truth'
6. Loading the language – thought-stopping clichéd language
7. Doctrine over person – following the teaching is more important than an individual's well-being
8. Dispensing of existence – you have no right to exist if you are not confluent and compliant

Although these may be challenging to understand initially, we will chew over their meaning and how they may apply to your experience.

> All the eight components work together, they are a system, a machine, not independent processes – although some may be more applicable than others. It is not necessary for every component, or every aspect of a component, to apply for thought reform to work and control to occur – but often they will all apply, even if some are hidden at first.

Before we unpack each component of thought reform, I will provide some guidance on working through this Milestone.

M10.0.3 Working through the components

At this Milestone, I provide the opportunity for you to reflect on how each component applies to your experience – and how it does not – and this will help you not to miss any of those blind spots!

For each component, I will provide a description, with examples. As you read, you can consider whether you recognise your experience and whether the explanation accurately describes it. If so, you may like to tick the sentence or paragraph. If your experience was a little different, you could amend or add to the text to more accurately describe your situation, or write in your journal.

The examples from former members' experiences illustrate certain points and may help you recognise, make sense of and apply them to yourself. If you do not relate to a particular example, see if you can think of anything similar from your, or another former member's, experience. Each person's experience is different, even from the same setting, but my hope is that you can identify with and apply at least some of the examples.

There are Worksheets for each component, including opportunities to write down specific incidents and examples of how it applies to your experience. You don't need to think of every single example, one or two may suffice. You can use either the spaces allocated or your journal.

There is also an opportunity to reflect on how often each component applied to your experience. Other Worksheets are there to help you 'chew over' your experience of thought reform. As you work through this Milestone, you will gain a greater understanding of coercive, cultic and spiritually abusive dynamics and how they apply to you personally.

As there are many connections between the components of thought reform – and because they work as a system – I have indicated some of these connections by naming other components in brackets next to particular points, for example '(milieu control)'.

If you were required to read through texts in your cultic setting, remember that this is different! There, you were almost certainly learning by rote, taking in and introjecting beliefs without chewing the ideas over. Here, the purpose is to use your critical thinking (M5) and tell your story as it was for *you* – you are in control. You might also like to refresh your memory on navigating the Workbook generally (P1.6).

You may find parts of this triggering. Please take your time, and if you find any aspect too hard, then you can leave it and return to it at another time; or revisit the sections on looking after yourself and your Safe Enough Space (P3.1) and understanding traumatic stress (M7); or consider speaking with a safe enough friend or therapist (P5). Self-care, including listening to and regulating ourselves, is of utmost importance.

I will now introduce you to each of the eight components, starting with milieu control.

M10.1 Milieu control

We have now reached the top of the hill on the Roadmap that addresses milieu control! There is a bench for you to sit and reflect on how this affected you in your cultic setting. We will spend more time on this than other components.

Milieu control is the overarching term describing the limitation and control of the member's environment and personal life, communication with the outside world and inner dialogue. Lifton (1989, p. 420) refers to it as the *"psychological current"* upon which all else in the thought reform environment depends: it *sets the whole process in motion*. It has many aspects and is worth exploring in detail.

A 'milieu' is a person's social environment and includes the individual and their personal life, other people, physical and social conditions, and events and routines that form this environment in which they act and live. As control of the environment and personal life – including time, energy and communication – is exerted on the unsuspecting, and often idealistic, individual, they become internally and externally entrapped, enmeshed and confluent.

This psychological current sweeps them into the thought reform milieu. I picture this as a strong current in the sea – if a swimmer gets pulled in, they are unlikely to be able to resist. Those who join a cultic setting may dive in, be pulled in or they may be groomed and swept in. Those who are born and/or raised are dropped into the current from an early age and have no choice.

In all cases, this current sweeping around them creates a psychological prison that ensures the whole thought reform process continues to exert control over them and, for many, takes years to recognise and break free from.

Max referred to this psychological prison as a *"marble edifice"*. When I think of this, I imagine a structure or building with no doors or windows, or just small high windows, with thick walls that are made of marble and seem impossible to break through. Often mausoleums or tombs are referred to as marble edifices. This is a picture of the psychological prison that constrains and squeezes us, resulting in us being suppressed and suppressing ourselves, and feeling stifled and suffocated. It is hard to penetrate a marble edifice once it is set in place: it is hard to face our doubts, crack it open and escape.

So, how does the marble edifice or psychological prison form in practice? The details will vary according to circumstances, but the strategy and results tend to be similar in many settings, including some which are assumed to be less 'cultic'.

Milieu control happens where various coercive and controlling strategies are in place and is the *purposeful limitation and control* of

- the environment, physical energy and personal life
- communication with the outside world
- internal communication within the individual

I will explain each of these.

M10.1.1 Limitation and control of the environment, physical energy and personal life

This can touch almost every aspect of the member's life, including:

- physical energy
- time
- sleep
- personal space and privacy
- food and diet
- clothing choices
- physical and mental health needs
- money and employment
- social life and celebrations
- sex, marriage and sexuality
- having and bringing up children
- access to legal protection

I will discuss each area and give some examples, both from others' experiences and my own (in the Community, all of these areas were controlled).

The member's physical energy is required in the service of the cultic group or relationship, restricting their time, work and social life. Members may be expected to work long exhausting hours on little food (see below), including late nights and early mornings, leading to sleep deprivation. This happens because the mission is deemed to be more important than our personal needs (doctrine over person). Members may not even realise they are suffering burnout because they have rationalised that it is more important to keep working for the leader and the cultic setting, than to 'waste' time on rest or sleep. When we suffer from sleep deprivation, we are more easily influenced and less able to think critically. The introjects flow in, and we are likely to be kept in the 'freeze' zone.

It took me a long time to realise that working at my job all day, and then being expected to labour till 3 a.m. decorating community households, was milieu control – we were overworked, sleep deprived and exhausted, and it aided self-suppression. Others have told me they had to go to work and then spend their evenings delivering Bible studies or seeking recruits, leading to exhaustion and burnout. In some cultic settings, members are woken randomly, purposely disrupting their sleep patterns so they cannot respond naturally to their circadian rhythms, which regulate sleeping and waking.

The lack of available time and the expenditure of physical energy results in members having little or no personal space, or insufficient energy to use it for their own benefit and well-being. Consequently, they have little or no time to use their critical thinking (M5), reflect and chew over what is happening and what they are hearing – so negative introjects can flow in unchecked. In the Community, our personal boundaries were denied us, for example, we had to share bedrooms and had no choice with whom. This lack of privacy is true of many cultic settings. Privacy for personal care and shutting doors on the bedroom, bathroom or toilet may be prohibited. Children may not be taught about personal boundaries and may have no personal space for reflection, recreation and play.

When we lack energy and the needed fuel for our body, we are more easily influenced, and so a powerful strategy to keep members weakened and introjecting is to control food. Low physical energy may keep us in the 'freeze' zone (M7). Whilst the food in the Community did not lack nutrition, what, when and how much we could eat was controlled – I remember often feeling weak and faint due to lack of food. In other cultic settings, members are told they must be vegan or vegetarian, or they have an unbalanced diet lacking in nutrition, disgusting to eat or a small amount. This can lead to depleted energy, malnutrition, digestive disorders and difficulty monitoring body weight.

Being told what to wear can have a huge impact on our identity because we cannot show our individuality through our clothes, as many people do outside of cultic settings. Sometimes what members wear is almost a uniform that identifies them with the setting, such as orange robes, suits for men or long dresses and head coverings for women. Meanwhile, certain clothes are banned, such as trousers for women. In some, the children have to wear homemade clothes, hand-me-downs, second-hand or substandard clothes. In one, everyone had to share underwear from a communal drawer – they had no choices and nothing they could call their own that would identify them as themselves.

Many members are restricted from taking care of their body, and physical and mental health – in fact, they are likely to suppress thinking about these aspects of their life, assuming it is selfish, 'egotistical', 'worldly' or 'sinful' to do so. Many settings have a belief that the body is less important than the 'soul' or 'spirit', leading members to dismiss their physical needs (sacred science, doctrine over person and dispensing of existence). This is dangerous, because our bodies matter, we live in them and need to take care of them. These beliefs result in us living in 'freeze', where we may harm ourselves by not attending to our needs properly.

Many members do not have access to adequate medical or dental care. Some cultic settings believe prayer, strange and unusual rituals, or herbal remedies, are sufficient for all ailments, but relying on these may be ineffective or dangerous. If someone has a disease that requires medication and treatment, but is prevented from receiving these, they may be in danger of dying or long-term harm. Mental health needs may be assumed to require a 'spiritual' solution, so access to professional help is denied.

Some settings only allow their members access to doctors who are approved by, or are members of, the cultic setting. These doctors may break patient confidentiality and report back to the leadership. The leader may control the member doctor and expect them to give the treatment the leader, 'God' or other higher being, has 'prescribed', rather than sound medical advice.

Those joining a cultic setting are often expected to hand over their possessions and savings. If members are allowed to work in jobs outside the cultic setting, they may be required to pass all or most of their earnings to the leadership or central organisation. This ensures confluence and dependency – members cannot easily leave if they do not have the resources to do so. When I worked outside the Community, I handed over all my earnings. Some have to secretly save their wage rises over years before they can leave.

Many cultic settings have their own businesses and expect members to work for years with little or no pay. Consequently, they have no pension, savings or financial security in old age. If they leave, they may live in poverty, and it is likely that many therefore stay.

Many cultic and spiritually abusive leaders have double standards in relation to finances, assuming they personally deserve to live well because of their status, whilst members struggle financially.

Many cultic settings do not allow their members to celebrate festivals such as Christmas, birthdays or other occasions valued by society in general – these are viewed as 'worldly' or something similar (depending on the language of the setting). This further separates members from society. If they attend mainstream school or work, they are likely to be barred by the cultic setting from acknowledging these festivals and celebrating with others, and this is likely to leave them feeling they are 'not normal', 'weird', different or outcasts.

> In the Community, we did celebrate birthdays – too much. We were living in an abusive and fearful setting where we could be 'rebuked' at any time, but then on birthdays, we would receive cards signed by all the members with their messages telling us how lovely and beautiful we were, and how much everyone (including the leaders) loved us. It was another way of controlling our environment. It was deeply confusing and designed to lure us into trusting and being open – before the next round of abuses. Messages from some of the other members were heartfelt, which made it even more confusing.

Sexual practices vary widely between different cultic settings, but are often used to control, including restricting choices over whether one can have sex and/or who one can have sex with. Some encourage or even require sex for various reasons, such as a 'spiritual practice' or route to enlightenment, a means of recruitment, or the creation of a new 'perfect' generation of children. Some leaders say that having sex with them will bring healing to the individual and to the world. Marriage and sexual partners may be chosen by the leader, or polygamous marriages may be expected.

Other cultic settings control sex by restricting it. In some, celibacy (abstaining from marriage and/ or sex) is a requirement for all; and in others just for a 'chosen' few. Some cultic settings outlaw any form of sexual contact, and masturbation may be forbidden or viewed as a 'sinful' practice. Birth control may be prohibited or required, and the members' rights to decide for themselves when they have children, and what happens to their children, may be removed from them. Sex and marriage were controlled within the Community. The leader discouraged new marriages and separated married couples, requiring them to sleep in shared men's and women's bedrooms. Few children were born in the Community as he had a negative view of women, pregnancy and childbirth.

Sexuality and sexual orientation may be controlled and prescribed. For example, in some cultic settings, everyone is expected to be gay or lesbian, and in others, homosexuality is punished and only heterosexuality permitted. The topics of sex and sexuality will be discussed further, in relation to the demand for purity, at M10.3.3. The point here is that, whatever the particular restrictions, this is a key area of control of members' lives.

It can be nearly impossible to report crimes because 'worldly' legal systems are not respected. Sexual and other crimes may occur without redress or protection because many cultic settings are reluctant to involve the authorities, including the police. Some groups move members, including children, and deliberately operate in countries with weaker law or enforcement systems. Although apparently for legitimate reasons, including 'missionary' work, the real reason for this may be to escape stricter laws and to ensure that members are not protected by the authorities. In the Community, we could have gone to the police and reported the abuses, but it did not occur to us because the milieu control was deeply effective.

Worksheet M10.1: Milieu control: limitation and control of the environment, physical energy and personal life

This Worksheet is an opportunity to consider how aspects of your environment, energy and personal life were controlled in your cultic setting. There are spaces for any aspects you might like to add.

Date _____

Aspect of life	Was this controlled?	Could you give an example?
Physical energy		
Time		
Sleep		
Personal space and privacy		
Food and diet		
Clothing choices		
Physical and mental health needs		
Money and employment		
Social life and celebrations		
Sex, marriage and sexuality		
Having and bringing up children		
Access to legal protection		

We will now look at the next aspect of milieu control.

M10.1.2 Limitation and control of communication with the outside world

This includes:

- friendships and contact with family
- information that might conflict with the setting's purposes
- choices as to what to watch, read, etc.
- TV, radio, newspapers, internet, etc.
- access to information including education

Cultic settings have several ways of limiting and controlling communication with the outside world, including preventing or reducing meaningful contact with outsiders. They do this by negatively labelling outsiders, often including those in the family who are not members, so members do not value or listen to what they have to say. Other people and organisations may be labelled as wrong, deceived, enemies or 'of the devil' (dispensing of existence). It is assumed that only the cultic setting has the 'Truth' (sacred science).

Consequently, members are unlikely to look outside for information or advice, including spiritual information. Some settings may restrict communication by maintaining their physical separation, or by ensuring members never see outsiders alone. This control over who members can listen to, see or talk to may result in a significant degree of isolation from surrounding society.

Since new information, or anything contradicting the setting's beliefs, is restricted or dismissed, members cannot make critical, rational judgements about what they are being taught. This is intensified by personal controls, overwork, busyness, multiple lengthy meetings, etc. Some cultic settings restrict access to news, television and the internet, either generally or only permitting access to approved services or websites.

> When I was a member of the Community, limitation and control of communication with the outside was prevalent, even though I and others had jobs outside the group for some of the time. For example, we thought we were the most important church in the area (probably in the world!) and that others were inferior to us, so we didn't respect them or listen to them (dispensing of existence). We didn't have a television in most of the community houses, and watching TV was an occasional treat. We didn't have regular newspapers, although we weren't prohibited from reading them, we just didn't have time – we had more important things to do!

This limitation and control also have an impact on education. This is often not valued, or only certain types of education are valued, so the member is likely to dismiss it as being unimportant. Some cultic settings operate their own schools and educational programmes or expect members to provide home schooling. Often the normal curriculum is ignored, ensuring that children are indoctrinated and the thought reform system is constantly imposed and reinforced.

Many prohibit further education and university, especially cultic settings that have an 'end time' philosophy: why waste time on education (or anything else outside the setting) when the world is going to end in the near future? In the Community, higher education was deemed to be pointless. Few members attended university, and some left it when they joined.

If the individual joined, they may have had to cut off from family and pre-membership friends. If they were born and/or raised, they may never have known those in their family who are not members, such as grandparents, with serious consequences as they might have been better protected if they had been allowed access.

We were also taught in the Community that our family and friends were 'going to hell', and the only point of talking to them was to try to get them to become members. Of course, they didn't appreciate this, and it resulted in us becoming more estranged. I lost contact with many people I was close to before I joined, such as school friends, and we had no contact for years.

Daphne's cult worked hard to ensure she did not have contact with her family. They hid her from them, moving her from one location to another to ensure the family could not track her whereabouts, and warning her that she would become a 'spiritual vegetable' if she had contact with them! There was always an apparently logical reason for these moves, such as needing staff in another office, but the result was that she lost contact for years.

Members may be told that they are not allowed to make friends or have any social life outside the setting; or that the only purpose of getting to know someone is to recruit them. This is likely to keep them isolated and alienated from society.

I know some who were born and/or raised whose school friends never knew they were growing up in a cultic setting – it was too embarrassing to admit and they wanted to keep the two lives separate. This had a big impact on them, and on how they felt about themselves, as they had to form two identities – one for the cultic setting and a 'mask' for their friends (also see M6). Constantly switching between these can be a terrible strain.

In some cases, the member has some contact with their non-member family, but the setting attempts to destroy their relationship by implying their family does not love them. Fred had a loving family that he had lost contact with while a member of a cult. He says:

> One of the things the community tried to do was destroy the sense of family, and vilify your family. So, your family somehow were against you, they didn't love you.

This gaslighting (M11.3) can have the effect of reversing our sense of reality. Marjorie reflected on a well-known psychological experiment, the inverted vision experiment. In this, the participant puts on a special pair of glasses containing mirrors, which turns the room upside down. The experiment illustrates how quickly the brain becomes used to this. Although the eyes are seeing the world upside down, the brain learns to turn it back. Marjorie says that this was like her spiritually abusive experience. Her reality was 'upside down' but she came to feel it was normal because she had no conflicting information or outside contacts to tell her otherwise. It was only on leaving that she recognised how her reality had been reversed.

Worksheet M10.2: Milieu control: limitation and control of communication with the outside world

This Worksheet is an opportunity to consider how aspects of communication with the outside world were controlled in your cultic setting. There are spaces for any you might like to add.

Date _____

Aspect of communication	Was this controlled?	Could you give an example?
Friendships		
Contact with family		
Access to conflicting information		
Choices as to what to watch, read, etc.		
TV, radio, newspapers and internet		
Access to education		

M10.1.3 Limitation and control of communication within the individual

This leads to self-suppression and includes:

- personal internal life and communication within the self, such as facing doubts, thinking critically, etc.
- internal dialogue
- acknowledging and listening to our feelings

The most personal aspect of milieu control is also the most subtle. We are not only disconnected from the outside world (including our non-member family and friends, and, for those who joined, from much that was familiar) but also within ourselves, as the crucial inner dialogue within our authentic identity is cut off.

In normal healthy living, we keep in touch with our authentic identity, and with our own needs and wants. There is an interaction between who we are within and how we live in society. We adjust creatively to life and are able to grow. However, the effect of milieu control is to block this communication and contact within ourselves and our self-regulation. So, we become confluent and fixed, dependent on the cultic setting and no longer growing.

In this dependence and confluence, we are likely to end up becoming an integral part of the process of our own control, because we buy into the commitment to the setting and the leader (we feel sure we are doing the right thing) and suppress our authentic identity. As our authentic identity is no longer creatively adjusting (M6.3), the inner dialogue is replaced by introjects from the cultic setting. We continually rehearse and reiterate the negative introjects (confession), suppress our doubts and block our authentic independent thought, creativity and critical thinking. We suppress the desire for personal space, to think for ourselves, reflect, daydream, be creative and make our own choices. We also block our authentic feelings that could give us important information about our state of well-being – the pseudo-identity takes charge.

So, with milieu control, we are deprived of both external information, *and* our personal inner reflection, either of which could moderate our thinking. Both are necessary if we are to test reality and maintain our separate authentic identity. Without them, our worldview becomes polarised, split between what is regarded by the cultic setting as "real" (the cultic culture and belief system) and "unreal" (everything else outside) (Lifton, 1989, p. 421). We lose, or never develop, the ability to think critically about the subtleties of what is true and what is not. Instead, we introject, or swallow whole, what we are told.

Without critical thinking skills, we end up resorting to this all-or-nothing approach. We are no longer thinking for ourselves but thinking for and as the cultic setting (introjection and confluence). Because of the pressures put on us, we can feel some relief in doing so. Life, 'Truth' and reality seem straightforward and clear cut – we know what we are expected to do to save and heal ourselves and 'the world'. But there is a high cost to this certainty, and we end up encountering a "profound threat to [our] personal autonomy" (Lifton, 1989, p. 421) as we become increasingly confluent and controlled.

Combined with control of our environment and external communication, the self-suppression of our internal dialogue entraps us in the thought reform system. This does not just happen once: the system ensures the constant maintenance of the pseudo-identity, and suppression of the authentic identity, along with our thoughts and doubts. As a result, the psychological current continues to sweep around us, maintaining control and keeping us trapped in a psychological prison – the marble edifice.

Self-suppression, to keep us trapped, may be maintained in many ways. In Marjorie's Bible-based group, a strong precept was:

Do not think for yourself, those thoughts are from the enemy [that is, Satan].

This applied to any independent thought, but particularly anything critical or independent of the leader. Another participant was warned that any thoughts that were negative towards the leader were tantamount to killing the leader. This caused him to block and suppress his critical thoughts.

> I was so often afraid to think certain thoughts, believing that if I did someone would know – as if they could read my mind. I also learned that certain feelings were outlawed, particularly anger and anything that they deemed 'negative', and so I would suppress them to avoid being punished. I don't really remember having any doubts about what was happening in the Community. I was so afraid and self-suppressed that I could barely think.

Those who are born and/or raised and do not agree with the belief system may struggle deeply, feeling torn between their authentic and pseudo-identities, and learn to self-suppress from an early age. Children who may receive harsh punishments for minor, perhaps arbitrary reasons, also learn to self-suppress to cope.

Self-suppression is also maintained by exhaustion, hunger, lack of time, energy and space and all the other aspects of milieu control. As we will see in relation to mystical manipulation (M10.2), trance states, including drugs, speaking in tongues and meditation, can also assist self-suppression.

Worksheet M10.3: Milieu control: limitation and control of communication within the individual

This Worksheet is an opportunity to consider how aspects of your internal communication were controlled or self-suppressed in your cultic setting. There are spaces for any you might like to add.

Date _____

Aspect of internal communication	Was this controlled?	Could you give an example?
Facing doubts		
Thinking critically		
Internal dialogue		
Daydreaming		
Thinking creatively		
Acknowledging and listening to feelings		

You now have an opportunity to consider in more detail how some aspects of milieu control apply to your life story.

Worksheet M10.4: Tell your story – milieu control

What events or practices come to mind that seem to involve milieu control? You could write your experience in the space below or in your journal.

Date _____

_____

_____

_____

_____

_____

_____

_____

_____

_____

_____

_____

You could reflect on how frequently milieu control occurred in your cultic setting.

Worksheet M10.5: Frequency – milieu control

Date _____

Was milieu control applicable to your group/relationship?

Never	Seldom	Sometimes	Frequently	Always

We will now look at mystical manipulation.

M10.2 Mystical manipulation

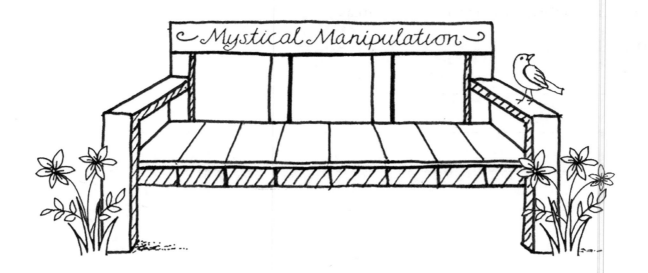

We have now reached the top of the second hill, which addresses mystical manipulation! You could imagine yourself sitting on the bench and reflecting on how this affected you in your cultic setting.

Once the milieu control is established and the marble edifice is in place, the inevitable next step is mystical manipulation which is "extensive personal manipulation" (Lifton, 1989, p. 422).

Mystical manipulation

- creates a 'mystique' that elevates the leader and seemingly proves their power, resulting in control
- elicits "specific patterns of behavior and emotion" in the member that "appear to have arisen spontaneously from within the environment" (Lifton, 1989, p. 422)
- induces trance states with an addictive element
- encourages members to go along with 'group think' and peer pressure and
- leaves members feeling they are chosen to play a special role, along with the leader and other members.

I will look first at how the leader creates mystique, and then at how mystical manipulation is reinforced by trance states and psychological factors.

M10.2.1 The leader and mystique

Mystical manipulation is a way of elevating the leader in the eyes of the members by purposely creating 'mystique' around them. This has several elements: constructing beliefs that the leader has special powers, importance or value; combined with a sense of mystery and secrecy, keeping ordinary members unsure about the full extent or nature of those powers or value.

Some leaders create this mystique by remaining hidden, operating behind closed doors, so the members project an image onto them, assuming they are perfect and trustworthy. Others are more public. At M12, I discuss different categories of leader and give you an opportunity to focus on and unmask your specific leadership. This is important so you begin to see them as the flawed human being they are, rather than an elevated being, god, or representative or reincarnation of a god, that they may claim to be!

In charismatic groups, whilst mystical and supernatural phenomena appear to arise spontaneously within the group, and more usually from the leader, they are often worked out in advance, with an "element of planned spontaneity" (Lifton, 1989, p. 422). This is unknown to the members, for whom they appear as evidence of divine intervention and affirmation, or of superhuman power. These apparently miraculous or psychic events provoke a sense of awe, convincing the members that something mysterious and incredible is really happening.

In other words, the leader does things that look impressive and spontaneous, but are actually stage-managed and pre-prepared. These phenomena have a powerful effect on the members emotionally, which results in them being manipulated into feeling and behaving in certain ways. They are often ascribed to a 'god' or higher being, channelled through the leader. The members do not know that the leader is orchestrating events which appear to confirm their special abilities, divine authority, charisma and spiritual advancement. Therefore, the member continues to be caught in the psychological current (milieu control) sweeping around them.

Mystical manipulation keeps the member confluent and dependent, and maintains their belief that the leader is special or great, and certainly far superior to the member.

In some groups, there is an inner circle of members close to the leader, who are aware of how the tricks are performed but are trusted to maintain secrecy about this. The tricks may be rationalised as necessary to maintain the conviction and passionate interest of the 'weaker' members, whilst those in the inner circle are apparently 'strong' enough without them.

There are numerous examples of mystical manipulation, varying according to the setting and the leader. Some leaders 'prophesy' or give 'words of knowledge' (supposedly messages channelled from a god or other higher being). These appear to be supernaturally inspired, for example, they may involve, or appear to include, personal secrets that the leader would not be expected to have known.

The leader may say, for example, that God has given them a message for someone in the audience or congregation with a specific type of illness or problem, and ask for that person to raise a hand. They also create an atmosphere of expectation, perhaps with music or preaching, and emphasise the urgency of responding. Usually, the description of the problem is sufficiently vague that someone will eventually respond and will be given the 'message'. This may be combined with claims of performing divine or spiritual healing. All this apparently proves the leader's power. If no one responds, the leader may subtly change the question or suggest that the people need to exercise greater faith. The management of the process ensures that, whatever happens, the sense of awe about the leader is increased.

In some cases, it has been shown that the leader gleaned information about the attendees before the meeting, for example, by being notified by trusted aides or by getting people to fill out information sheets. They could then appear to have received quite specific messages from a god or higher spiritual being, and be elevated in the eyes of their followers.

Some claim to 'manifest' (produce out of thin air) objects or matter, such as expensive watches, gold dust or 'holy ash', as evidence of their power or special access to a higher being. One former member told me he saw a ball of light, about two-foot-wide and two-foot off the ground, moving up the aisle between the other members and disappearing into the cult leader. Shortly afterwards, the leader started 'prophesying'. Others believed they saw their leader walk through walls; or were confused by the way their mind went blank in the presence of the leader, believing it was evidence of the leader's power.

I suspect these all happened because the member was confluent, and in a manufactured atmosphere of heightened awe, tension and often sheer terror – a trance state - and therefore especially suggestible. I will discuss this at M10.2.2.

These phenomena are mind games or magic tricks that many stage magicians can perform. For example, Derren Brown, a British mentalist and illusionist, illustrates many aspects of mystical manipulation in his stage and TV shows. These include convincingly appearing to be psychic, or a healer or Messiah, as well as more conventional magic. His website includes the question, "Does Derren possess god-like or psychic skills and have messianic abilities?", with the answer, "Watching Derren's shows may lead you to think that; however, Derren fuses magic, suggestion, misdirection, psychology and showmanship to appear to have god-like skills" (Brown, 2022). These phenomena have a down-to-earth explanation and are not 'spiritual' or from a higher being.

Mystical manipulation raises the issue of the leader's motivation. We will look at this in more depth at M12.

To consider:

Did your leader create a mystique around themselves, and how?

You may like to reflect on this in your journal.

We will now look, in more detail, at what is happening to the member who is subjected to mystical manipulation, starting with trance states and addictive elements.

M10.2.2 Trance states and addictive elements

One way that cultic settings make mystical manipulation so effective is to induce trance states in members. These can, for example, be induced by drugs, or brought on by meditation, chanting, repetitive singing or dancing, speaking in tongues or sheer boredom! Cultic settings use such methods, because in a trance state, we lack critical thinking, becoming suggestible and more vulnerable to manipulation.

A 'confluential trance' (Jenkinson, 2019) can also result from not chewing over and using our critical thinking, but from continually introjecting while we are confluent. We can become desensitised, not fully aware of or interacting with the environment, and more open to manipulation.

Trance states dull psychological contact with others and the environment. They can also result in a 'high' which keeps the individual coming back for more, and so there is also an addictive element to mystical manipulation – it may feel good!

This 'high', 'spiritual' or powerful emotional experience helps to convince the member that the apparent spiritual or otherworldly power of the leader is real, and perhaps truly 'divine' or 'enlightened'. It serves to distract, desensitise and suppress the individual, numbing them from the emotionally painful abuse that being a member and following the doctrine involves. That is, it stops them from feeling the full impact of some of the abusive and terrifying doctrines and practices of the cultic setting. Instead of resisting and questioning, they are manipulated to accept and introject.

In mystical manipulation, trance states and emotions are managed and induced from outside us, rather than being genuine, healthy, emotional or spiritual experiences coming from within.

The 'high' and emotional numbing, which helps to ensure the mystical manipulation continues, have been reported to occur through various practices, including:

- drug use (often illegal depending on the country) e.g. ayahuasca, LSD (lysergic acid diethylamide), MDMA (methylenedioxymethamphetamine or 'ecstasy'), psilocybin or a mix
- repetitive music, chanting and speaking in tongues
- meditation

I will address these in turn.

Thought reform on drugs

When someone is already in a thought reform milieu and exposed to a leader with 'mystique', there is increased impact if they are also using mind-altering, psychotropic and hallucinogenic drugs. (The setting may refer to these as 'medicine'.) Members are likely to be affected more deeply and to be even less able to resist the mystical manipulation, control and abuse from the leader, and peer pressure from other members. They are more open to suggestion and may have no filters or critical thinking whatsoever.

Once the former member has left, the effects on their mind may mean that they struggle to chew over what happened as a member and take much longer to access those memories. They may experience powerful triggers and emotions that are hard to regulate, and which stop them from being able to process their thoughts and emotions. They live outside the window of tolerance.

I mentioned in relation to milieu control (M10.1.2) that life in a thought reform environment is like being turned upside down, and it is hard enough to make sense of and understand the experience of coercion and control. However, when it has occurred on drugs, it has an added dimension. The experience is somehow foggy, far away, deeply out of awareness and wrapped in the distorted logic of the thought reform system. If this happened to you, then please be patient with yourself and consider asking a safe friend or therapist, especially one who is aware of the impact of drugs, to help you as you process your experience alongside the Walking Free journey.

Music, chanting and speaking in tongues

Music is a powerful tool that can inspire intense, often pleasurable, feelings. It affects our brains chemically when we hear and perform it (Smith, 2018). Many cultic settings have beautiful music, rousing revolutionary songs, repetitive choruses or chanting mantras. These can put the member into a trance state, especially when endlessly repeated, rendering them more vulnerable to mystical manipulation. Repetitively speaking in tongues can have a similar effect.

Meditation

Meditation, although helpful to many when practised safely, can be dangerous in a thought reform environment and render the individual more open to influence, mystical manipulation and thought reform in general. Intense meditation without safe and ethical boundaries can also lead to difficult and challenging symptoms, including blackouts, anxiety attacks, memory difficulties, sudden bursts of energy, visual hallucinations and other symptoms (Singer, 2003, pp. 139–149).

> **To consider:**
> Did your setting induce trance states?
> How did they create these?
> Did this leave you more open to manipulation?
> You may like to reflect on this in your journal.

M10.2.3 Psychological factors

In addition to trance states, there are some psychological factors that help make mystical manipulation effective.

Group pressure

Mystical manipulation can happen more easily because, in a cultic setting, we are likely to get caught up in the mood of a group or gathering. As a result, we feel pressure to conform and so we are more easily manipulated. If we see those around us accepting what is happening, and enjoying a 'high', it is difficult to resist and easy to join in. We want to belong and know that disagreement, or even doubt, will have negative consequences.

Cognitive dissonance

In the cultic setting, there are likely to be contradictions between the individual member's ideals and ethics, their beliefs about the leader and the setting, and what the leader actually does. These create psychological stress and render the member more open to mystical manipulation. This is cognitive dissonance (for more see M11.2).

Confluence and projection

When we are confluent with the leader, we are likely to project an ideal image onto them (M4). As a result, we believe the introjects about how weak we are, and the leader gets built up in our minds into someone strong and powerful. Figure M10.1 illustrates this process – we project onto the leader their message that they are strong and powerful, and we introject the belief that we are weak (as we cannot stand up for ourselves). I will return to the idea of projection in relation to the demand for purity (M10.3).

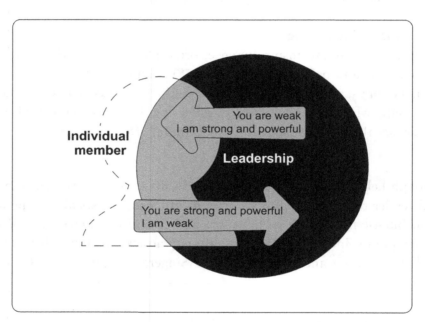

Figure M10.1 The dynamic of introjection and projection in mystical manipulation

The distracted mind

When we are focussed intensely on one thing we are, of course, less aware of other things. Even in normal circumstances, this applies, for example, when walking and using our mobile or cell phone in a public space, we are less aware of where we are going.

As the leader directs the member's attention onto them, and as the member is in a trance state, focussed on the leader and their apparent miracles and mystical power, attention is diverted away from what is actually happening – the mystical manipulation, unethical practices and abuse.

Member's special role

Because members are taught the setting has a special purpose, they often believe they have been chosen to play a special role in fulfilling this purpose along with the leader. This gives a rationale for believing the mystique. Pursuing this purpose overrides "all considerations of decency or of immediate human welfare" (Lifton, 1989, p.422) (doctrine over person and dispensing of existence). Members are likely to comply in working towards the setting's aims since all of life appears to support the claims of the leader.

For example, when I was a member of the Community, I felt special, believing what we were doing was going to make a difference in the world. (It didn't!) All the former members I have known, from many settings, had a similar feeling – we have often made jokes about "my group was more special than yours"! (I addressed some of these issues of being special at M9, particularly in relation to being 'grandiose'.)

To consider:

Did your setting use psychological factors such as group pressure, cognitive dissonance, confluence and projection, the distracted mind and the member's special role?

Did this leave you more open to manipulation?

You may like to reflect on this in your journal.

You now have an opportunity to apply mystical manipulation to your life story.

Worksheet M10.6: Tell your story – mystical manipulation

What events or practices come to mind that seem to involve mystical manipulation? You could write your experience in the space below or in your journal.

Date _____

_____

_____

_____

_____

_____

_____

_____

_____

_____

_____

_____

_____

You could reflect on how frequently mystical manipulation occurred in your cultic setting.

Worksheet M10.7: Frequency – mystical manipulation

Date _____

Was mystical manipulation applicable to your group/relationship?

Never	Seldom	Sometimes	Frequently	Always

We will now look at the demand for purity.

M10.3 Demand for purity

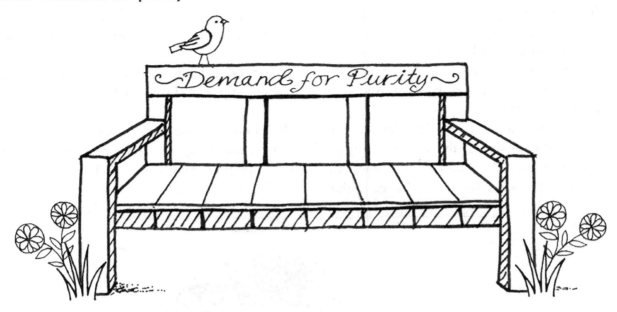

We are making progress! The third hill on the Roadmap represents the demand for purity, and again, there is a place to sit and reflect on how this affected you in your cultic setting.

The demand for purity refers to the requirement that all members be 'pure', as defined by the leader and cultic setting. If something is pure, it is without blemish or contamination – people refer to water or metals being pure, or not.

The assumption that people and their actions are either 'good' or 'bad', 'pure' or 'impure' indicates polarised, 'all or nothing' thinking (sometimes referred to as 'black and white' thinking). This way of thinking is introjected by the members, who are likely to think they are 'impure' and 'bad', and the leader is the only one who can be completely 'pure' or 'good'. Nigel elaborates:

> There's this whole trap of being taught about the fall of man and original sin, that we are full of original sin and the only way to be blessed is by [the leader], 'you are all unworthy and I am the only pure worthy one'.

Absolute 'purity' or perfection is, therefore, assumed to be attainable, but only within the confines of the cultic setting (milieu control). All that members are, and all that went before, must be rejected. They must all be convinced of their current intrinsic 'impurity'; and those who joined (and those who believe they have been reincarnated) of their previous impurity. They are expected to reject this impurity in themselves and in society and to embrace purity. However, as this can never be achieved, and the member constantly fails, they are plagued with guilt and shame and must continually strive for purity.

The introjects around being bad or impure (sinful, rebellious, unclear, mentally unstable, bourgeois – or whatever the loaded language is within the setting) impact on our guilt and shame systems, making it hard to have an "inner sensitivity to the complexities of human morality" (Lifton, 1989, p. 425).

Matt, who struggled with addiction, had to 'make amends' and ask for forgiveness for any 'mistakes' or 'sins' (impurity) prior to joining – and to work hard not to make those mistakes again. The rationale was that his addiction was caused, in part, by these mistakes and 'sins' weighing on his conscience, so he had to become 'pure' as defined by the cult. He says that making amends would:

> ...keep me on the straight and narrow, it was like, anything that happened after I joined was good and positive. Now it's okay, you're a good person because you are in the cult.

The result of the struggle to maintain purity is that the member remains confluent with and dependent on the cultic setting, and especially the leader – fearing disaster (personal or global) may result if they do not. In Matt's case, the disaster would be that he would return to his addiction and would end up mentally ill, living in a box under a bridge.

This gives an inordinate amount of power to the leader, because in many cultic settings, it is assumed that only they are truly 'pure', and able to "forgive" impurity (Lifton, 1989, p. 424) and thus make the member 'pure' again.

As previously noted in mystical manipulation, within a cultic setting, we project onto the leader (Figure M10.1). A similar dynamic is set up in the demand for purity, where we project our 'purity' or 'goodness' onto the leader, and introject the leader's 'impurity' and 'badness'. This is a complex psychological process, but the exchange is illustrated in Figure M10.2.

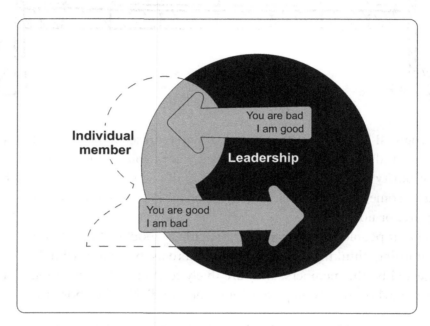

Figure M10.2 The dynamic of introjection and projection in demand for purity

This dynamic ensures that demand for purity (from the leader or other members) results in guilt and shame, leading to confession (by the member to the leader or other members) (see M10.4), in an attempt to feel better. In a thought reform milieu, the pressure to be the person you are expected to be (and the pressure *not* to be your authentic self) ensures that the pseudo-identity is reinforced by the demand for purity, as it builds layer by layer.

In a thought reform system, we can try to do our best but it is never good enough, either in our own eyes or the leader's. For some, the demand for purity can, therefore, lead to a sort of **perfectionism**, where we feel we should be 'perfect' – and this may continue even after leaving. This introjected belief leads to shame, self-blame and judgement, and a feeling of 'not being good enough' when we find that we cannot live up to our own introjected expectations. These introjects need challenging (M5).

This is what Sean has to say as an antidote to being perfect:

> I think, that being human is a good thing and one does not need to be a saint or perfect etc. - you know, **being a human being is good enough**.

Demand for purity is inescapable within a thought reform milieu and shows itself in many ways. I will look at some aspects in a little more detail:

- Guilt and shame
- Feeling stopping and thought stopping
- Sex and sexuality

M10.3.1 Guilt and shame

So, if demand for purity leads to guilt and shame, what is the difference between them, and when are they a problem?

Healthy normal guilt (as opposed to cult-induced guilt, covered below) is a focus on our behaviour, and how we feel as a result of that behaviour.

In healthy guilt, the individual is "able to make a conscious, cognitive distinction between the self and behaviour". In evaluating our actions, we are focussed on the mistake or act of wrongdoing, and not on our core authentic identity, which remains "relatively unscathed and intact" (Sanderson 2015, p. 31). We don't 'wipe ourself out' because of what we did.

With healthy guilt, we take responsibility for our actions and work to not repeat the behaviour. For example, we may acknowledge that we have hurt someone's feelings. It is healthy to be able to identify genuine guilt if we have caused harm, and to make amends and apologise – even if it is uncomfortable.

However, it is different if we break the imposed standards of purity and perfection that come from thought reform and the leader. We then experience cultic, not genuine guilt, which cannot be resolved, but keeps recurring and plaguing us until we comply with the demand for purity and confess (M10.4) – which brings only temporary relief.

Shame is different from guilt. Shame is a focus on self – I am bad – I am a mistake. It is an emotion that all people naturally experience, and we are particularly vulnerable to shame in social groups. Within a thought reform milieu, shame is purposefully and specifically induced. We will come back to this in relation to doctrine over person (M10.7).

Some shame can lead to good outcomes. If we can respond in a healthy way to mistakes and embarrassing errors, it can help us to connect with others, and have humility, modesty, empathy and compassion (Sanderson, 2015, p. 23). It can help us respond with gratitude and respect for others, and be a powerful motivator for personal change.

Toxic shame, on the other hand, severs connections with others and is a result of "humiliation, denigration, dehumanisation and mortification" (Sanderson, 2015, p. 22). Our authentic identity is attacked and the pseudo-identity builds as we introject negative messages in the abusive environment.

With toxic shame, the focus is entirely on our self and the belief that the whole of our identity is inferior and defective. We believe the introjects that we are sinful, unenlightened, toxic, worthless, worthy of punishment, deserving of abuse, etc. In toxic shame, we withdraw and shut down to try and avoid more exposure to shame (Sanderson, 2015, p. 32). However, this does not help because "the less you talk about it, the more you have it" (Brown, 2010). Brené Brown describes shame as "the intensely painful feeling or experience of believing that we are flawed and therefore unworthy of love and belonging" (2015, p. 69).

Toxic shame, therefore, includes an introjected belief that we are inherently bad, we are a mistake and we are unacceptable and unlovable. It indicates that "I believe I am not okay as I am and I am sorry for who I am". When we try to believe in our own worth, there are many possible shame-driven introjects to remind us that we are not good enough, and how often we have failed. This, of course, happens outside cultic settings, but the demand for purity multiplies and strengthens these introjects, and purposely induces them in members, specifically to control them.

In these controlling and coercive situations, it may feel safer to accept the shame and believe we are bad than to blame others. Blaming ourselves instead of the abuser helps us feel more in control and less at the mercy of others – but in the long term harms us further.

To consider:
How did your setting use guilt and shame?
How does this still affect you?
Can you identify any introjects you are left with?
Can you chew over and challenge these?
You may like to reflect on this in your journal.

If we feel judged, having introjected the need to be perfect, we will most likely be judgemental of ourselves. This, in part, shows itself in a shame-bound harsh inner voice (see M5 and M8.4).

If we judge ourselves, then we are likely to judge others. For example, if I feel I 'should' do something 'right' then I am likely to think you should similarly do it 'right'. After being in an abusive cultic setting, where no one can do things 'their way', it can be quite an adjustment. It is important that you know you can do things your way – and that others can do things their way!

M10.3.2 Feeling stopping and thought stopping

The demand for purity extends far beyond our actions and includes our thoughts and feelings.

In order to be 'pure', we have to suppress certain feelings and we become used to 'feeling stopping' and self-suppression (milieu control). As a member, we are likely to associate 'purity' with an absence of so-called 'negative' feelings (feelings that we 'shouldn't' feel). We may, therefore, assume that if we only feel so-called 'positive' feelings (those permitted by the setting), or have no feelings, then we are pure. (We will come back to suppression of feelings in M13.)

Our authentic feelings may be construed as 'rebellion', 'lack of obedience' or 'sinfulness' – and so, we introject that we should not have these feelings. Suppressing our feelings leads to both dissociation and the formation of the pseudo-identity, as it adds another layer over the authentic identity, suppressing and squeezing it.

A similar sort of suppression applies to thoughts, and I will revisit this in relation to loading the language (M10.6).

The demand for purity means that members learn to fear, and dissociate from, their authentic thoughts and feelings, and to accept and expect punishment for their 'impurity'. This reinforces the control of the leader and the thought reform system.

M10.3.3 Sex and sexuality

The demand for purity in cultic settings may cover any aspect of life, but many settings, especially religious ones, have a particular focus on sex and sexuality as areas where 'purity' is required and tightly defined (referred to as 'purity culture' in some religious settings).

Many cultic and spiritually abusive settings are obsessed with such matters as celibacy, virginity, masturbation and sex only in marriage. Their warnings often, ironically, raise children's awareness of sex long before it is healthy or necessary for them to even think about the subject, and long before they are mature enough to make decisions about it.

Teens and adults can become hypersensitive to any sexual thoughts, leading to self-suppression, because these are assumed to be 'impure' (milieu control). For example, in Bible-based settings, members may be told it is sinful to even think about fancying another member. Guilt and shame are inevitable.

Children and young people may be expected to 'buy into' and introject particular ideas. The setting's concept of sexual purity may be presented as the ideal (and only acceptable) way to live – and they may have little choice. If they do not agree and comply, they may be shamed or shunned. Some have said that these practices and teachings were extremely harmful, and left them with hang-ups about sex, including masturbation and physical problems having sex, for many years after.

In some settings, if members, including young people, have sex they have to 'confess' to a group of leaders or 'elders' – this may involve giving graphic details about what occurred. This is voyeuristic, intrusive and abusive for many. For some, having sex before marriage has led to a requirement to marry someone quite unsuitable so 'purity is restored', but resulting in years of heartache for both parties.

Many settings require heterosexuality as part of 'purity'. Some use 'conversion therapy', which is designed to 'heal' someone of homosexuality. (This is now banned in some countries as abusive.) However, other settings require homosexuality and regard heterosexuality as impure.

You may have been in a setting where sexual purity was viewed in very different ways. Some settings teach sexual 'freedom' in which members are expected to have sex with multiple partners, encourage sex as a 'spiritual practice', use sex for recruitment or even allow sex with children. These different approaches do not mean that the demand for purity did not apply, but that it was defined in a different way by the doctrines and practices of the setting. In many settings, the precise rules and expectations may be unclear or change without warning, so members are left unsure about what is acceptable, and when they may be punished.

To consider:
Did your setting have particular expectations or requirements about sex and sexuality?
How did these affect you?
How does this still affect you?
You may like to reflect on this in your journal.

You now have an opportunity to apply demand for purity to your life story.

Worksheet M10.8: Tell your story – demand for purity

What events or practices come to mind that seem to involve the demand for purity? You could write your experience in the space below or in your journal.

Date _____

_____

_____

_____

_____

_____

_____

_____

_____

_____

_____

_____

_____

_____

_____

You could reflect on how frequently demand for purity occurred in your cultic setting.

Worksheet M10.9: Frequency – demand for purity

Was the demand for purity applicable to your group/relationship? (please circle)

Never	Seldom	Sometimes	Frequently	Always

We will now look at confession.

M10.4 Confession

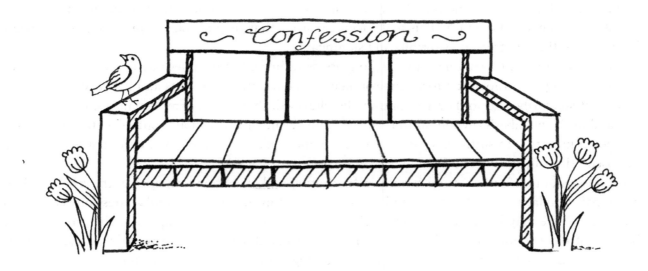

The fourth hill on the Roadmap addresses confession. There is a bench for you to sit and reflect on how this affected you in your cultic setting.

Confession is the natural progression from the demand for purity because, when our tendency towards guilt and shame is activated, we feel uncomfortable and need to do something about it. The two, therefore, work together creating a cycle where guilt and shame, held and expressed within the introjects, lead to feeling 'bad' about our 'impurity', followed by the need to get the resulting 'bad' feelings and thoughts out. This is done through 'confessing' or sharing those introjected 'bad' feelings and thoughts – both to others and ourselves – to relieve our discomfort, try to rid ourselves of the guilt and shame, and feel better.

Ideally, when people see a therapist, priest or lawyer and they 'confess' and talk openly about their lives, there are professional ethical boundaries in place to protect them. This is not the confession we are discussing here: within a cultic and spiritually abusive setting, there is an expectation that members are open, but ethical boundaries are weak or non-existent. This creates vulnerability, which is then used against the individual.

Within thought reform, confession is:

- oversharing, in an attempt to resolve the guilt and shame arising from introjecting the belief that we are 'impure' (Lifton calls this a "psychological purge" (1989, p. 425))
- a way of proving to ourselves, the leader and other members that we are fully committed and open, leading to confluence
- a way for leaders to elicit total openness and learn about members' personal lives, and especially their weaknesses and 'impurities', which gives them ammunition with which to control and manipulate them (Lifton describes this as an "ethos of total exposure" (1989, pp. 425–426))
- a way to maintain the introjects as the member reiterates their 'badness', failings and vulnerability, in confession to others and themselves (reinforcing the pseudo-identity)

Confession, therefore, works in several ways to reinforce thought reform and cultic control.

M10.4.1 Dynamics of confession

In confession, the member is expected to let down their barriers and openly discuss their "life experiences, thoughts and passions" (Lifton, 1989, p. 426), their "innermost fears and anxieties" (Andres and Lane, 1988, pp. 3–12) and their 'sins' and impurities – either publicly to the wider membership or privately to a personal monitor. This may include matters that general society might regard as trivial, but in the setting are treated as serious and significant.

This is not limited to genuine actions, thoughts or feelings, but includes introjects from the leader and the setting. In a thought reform environment, these negative introjects and beliefs cannot be resolved satisfactorily, and so they are continually rehearsed, shared and reiterated in confession to others, and in the member's own mind to themself. This results in individuals confessing to "crimes one has not committed, to sinfulness that is artificially induced, in the name of a cure that is arbitrarily imposed" (Lifton, 1989, p. 425).

Confession, in the cultic setting, results in frustration and alienation, rather than the relief, healing and repair of relationships (with self and others) that healthy genuine guilt and confession is meant to facilitate. There may be some temporary relief from confessing, and perhaps receiving 'forgiveness', but the introjects remain unresolved. The impossible demand for purity means that the discomfort of cultic guilt and toxic shame will soon return, requiring another round of confession.

In fact, the cycle may get worse, because information about the member's personal life given in confession provides the leader and others with more ammunition to understand the member's vulnerabilities and point out their failings. Also, as confession has not removed the discomfort of guilt and shame, the member may search ever deeper into their own life, trying to diagnose the root of their 'problem' within themself.

In summary, the leader creates the 'problem' through the demand for purity and then offers the apparent solution in the form of confession.

Figure M10.3 illustrates the exchange between the member and the leadership in terms of projection and introjection, showing both the demand for purity and confession. (This builds on Figure M10.2 in Section M10.3.)

Through the practice of confession, the abusive cycle is therefore maintained.

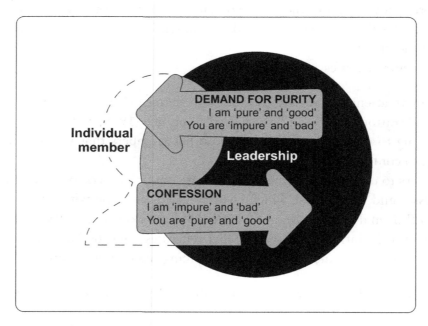

Figure M10.3 The dynamic of introjection and projection in demand for purity and confession

M10.4.2 Experiences of confession

The means of ensuring confession differs, but it is nearly always psychologically dangerous to confess in a cultic setting and may lead to abusive 'punishment'. The invitation to confess is a trap that often leads to more abuse.

> In the Community, a culture of oversharing and total openness was unavoidable. If someone did something 'wrong', they were expected to 'confess', whether it was a genuine wrong or not. When the leader of my household squeezed his hand and said it hurt "because of sin in the house", I freaked out and thought, "It must be me at fault". Even though there were others present, and the leader's comment was not directed at me specifically, it acted as a trigger for me to confess. In this case, I confessed to resentment because I couldn't think what my sin was. This resulted in physical punishment, which then apparently 'cleansed' my so-called sin – and then the leader 'forgave' me for this 'sin'.
>
> Although this was traumatic, at the time I was grateful for the forgiveness and more committed than ever to the Community and the leader. This type of response is known as a 'trauma bond' (Stein, 2017).

In the therapy field, 'encounter groups' have been popular for decades, and some of these have become cultic. There have been reports of harm resulting from confession and punishment sessions, usually in the form of shouting and 'putting people down' – and in some cases, even hitting people or throwing them against the wall. This type of session also occurs in other types of cultic settings.

When Shannon's mother died, leaders of a small group within the cultic school she attended asked her how she felt. She told them truthfully how upset she was, but they turned this against her, reversing the meaning of her words, implying that she was unfeeling rather than expressing her grief. This gaslighting (M11.3) shocked her as they:

> ...all started like a feeding frenzy and coming up to me and spitting on me and pushing me.

Matt and Fred show how the leader would encourage them to talk openly, with negative consequences:

> They encouraged me to talk about things I never dared speak about before, but looking back retrospectively, they would store it up and use it against me. [Matt]

> He got us to reveal all the issues that were affecting us so he was able to very easily manipulate us by bringing up all the things that we had basically told him about our situation. [Fred]

Dillon said that his leader would invite members to speak openly, asking:

> Has anyone got anything to talk about?

This was shorthand or loaded language (M10.6) for:

> Is there anything going on in your life that is distracting you from being able to pay attention to God and what you are supposed to be focussing on?

This invitation resulted in church meetings turning into:

> ...a big soap opera all of the time when you were always dealing with people's problems because these problems were apparently always interfering with their ability to perfectly hear the word of God. So, people would confess.

The need to respond to the invitation to confess can be compulsive and almost obsessive because it is driven by the induced cultic guilt and the need to feel better. But, as in the case of Dillon above, confession does not resolve people's problems but instead contributes to the maintenance of control and attachment to the leader.

Confession results in humiliation for many. Joe says:

> They knew intimate stuff about me, they were trying to use that against me to make me look stupid.

After leaving, the habit of confession may continue, as a compulsion to be too open (our boundaries are weakened or non-existent) or to put ourselves down and reiterate negative introjects. This often happens as a response to guilt or shame feelings, which can act as a trigger. If you find yourself doing this, I suggest you consider what introjects are involved, and whether they need challenging.

To consider:
How did your setting use confession?
In what ways were you required or manipulated to confess?
What sort of things did you confess? Were they introjected 'wrongs'?
Did confession make you feel better, and if so, did this feeling remain?
Did confession resolve issues or did the same or similar issues keep returning?
You may like to reflect on this in your journal.

You now have an opportunity to apply confession to your life story.

Worksheet M10.10: Tell your story – confession

What events or practices come to mind that seem to involve confession? You could write your experience in the space below or in your journal.

Date _____

_____

_____

_____

_____

_____

_____

_____

_____

_____

_____

_____

_____

You could reflect on how frequently confession occurred in your cultic setting.

Worksheet M10.11: Frequency – confession

Was confession applicable to your group/relationship? (please circle)

Never	Seldom	Sometimes	Frequently	Always

We will now look at sacred science.

M10.5 Sacred science

We are well on our way to understanding the system of thought reform. We have now reached the top of the fifth hill on the Roadmap, which addresses sacred science.

Sacred science refers to the belief system and ideology held in the cultic setting, whether it be religious, spiritual, therapeutic, political, business orientated, etc. Lifton states that:

> The totalist milieu maintains an aura of sacredness around its basic dogma, holding it out as an ultimate moral vision for the ordering of human experience.

> (1989, p. 427)

The term 'sacred science', as it is used here, implies that the cultic setting and the leader are assumed to have THE Truth, which must not be questioned and must be treated with reverence; and also that their beliefs are 'scientific', and therefore accurate, impartial, rational and trustworthy. The sacred science is claimed to be more relevant and accurate than any other 'science' or explanation of the meaning of life that can be found anywhere – it is the *ultimate* 'Truth'! In some settings, it is simply referred to as "the truth", which is loaded language.

Cultic belief systems tend to involve a mixture of insights or revelations received by the leader or founder, and apparent rational, logical argument. Cultic settings assert that they have the only valid belief system, and its assumptions cannot and must not be questioned. In addition, leaders are above criticism and deserve reverence as the keepers and providers of that 'Truth' (Lifton, 1989, pp. 427–428).

Despite the 'sacred' nature of the beliefs, if the occasion requires it, and if it suits the powerful leadership and their purposes, they may simply change this 'Truth'. For example, the internet was banned by many groups, until they realised it could serve their purposes to recruit new members and influence current members! In order to allow members to use the internet they had to invent a 'new Truth', for example, by claiming to have received a new 'revelation'. When the end of the world was predicted to happen on a certain date, which then comes and goes, leaders have to change this 'Truth' and invent a new one (usually a new date, combined with a 'spiritual' explanation for the change!).

This is very different from the process in scientific research, where it is normal and healthy for knowledge to be continually updated as new information becomes available. In the cultic setting, the 'Truth' is updated to suit the leader, although usually without any admission that the previous version was wrong. This creates cognitive dissonance (M11.2). The mixed messages can be confusing for members who may feel out of control and at the mercy of an all-powerful 'god', higher being or leader, who can apparently change their mind at any moment, 'moving the goalposts' whenever they want to, but always demanding that their 'Truth' is revered.

The sacred science has implications for every aspect of life. Lifton says that in a totalist, thought-reform, environment "there is no thought or action which cannot be related to the sacred science". Milieu control ensures the individual has little access to alternative beliefs, so any open discussion or critical thought is cut off and "there is virtually no escape from the milieu's ever pressing edicts and demands" (1989, pp.428–429).

The origins of the sacred science vary according to the setting. In some cases, the leader uses an established ideology, borrowing from it and elaborating on it. In others, they devise a complex (and at times clever) philosophical system that is convincing to outsiders and members alike. Some leaders borrow from long-established belief systems, such as Christianity, Buddhism or Marxism, and make their own special interpretations, perhaps adding elements from elsewhere, resulting in an attractively varied and wide-ranging mix of ideas. Others take ideas from the worlds of business or psychology.

Sometimes, the ideology is physically dangerous. For example, it may lead the individual to believe their body is not important because only the soul matters. They may then dismiss their physical needs and the importance of their life. This can lead to self-neglect, illness, suicidal ideas and in some cases suicide (dispensing of existence).

Anyone who questions the ideology, or has some different beliefs, has two problems within the cultic setting: they have failed to revere the sacredness of the 'Truth', and they are "unscientific" (Lifton, 1989, p. 428). If a member begins to feel attracted to ideas which either contradict or ignore the 'Truth', they may become guilty and afraid, and feel the compulsion to confess.

However, if the member fully accepts the sacred science, this can feel like a relief. The sense of certainty about the world is comforting – but at the cost of psychological imprisonment.

The personal quest for knowledge, therefore, becomes self-suppressed, as do the member's doubts and critical thoughts, and the sacred science provides a rationale for this. This enables the leader to maintain their position of power and to justify their actions; even, in some cases, violence (doctrine over person and dispensing of existence).

In the quote below, Nigel shows the suppressive nature of the sacred science, the ideology, and how it can maintain the leader's status. This leader elevates their status by referring to and aligning themself with characters in the Bible. Cain was the first son of Adam and Eve, and he killed his brother Abel:

> Another whole dynamic is the 'Cain and Abel dynamic'. So, the leader is always in the position of Abel and you are in the position of Cain, so you have to overcome your desire to kill your leader, or rebel against your leader. So this is more of your 'fallen nature'. So if you have 'Cain thinking', 'Cain thoughts', or the Cain type desire to kill your leader, or criticise your leader, or judge your leader, then you are 'multiplying the sin'.

This leader is using sacred science to ensure that members suppress their internal dialogue, and their critical thinking, doubts, thoughts and feelings (milieu control), which they interpret as 'impurity' (demand for purity). The sacred science provides a rationale for the maintenance of confluence, introjection, projection and compliance and the smooth working of the entire thought reform system.

Because members introject the sacred science it needs to be unpacked, carefully chewed over and challenged.

You now have an opportunity to apply sacred science to your life story.

Worksheet M10.12: Chew over the sacred science

In this Worksheet, you have an opportunity to chew over some of the beliefs from your setting – and note what they meant in, and what they mean to you outside. Depending on your setting, you might consider beliefs about God or gods; the leader's special nature; the meaning of life; human nature; body, soul and spirit; the future of society, etc. You may notice that many of these look like introjects which need challenging! Here are a couple of examples:

Can you list (some of) the beliefs?	How was this applied?	What do you believe now?
The world will end on date xxxx.	Members were terrified of the world ending, which increased obedience and fear.	I think it is a ridiculous idea and that the world will not end on any date!
God called our leader and gave him unique revelations about the physical and spiritual worlds.	We had to listen carefully to everything the leader said, since only he could tell us how to live and what to do.	The leader is an ordinary person without special powers or revelations, and what he said was harmful to us and just served his own purposes.

You could note your own examples in the table below or in your journal.

Date _____

Can you list (some of) the beliefs?	How was this applied?	What do you believe now?

Worksheet M10.13: Tell your story – sacred science

What events or practices come to mind that seem to involve sacred science? You could write your experience in the space below or in your journal.

Date _____

_____

_____

_____

_____

_____

_____

_____

_____

_____

_____

_____

You could reflect on how frequently sacred science occurred in your cultic setting.

Worksheet M10.14: Frequency – sacred science

Was sacred science applicable to your group/relationship? (please circle)

Never	Seldom	Sometimes	Frequently	Always

We will now look at loading the language.

M10.6 Loading the language

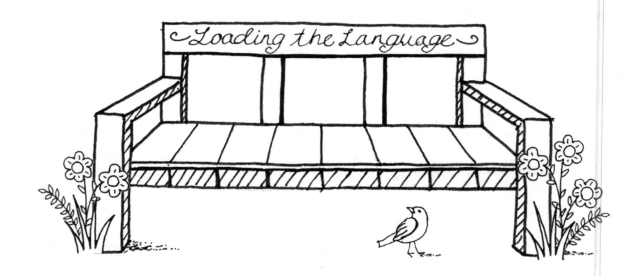

We have seen how cultic settings restrict communication, but they cannot do without language. Instead, they 'load' language with specific meanings to suit their purposes – which include controlling the milieu, mystically manipulating, defining purity, facilitating confession and laying down their sacred science.

We will now address how the language is loaded, and there is a bench for you to sit and reflect on how this affected you in your cultic setting.

Loading the language means limiting or altering the meaning of words and phrases to affirm the beliefs and ideology of the cultic setting. Language is changed so that it serves the sacred science and prevents alternative views from being spoken or thought. It is made up of what Lifton refers to as "the thought-terminating cliché" (1989, p. 429). A cliché is an overused saying that has lost its original meaning.

Whilst many areas of society creatively develop language to assist understanding, for example, medicine or social psychology, they generally do so to educate and explain, and not to manipulate, impose an ideology or restrict thinking.

With loaded language, "the most far-reaching and complex of human problems are compressed into brief, highly reductive, definitive-sounding phrases, easily memorized and easily expressed" (Lifton, 1989, p.429). It stops the member from thinking critically and also results in feeling stopping as the member suppresses their authentic identity (milieu control).

Loaded language consists of numerous words and phrases, which only the members understand, or think they understand. It gives new and particular meanings to familiar words and phrases, or creates new words with special meanings. Thought-provoking complexities are, therefore, bypassed and the ultimate truth is expressed in a single phrase or word.

The precise loaded language varies enormously between different cultic settings, but it typically puts people and things into simple but polarised categories. For example, those within the setting may be 'the chosen' and those outside 'the lost'. This leaves no room to consider subtleties and complexities, and it is easy to dismiss outsiders. Thoughts, feelings and actions may be either 'of God' (approved) or 'not of God' (disapproved), with little or nothing between. This reminds members that they need to ensure that their every thought, feeling and action is in the 'approved' category, and that anything 'disapproved' is swiftly prevented and suppressed.

Loaded language closes the member's mind, as these thought-stopping clichés dull the ability to engage in critical thinking. It also intensifies trance states (mystical manipulation), as the individual is not thinking for themselves, but for and as the cultic setting (their pseudo-identity) and is therefore likely to be automatically obeying (Cialdini, 2001).

Loading the language also adds to the sense of being important and special, a person who is a party to inside information – because they have 'THE Truth' (sacred science) and the language that backs it up. Also, because this jargon is, in many ways, unique to the cultic setting, outsiders cannot understand it and are excluded from the superior knowledge available to members (milieu control and dispensing of existence).

Here are some examples from various sources and settings.

M10.6.1 Examples of loaded language

Political

'Bourgeois mentality': any thinking that does not support the aims of the group/leader.

'Fighting for freedom': Freedom "meant freedom from within and not without, freedom from personal wants and desires, freedom from personal needs and instincts, feelings and emotions, freedom from self and individuality" (Banisadr, 2014, p. 317).

'Democracy': "...no longer meant the right to vote for our leaders and to decide on the future course of our society. Here it was defined according to the ideological merit of a member; he or she had the right to vote, to speak and make decisions, if he or she had the ideological merit for doing so. And who judged whether a member had merit or did not have merit? Of course the leadership" (Banisadr, 2014, pp. 317–318).

'Ideological merit': those deemed worthy.

Bible-based

'Cain thoughts': any thoughts not supportive of the leader (implying that such thoughts equate to a desire to kill the leader, leading to self-suppression – see Nigel's quote in M10.5).

'Fallen nature': all humankind is inherently corrupt and tainted by sin (which started when Eve ate the apple in the Garden of Eden – sometimes used to blame women for all wrongs!), which is why not everyone follows the cultic leader.

'Soulish': indulging your personal tastes (for example, playing music for pleasure) instead of working for the benefit of the cultic setting.

'Common purse': all money (including wages and gifts) to be handed to leadership (to share with everyone in theory, but not always in practice).

'Being in the spirit': agreeing with the current teaching.

'Not in the spirit': not agreeing.

Therapeutic and new age

'A princess': you are ungrateful, spoilt and useless.

'Ego-centred': concerned with yourself.

'Having needs': being weak and selfish (instead I must *'deny myself, be strong'* and concentrate on others).

'Dependent': you are rubbish and incapable.

'Social': you are *'superficial'* if you socialise, and if people like you.

'You must learn to deal with it': you are deficient and on your own.

'*Be grateful*': you are ungrateful, so suppress yourself and get on with it.
'*Off purpose*': not fully behind the aims of the organisation.
'*Raw meat*': potential members.
'*Green*': new members.
'*We love you*': you are special to us – if you do what we say!
The list of loaded language could be endless, and you will have many more examples of your own.

I expect you have noticed that much of the loaded language looks very like the introjects we looked at in M5. It is important to develop a 'nose' to sniff out the loaded language of your cultic setting *because* it is introjected. This clichéd, thought and feeling-stopping language needs to be analysed to get behind the meaning and implication of each word – it needs 'chewing over' and challenging as you would any introject. You could use Worksheet M10.15 to highlight and challenge your introjected loaded language.

Loaded language also acts as a traumatic trigger for many, and being aware of the pattern match between the words, and the memories which come to mind when the words are spoken, can make life easier and help us stay in the window of tolerance (M7).

Worksheet M10.15: Identify and chew over the loaded language

In this Worksheet, you have an opportunity to:

- identify some of the loaded language from your cultic setting
- say how the word or concept was applied
- note what the common usage of the word is in society outside and
- challenge the cultic interpretation

If you are struggling to think of loaded language from your setting, you could consider whether the examples above or below suggest anything similar from your experience. It is also likely that if you think about the belief system (sacred science), this used loaded language.

Loaded language consists of introjects, and it is vital to challenge these so we don't simply reiterate them!

I suggest you see if you can make this light-hearted because some of the loaded language sounds ridiculous from an outsider's perspective (like the second example below). I have often had a laugh with clients, once we have moved through the seriousness of it!

First example:

Identify the loaded language: *The world*

How was this applied? *Sinful unsaved society outside – all are doomed and going to hell*

What is the common usage? *The actual earth we live on or the society we live in*

Can you challenge the cultic use of the language? *I do not want to reject outsiders; and the word has no negative, spiritual, judgemental or existential meaning or value to me anymore.*

Second example:

Identify the loaded language: *Sin crystals*

How was this applied? *This refers to sugar, which was seen as indulgent and a luxury. If you have any you are selfish – it will lead you into 'sin' and you will be doomed!*

What is the common usage? *Sugar is a natural sweetener that is a pleasure to some, and it has some negatives in that it can harm teeth and cause weight gain.*

Can you challenge the cultic use of the language? *Ha, this is ridiculous! It has no spiritual, judgemental or existential value to me, and I will definitely not be doomed if I have some (although I may put on weight!).*

You could try this for yourself here and continue your reflection in your journal. You may wish to copy this Worksheet.

Date _____

Can you identify some loaded language from your cultic setting?

_____

_____

_____

How was this word or concept applied?

_____

_____

_____

What is the common usage of the word?

_____

_____

_____

Can you challenge the cultic use of the language?

_____

_____

_____

You could reflect on how frequently loading the language occurred in your cultic setting.

Worksheet M10.16: Frequency – loading the language

Was loading the language applicable to your group/relationship? (please circle)

Never	Seldom	Sometimes	Frequently	Always

We will now look at doctrine over person.

M10.7 Doctrine over person

We are making good progress in building the picture of the thought reform system. We follow on from the sacred science, and the loaded language that backs it up, with doctrine over person, which elevates the teaching so it is seen as more real and important than anyone or anything else. There is a bench for you to sit and reflect on how this affected you in your cultic setting.

Doctrine over person means convincing the member that the doctrines, the sacred science and set of beliefs held are not only THE 'Truth' but *the only reality that matters*. The doctrines are assumed to be "ultimately more valid, true, and real than is any aspect of actual human character or human experience". The 'logic' of the sacred science and the cultic setting's *interpretation* of reality can be "so compelling and coercive that it simply replaces the realities of individual experience" (Lifton, 1989, p. 431).

Apparently contrary experiences and inconsistencies must be denied, self-suppressed or reinterpreted to fit the doctrine; accounts of past events are "retrospectively altered, wholly rewritten, or ignored, to make them consistent with the doctrinal logic" (Lifton, 1989, p. 431). This gaslighting (M11.3) results in cognitive dissonance in members (M11.2). They are told that what they may think happened, or is happening, is unreal and something more aligned with the sacred science actually happened. In the thought reform environment, they learn to substitute this alternative reality without having to be told.

For example, the member may be told, and later tell themselves, that all good things in their life resulted from their membership and from the leader, even if that is the opposite of what actually happened. Their true history is treated as unreal.

Doctrine over person underlies the practice of punishing individuals, including excommunicating, ostracising, shunning, beating and subjecting to group confession sessions. Following some so-called wrongdoing, punishment is justified as being necessary to cleanse this impurity (demand for purity). When I was physically punished for 'sin' in the Community, the doctrine and 'purity' were more important than my well-being or any need for understanding, kindness and safety. The harm done to me was simply treated as unreal, and substituted with a narrative that this was good for me and that I had benefited. This is a powerful control – I did not know I was being abused, I thought the punishments were necessary and justified.

When illegal practices are in danger of being exposed (such as beating children for disobedience, child sexual abuse or abuse of adults), the leader may assert that these practices never happened or were unreal in some way. For example, this happened in the Community, when a journalist attended and the leaders feared the abuses would be reported. They simply asserted that they didn't happen, because Christ died to remove the record of all (their) wrongdoings! This had the effect of turning my reality upside down. My physical beatings had (apparently!) never happened, and I had to get used to this changed reality, as in the inverted vision experiment (M10.1.2).

The individual, therefore, has to do more than suppress their doubts: they have to suppress and change their reality and their identity. To remain a member, they must obey, comply, submit and self-suppress to fit the rigid mould the doctrine creates (Lifton, 1989, p. 431). They shape or reshape their authentic identity into a pseudo-identity – like a mould for molten metal or plastic. Thus the introjected doctrine takes precedence over the authentic identity and all that individual is, and knows – their identity, life, loves, abilities, creativity, well-being, history, experience and reality.

The cultic setting treats any individual attempts to retain independent thought and identity as "deviant tendencies" that come "entirely from personal problems" (Lifton, 1989, p. 432). The doctrine is always more important than the individual, and the personal experiences of members are subordinated to the sacred science, 'The Truth'.

In some cases, the individual's reality is replaced by false memories, resulting in "false confessions" (Lifton, 1989, p. 431). This can be especially toxic. For example, being told by the leader that they were sexually abused as a child, by a parent who was actually non-abusive, can cause further alienation from their family and worsen their mental health problems.

There are many examples in the milieu control description (M10.1) that indicate doctrine over person, such as the control and limitation of food and what people can wear – all putting the sacred science above the individual.

Matt shows how, even though he was seriously mentally ill and needed to see his doctor, the other members rationalised that he had all he needed in the cult, with the implication that he would be a failure if he sought outside assistance. This resulted in him not seeking this help:

> I was experiencing clinical depression, and the members of the cult that I was close to were discouraging me from getting help. They were telling me that my problems could be solved within the cult, and that if I were to go to outside help, the GP, and get medication, which is what I was wanting to do, that I would actually be a failure. There was a sense that everything that one needed in life could be provided by the cult. At the time I was, I was VERY [mentally] ill.

Nigel was told, prior to joining, that the doctrine valued marriage and would support his relationship. This was a lie to recruit him and his partner, however, because when they joined, the doctrine apparently changed:

> They said 'oh yes, you know, we can bless people in marriage and sanctify your relationship before God and all of that' and of course, as soon as we joined and moved in, very quickly we were sent to different cities and separated, which is, you know, part of the whole thing of cults, it is to separate people from their families, from their backgrounds, from all their attachments, so the attachment is toward the guru.

The doctrine, in this case, was that the leader was the only one who could choose marriage partners for members, but this information was hidden from potential recruits and they were lied to. The doctrine of choosing marriage partners for members took precedence over the individual's personal preferences and well-being.

> **To consider:**
> Did your setting put its teaching above the well-being of members – or outsiders?
> Were events in your life, or in the group/relationship, denied or reinterpreted to fit in with the doctrine (sacred science)?
> Was a new 'history' created?
> Was individuality treated as a problem?
> You may like to reflect on this in your journal.

You now have an opportunity to apply doctrine over person to your life story.

Worksheet M10.17: Tell your story – doctrine over person

What events or practices come to mind that seem to involve doctrine over person? You could write your experience in the space below or in your journal.

Date _____

_____

_____

_____

_____

_____

_____

_____

You could reflect on how frequently doctrine over person occurred in your cultic setting.

Worksheet M10.18: Frequency – doctrine over person

Was doctrine over person applicable to your group/relationship? (please circle)

Never	Seldom	Sometimes	Frequently	Always

Finally, we will look at dispensing of existence.

M10.8 Dispensing of existence

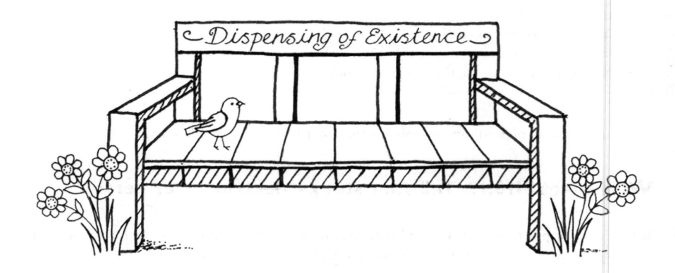

We have now reached the top of the last hill on the Roadmap – dispensing of existence! This final view builds on all the others, to complete our perspective on thought reform.

Dispensing of existence is when the leader and the setting decide who has the right to exist and who does not. Although this sounds extreme, it is a logical outcome of the thought reform system. Sacred science and demand for purity provide a clear distinction between those who are 'good', or on the 'right' path, and those who are 'bad' or 'lost'. Doctrine over person elevates the teaching above human life and existence. It is, therefore, only a small step to say who deserves to exist and who does not.

This can take a variety of forms, including:

• predicting an early or unpleasant death for outsiders and those who leave the setting
• teaching that outsiders are spiritually dead or less than human
• putting members' lives and health at risk, for example by lack of care
• saying who will survive an apocalypse or world crisis and who will not
• saying who will exist in an afterlife or subsequent existence, and who will be annihilated or suffer eternal punishment
• in some extreme cases, physical violence, killing outsiders or members, or requiring suicide

In the case of the Japanese cult, Aum Shinrikyo, dispensing of existence was made to sound altruistic and selfless because the cult offered "a 'higher existence' to those it killed" (Lifton, 1999, p.26) – that is, if someone died as a result of their actions, resulting from the sacred science and beliefs, they would be 'saved' and become martyrs for the cause.

This power over whether one can live or die "stimulates in everyone a fear of extinction or annihilation" (Lifton, 1989, p.434). For example, for me, it was the idea of going to hell that kept me a member for many years – and left me feeling that death was lurking around the corner. I became very afraid of dying, and that I would become sick with cancer or some other serious disease if I left.

Many cultic settings limit the sense of a normal life span, for example, those that have an 'end time' philosophy, which teaches that the world is going to end soon. The member introjects the idea that it is pointless investing in education or planning for their future.

Others are made to live on the edge of life and death when the leader plays with their actual physical health, for example, limiting food to keep them weak and compliant, denying medical care, or drugging or poisoning. This is dispensing of existence on a literal and personal level, using the member's body to control them. It may be especially common in coercive control relationships.

Often outsiders are dispensed with by labelling them unspiritual, worldly, satanic, unconscious and so on, depending on the loaded language. To have value, they must be converted to the sacred science of the cultic setting. In dispensing of existence, therefore, non-members, or those who disagree with the teaching, are doomed or worthless. If individuals refuse to join, they must be rejected, including family members. If current members disobey, they are likely to be punished and rejected – ostracised or shunned.

All the components of thought reform work together to confirm that the member's very existence depends on the setting and the leader, and that if they stray, their "right to existence may be withdrawn" (Lifton, 1989, p. 435). They come to believe that their life is so bound up with the setting that, if they leave, they will die spiritually and, in some cases, physically.

Shannon was told she was a drug addict, although she had never taken drugs. People she knew prior to joining were also assumed to be addicts, and she was warned that there would be dire consequences if she ever contacted any of them because:

> ...they were my druggie past and they would lead me into death, institutions, jail; so it was like my past was erased.

Marjorie explains how terrifying it was, to leave, because of the threats related to spiritual death and going to hell, something she strongly believed in as a member of a Bible-based cultic church. On leaving, there is so much:

> ...fear involved, because up to now they frightened you with, you are going to the lake of fire.

Winnie had been taught, before she joined her spiritually abusive cultic setting, that God loved everybody, including her. However, once in, she was told something very different and was dispensed with through being unimportant and invisible:

> The [leader] would say 'why would he, the God of the universe, care about YOU? He only cares for the community, he doesn't care about you personally...that's the stupidest thing I have ever heard of...'.

Fred worked hard to fulfil the requirements and says of the leader's criticism:

> It was just a constant thing of, where am I going to go wrong, what am I going to do wrong, because nothing you ever did was right.

There was no let-up for Fred until he got to "breaking point". The leader would then begrudgingly acknowledge he had been somewhat helpful to the group. Fred was kept in a cycle of dispensing of his existence, but maintained by occasional encouragement. There was:

> ...some acknowledgement that some of what you have done has been important for the cult - and that was the reason why you were still there and not been cast away.

He worked even harder, believing that he needed the group and the leader if he was to achieve enlightenment. He worked from 7 a.m. to midnight over several years, including offering therapeutic services and cleaning the centre where they lived and worked. His well-being and need for self-care were dispensed with, as the extreme hard work was rationalised as being vital for the health and salvation of mankind!

To consider:

Did your setting:

- predict an early or unpleasant death or serious illness for outsiders, and those who left?
- teach that outsiders are spiritually dead or inferior?
- put members' lives and health at risk?
- say who will survive an apocalypse or world crisis and who will not?
- say who will exist in an afterlife and who will be annihilated or suffer forever?
- believe that their purposes meant that violence was justified?

You may like to reflect on this in your journal.

You now have an opportunity to apply dispensing of existence to your life story.

Worksheet M10.19: Tell your story – dispensing of existence

What events or practices come to mind that seem to involve dispensing of existence? You could write your experience in the space below or in your journal.

Date _____

_____

_____

_____

_____

_____

_____

_____

_____

You could reflect on how frequently dispensing of existence occurred in your cultic setting.

Worksheet M10.20: Frequency – dispensing of existence

Was dispensing of existence applicable to your group/relationship? (please circle)

Never	Seldom	Sometimes	Frequently	Always

We have now completed the eight components of thought reform. As I said at the beginning of this Milestone 10, they all work together as a system, to keep members compliant and confluent. I find they provide a powerful way of understanding how cultic settings operate. There are, however, some additional ways of understanding cultic dynamics, and we will look at these in Milestone 11.

Recognising other controlling dynamics

Although thought reform (M10) explains and covers most aspects of control that occur in a cultic setting, there are other helpful ways of understanding the controlling dynamics. At this Milestone, we will look at three ways in which deceptive control can be exercised, both in and out of cultic settings – double bind, cognitive dissonance and gaslighting. As with thought reform, understanding how these dynamics work is important for undoing their effects. This is an opportunity to sit and unpack any related baggage and reflect on how these dynamics apply to your experience.

We will start with double bind.

M11.1 Double bind

When there are two or more demands that conflict with each other so that it is impossible to meet one without failing to meet the other, this is a 'double bind'. The individual can't win whichever course of action is taken – they are "damned if they do and damned if they don't", and likely to be criticised, whatever they do.

For example, in the Community, we were told that we should be strong and confident; but at the same time, we always had to listen to the leader and could be punished for stepping out of line. So, we couldn't win and could be rebuked either for taking initiative or for not doing so.

DOI: 10.4324/9781003305798-17

In a non-cultic situation, it might be possible to discuss these conflicting demands and agree on which was the priority, or a reasonable compromise, but in a cultic setting there is no satisfactory solution, and we are set up to fail. The double bind also creates anxiety, as we desperately try to work out what to do, or simply freeze.

Being confronted with two irreconcilable demands, between two undesirable courses of action, is a feature of thought reform and makes cultic control more effective (Lalich and Tobias, 2006). Often, both demands will be introjected, and chewing them over will help undo their effects.

In Worksheet M11.1, you have an opportunity to reflect on examples of double bind in your coercive, cultic and/or spiritually abusive setting, and how you might challenge and counteract these.

Worksheet M11.1: Reflect on double bind in your experience

Do you recognise double bind in your experience? You could reflect on this in the table below, or in your journal. To help you, here are some examples of double bind and ways to challenge them:

Examples of double bind	Can you challenge and counteract the double bind?
I have to confess my 'sins' because it is required and I will feel less guilty. If I confess I may be punished for my 'sins'.	I do not have to confess to anyone, it is my choice whom I tell what to. These were not real 'sins' anyway and I do not need to fear punishment.
I have to work very long hours every day because it is required and necessary to 'save the world', even if it is exhausting. I have to always be cheerful and energetic because that is also required.	It is up to me to listen to my body and self-regulate. I can rest when I need to, and my work will not 'save the world' anyway! I do not have to be cheerful or energetic all the time.

You could add your examples in the table below.

Date _____

Examples of double bind in your experience	Can you challenge and counteract the double bind?

Another type of psychological disturbance created in cultic settings is 'cognitive dissonance'.

M11.2 Cognitive dissonance

Cognitive dissonance is that uncomfortable feeling we have when we find ourselves believing two or more things at the same time which contradict each other, or we recognise that our actions are contrary to our beliefs. For example, we may be thinking, "I need to lose weight to get healthy" and "I really want to eat this cake". If we cannot resist the cake, we feel the emotional discomfort of cognitive dissonance. To try and resolve this, we change our beliefs. We may say to ourselves, "I can always lose weight later", "This cake is not too fattening" or "I am reasonably healthy as I am". It is easier to change our thoughts, even if they become misleading or false, than to live with the inner conflict of the contradictions.

Cultic settings are full of contradictions between different beliefs and between beliefs and actions. For example:

- "We are bringing God's unconditional love to the world" and "Non-believers have no value and deserve punishment".
- "Our leader is the personification of goodness" – but I see them abusing and taking what they want.
- "Joining (or remaining) was the best thing I ever did" – but I am utterly miserable.

These contradictions agitate us and feel unbearable, so we try and resolve them in our minds. Using the last example, one option might be to decide we made a mistake and leave. But that means going against the whole system of thought reform and all we have been taught about why our setting is the 'right' place for us to be. It would also mean accepting that we have spent years investing our time, energy and money into something that only made us miserable. That feels too difficult.

So, we hold onto the belief that being a member was the best thing that ever happened to us, and try to make the rest of our thinking consistent with that. So we may say to ourselves, "My difficulties are only temporary and there are happy times ahead (in this world or the next)"; or "This misery is an attack from the devil (or sin, or the 'flesh', etc.) that I must overcome"; or "It is necessary that I suffer for the sake of mankind"; or "Maybe I am not really miserable after all"; or we just suppress all thoughts of what we really feel. However we do it, we end up reinforcing rather than challenging the idea that being a member was the best thing that ever happened.

> The theory of cognitive dissonance was first expressed by social psychologist Leon Festinger. With two associates, he infiltrated a cult whose leader 'Mrs Keech' had predicted that the world would end on 21 December, and that a flying saucer would come the night before to take them to safety. Some members had left their jobs, and given away their money and homes, because of this 'prophecy'. When the disaster and promised rescue did not happen, Mrs Keech had a new prophecy, which was that the world had been saved because of the faithfulness of the members.
>
> What was most interesting was the response of the members, especially those who had given up the most because of the prediction. Instead of seeing Mrs Keech as a fraud, they became more fervent followers and went out seeking new converts. It was too challenging for these members to accept that they had been wrong to believe in Mrs Keech and to give everything away. So, to cope with the cognitive dissonance caused by the prediction failing, they had to 'double down', resort to self-justifying behaviour, and become even more dedicated believers (Tavris and Aronson, 2013, pp. 12–13).

Cognitive dissonance is of course not limited to cultic settings, and it operates widely in individuals and society. Tavris and Aronson call it "the hard-wired psychological mechanism that creates self-justification and protects our certainties, self-esteem, and tribal affiliations" (2013, p. 10). They also report how MRI scans of the brain show that when people are trying to process conflicting and dissonant information, "the reasoning areas of the brain virtually shut down", but when the conflict was resolved, "the emotion circuits of the brain lit up happily" (2013, p. 19). *Cognitive dissonance makes rational, critical thinking much more difficult, at the time we need it most, and we may reach for irrational thinking to help us feel better.*

In cultic settings, cognitive dissonance is constantly at work. Doctrine and sacred science are presented with certainty, as the ultimate Truth, and all conflicting feelings, behaviours, ideas and even facts have to be changed to resolve the discomfort of dissonance. This, in turn, reinforces members' belief in the doctrine and keeps them loyal and compliant.

Cognitive dissonance helps explain why many of us remained members for so long, and why it is mentally and emotionally painful to face our doubts and to leave. Having dedicated our lives to something, perhaps for decades, facing that it is not what we thought it was can be both devastating and humiliating (Jenkinson, 2016). However, it is ultimately liberating! Maribel experienced cognitive dissonance and says that, as many incidents accumulated, they eventually led her to leave:

> Stuff that you don't wanna believe, and things that happen along the way that produce some cognitive dissonance, they go on the shelf and at some point, the shelf gets so heavy it collapses and then you leave.

It takes courage to face up to the dissonance and the discomfort it creates, and to decide we are going to engage our critical thinking about our beliefs and actions. These may include joining (for those who did), staying (perhaps despite doubts), things we did in the setting and things we believed. Even though we may have been coerced at every stage, there may be many regrets. However, if we can face the discomfort and pain (M13), and learn and grow from our experiences (M14), we can Walk Free and recover.

How do we avoid the traps of cognitive dissonance after leaving? After being in a cultic mindset, we are used to certainty. We have lived with 'the Truth' and have been taught that doubt is wrong. I think we need to retrain our minds to think critically. When leaders in society, religious leaders, politicians, activists and celebrities claim to have simple, appealing answers to the problems in society and the world, it is easy to be swept along, especially if they confirm what we already want to believe. Usually, the situation is more complex and nuanced. It may be wise to step back, listen to different opinions and think critically, recognise the complexity and be prepared to be flexible in our thinking.

In Worksheet M11.2, you have an opportunity to reflect on examples of cognitive dissonance in your coercive, cultic and/or spiritually abusive setting, and how you might challenge and counteract these.

Worksheet M11.2: Reflect on cognitive dissonance in your experience

Do you recognise cognitive dissonance in your experience? You could reflect on this in the table below, or in your journal. To help you, here are some examples of cognitive dissonance and ways to challenge them:

Examples of cognitive dissonance	Can you challenge these confusing ways of thinking?
If I give away all my money, 'god' will 'bless' and take care of me. Now I have given away all my money I am living in poverty, relying on others to subsidise me. The reason I am living in poverty is because it is good to suffer/I must be lacking in faith because 'god' would never let me down.	If I give away all my money, I will have nothing to live off – why would 'god' expect me to suffer/live in poverty or have to rely on others because I don't have any money? I can challenge the introject and take control of my own life.
The leader says they are 'good' and have my best interests at heart. The leader is cruel and greedy. I must be so bad I deserve this behaviour because they are perfect and I am flawed.	The leader's inconsistency and cruelty are evidence that they do not have my best interests at heart. I am not bad, and they are not perfect so I can do what I deem is best for me and get away from them without needing any excuse!
If I meditate all the time, it will end wars. Meditation is harming me, I am physically stiff, my back is sore and I feel mentally unstable. I cannot stop because it will have a negative effect on the world. I need to meditate more often.	Meditation is only good for me if I do it in a balanced way and it won't end any wars – I wish it could and this is my desire, but not my responsibility and I need to take care of myself first and foremost!

You could add your examples in the table below.

Date _____

Examples of cognitive dissonance in your experience	Can you challenge these confusing ways of thinking?

We will now look at the final controlling dynamic in this Milestone, gaslighting.

M11.3 Gaslighting

Gaslighting is a form of emotional abuse that makes us doubt our perceptions of reality (Gordon, 2022). The term comes from the 1944 film, *Gaslight,* in which a woman is driven to question her sanity because she was constantly undermined by her husband. For example, he would tell her that she did not say what she had said, or that what she observed was not true, implying she was mad. This seriously destabilised her and was cruel bullying. The term has become part of common usage because so many relate to it, and it has been acknowledged as coercive behaviour by the English Courts (Francis Hanna, 2022).

Whilst the term is often applied in coercive control and one-on-one relationships, it is applicable to most cultic settings. For example, when someone criticises or undermines us in private and then treats us warmly in public, it is gaslighting. When someone leaves us feeling attacked on an emotional level but says we are making a fuss about nothing or imagining it, it is gaslighting. 'Small t' traumas (M7.3.2) often include examples of gaslighting.

In Worksheet M11.3, you have an opportunity to reflect on examples of gaslighting in your coercive, cultic and/or spiritually abusive setting, and how you might challenge and counteract these.

Worksheet M11.3: Reflect on gaslighting in your experience

Do you recognise gaslighting in your experience? You could reflect on this in the table below, or in your journal. To help you, here are some examples of gaslighting and ways to challenge them.

Examples of gaslighting	Challenge
When I was concerned about how I and others were physically punished, I was told that it had not happened and that I had made it up.	The physical punishments did happen. I saw and experienced them. They were wrong and against the law.
When I was ill, I was told I was imagining it and just needed to have more 'faith'.	I was actually ill and needed to see a doctor, not 'have more faith'.

You could add your examples in the table below.

Date _____

Examples of gaslighting in your experience	Challenge

In the next Milestone, we will look more closely at someone central to cultic dynamics, the leader.

Unmasking the leader

We are nearing the end of Region 2, leaving psychologically. Having unpacked the baggage and looked in detail at thought reform and other controlling cultic dynamics, the final Milestone within this Region deals with unmasking your leader or leadership, or the other person in a coercive relationship. (I will use the term 'leader' to refer to all of these.)

Whilst leaders vary, in a thought reform system, they are the most influential person, and wield the most power. They often 'rule' by creating a sense of awe and adoration, mixed with terror and fear (Shaw, 2022; Stein, 2017). I learned from my research that if we are to fully recover and heal, it is vital that we undo all the effects of thought reform, including the mystical manipulation in relation to the leader (M10.2). There is often a magical or mystical quality ascribed to the leader, but within a coercive, cultic and spiritually abusive setting they almost certainly did not have our best interests at heart, even though they may have said or implied that they did (their actions speak louder than their words!).

Exposure to an abusive leader is almost inevitably harmful. These leaders often hide their true nature. They may present a mask of innocence and 'goodness', pretending to be a nice, kind, friendly person. Alternatively, they may appear confident, claiming to have great power, knowledge and wisdom, but they lack empathy and compassion. Their strength and malign motivation may be well hidden, but they are likely to have a predatory instinct for vulnerability, openness or defencelessness.

DOI: 10.4324/9781003305798-18

Abusive leaders have been referred to as 'wolves in sheep's clothing'. This term comes from the Bible verse, "Watch out for false prophets. They come to you in sheep's clothing, but inwardly they are ferocious wolves" (Matthew 7:15). In the face of such an individual, any defences we have are likely to be overwhelmed, and we may well freeze and 'submit' (M7.5).

Because most members fear *and* idealise their leader, and often love them, 'putting them on a pedestal', it is essential for our recovery that we see them as a flawed human being, rather than an elevated figure who is the answer to the world's problems, a perfect guru, politician, god or channel of a god.

This is, therefore, an important subject to address on the Walking Free journey. I have put it here, near the end, as it can be the hardest and scariest, because we are dealing with abusers and perpetrators.

This Milestone includes Worksheets designed to help you reflect on your situation and unmask your particular leader.

Although we will mainly look at abusive leadership, it is important to remember that not all leadership is harmful and that society and institutions couldn't run without it. Before looking briefly at what non-abusive leadership looks like, I will say something about the natural human tendency to look up to authority.

M12.1 The human need for authority

Robert Cialdini conducted research into how we are all influenced (whether in cultic settings or not). He discovered we are wired to obey authority and taught to do so from an early age (2001, p. 185). There is, therefore, strong internal pressure within us to comply with authority figures. I realise many of us also fight authority, but bear with me!

Obeying authority is generally beneficial when we are listening to genuine, non-abusive authority figures and good leaders. These may include many parents, teachers, police officers and recognised authorities who have expertise in their field and who are delegated by society to carry out their responsibilities.

Cialdini found that complying with authorities can occur unthinkingly and "in an automatic fashion", as a shortcut to decision-making, especially when we are under pressure. That is, we may simply do as we are told when an authority figure says we should, because of their status. He also found that people more readily respond to certain "symbols of authority" (2001, p. 201), rather than the more important, but less obvious, elements of someone's character, training and abilities.

Cialdini highlights three types of symbols which have been found to be effective:

- titles – 'Doctor', 'Father', 'Professor', 'Reverend', etc.
- clothing – a scientist's white coat, a suit or smart clothing, a guru's or priest's robes, etc.
- motor cars (automobiles) – smart expensive cars as symbols of wealth and power

He noted that people often respond to symbols of authority without realising that they are doing so, and are more likely to trust the authority figure without checking them out. Those possessing such symbols, without providing any other evidence of being trustworthy, "were accorded more deference or obedience by those they encountered". Also, people did not recognise how much they were influenced: "Individuals who deferred or obeyed underestimated the effect of authority pressures on their behaviors" (2001, p. 201). The actual symbols of authority may vary, and some are more subtle, but the effect is the same.

In addition, seeing others deferring to and obeying someone makes us more likely to do the same. Cialdini calls this "the principle of social proof", and it is especially powerful when people are unsure how to react: "When people are uncertain, they are more likely to use others' actions to decide how they themselves should act" (2001, p. 119). A cultic setting is likely to create much uncertainty, especially for those new to it.

We may, therefore, look up to the authority figure, and grant them deference and sometimes obedience, while underestimating how much they, and those around us, are influencing our behaviour. This is likely to happen in a cultic setting and was certainly true in my case. I thought the leaders of the Community were 'godly' men, had 'good hearts' and were genuinely interested in my well-being. After all, everyone else seemed to think so. In reality, they were two flawed individuals who wanted to build something for themselves that they could control, and who were ultimately abusive.

How do we stop ourselves from being unduly influenced by authority figures, especially those that are dangerous? Cialdini suggests asking two questions about anyone one is inclined to trust or follow:

- Are they a genuine expert? This "directs our attention away from symbols and toward evidence for authority status" (2001, p. 201).
- Regardless of their knowledge, are they truthful and trustworthy? Some deliberately appear modest and self-deprecating to gain our trust, so watch out for that tactic.

Let's consider now what good non-abusive leaders may look like.

M12.2 Non-abusive leaders

We have established that it is natural for humans to turn to authority figures and that some of these are harmful. Before considering abusive and dangerous leaders, it helps to have an idea of what a good and trustworthy mentor, teacher, advisor or leader looks like.

A non-abusive leader has a strong sense of their own identity as an individual authentic person and knows their own mind. They have a healthy level of self-love. On the continuum of self-love (M9.2), they are likely to be at the higher end of the healthy section. Healthy leaders have a high level of confidence, together with empathy and compassion.

When they need to assert their authority, they can use their healthy assertive anger, but they do not need to constantly assert their power and position to prove themselves. They may, therefore, be firm when needed, but are ultimately encouraging and supportive towards those they lead. They can also be aware of and admit when they are wrong.

Anthony Storr, a psychiatrist who has studied gurus, comments that good leaders are not authoritarian. They are committed to others' personal freedom and decision-making and are not controlling. They are "more interested in [their] subject and … pupil" than in themselves. They allow the individual to work things out for themself. They will "inform, suggest, advise" rather than impose ideas or doctrines. They are not threatened by their workers', colleagues' or students' success. Indeed, they hope for them to flourish and grow, realising that everyone is different and has to "discover their own paths and form their own opinions" (1996, pp. 224–225).

The best leaders show curiosity and empathy towards those they lead. Storr notes that it is important to find a leader who will "listen rather than preach; someone who will encourage [an individual] to look inward and find out what he as a unique individual thinks and believes, rather than accepting some guru's dogma" (1996, p. 233).

Brené Brown, a researcher and therapist, says leaders and teachers need to be "guardians of a space that allows students to breathe and be curious and explore the world and be who they are without suffocation" (2018, p. 13).

Non-abusive leaders are, in effect, the very opposite of the leaders we will be looking at in the next section!

Before we look at different categories of leaders, you have an opportunity to reflect on non-abusive leaders in Worksheet M12.1.

Worksheet M12.1: Your experience of good leaders

In this Worksheet, you have an opportunity to reflect on whether you can relate to the idea of a good leader. Can you identify anyone in your life who has acted as a good leader or mentor? What was good about them? If you cannot think of anyone in your life, have you come across any in history or literature, in movies or on TV? You could write here or in your journal.

Date _____

_____

_____

_____

_____

_____

_____

_____

_____

_____

_____

_____

_____

In this next section, we will look at different categories of cultic leaders.

MI2.3 The cultic leader – different categories

There are different types of abusive and dangerous leaders that I have placed in seven broad categories. I realise there may be more, and some leaders may belong to more than one:

1. Authority figures respected, endorsed and approved of by society, but who 'hide in plain sight' because society does not realise or recognise they are abusers.
2. Hidden 'puppet masters' controlling from behind closed doors.
3. Narcissistic powerful leaders not endorsed by society generally, who want to be seen and elevated for their assumed power and gifts.
4. Hidden subtle narcissists whose narcissism is masked by a kind of normality.
5. Founders who historically led the group, and who may have died, but still hold much influence over the members, who continue to follow their rules and edicts.
6. Dominant individuals in intense one-to-one relationships.
7. Dominant individuals in small family groups.

We will look at these in turn.

MI2.3.1 Authority figures endorsed by society

If the leader is an authority figure respected, endorsed and approved of by society, this may blind the member to their manipulative and deceptive actions. Society may not recognise that they are abusing because they are 'hiding in plain sight' – they are so bold and confident that it is hard to believe they are dangerous and abusive. Jimmy Savile, a famous UK television personality, was found after his death to have abused numerous vulnerable adults and children in the charities he supported both financially and by volunteering his time. Tragically, society, including the police and the television company he worked for, failed to recognise or act on indications during his lifetime, even though there were reports of abuse.

There are numerous examples of such leaders: gurus, priests or elders who abuse children or members of their congregation; televangelists (preachers with large followings on TV); political leaders who take advantage of their status; therapists who abuse and control their clients, etc.

A key question is how the leader's actions are interpreted. Members may interpret their leader's actions positively, even when they are being abused by them. The effects of thought reform are reinforced by society's positive view of the leader. Effective manipulators often conceal their intent behind normal appearances.

For example, a religious leader or priest may engage in a sexual relationship with a member of their congregation, explaining that this is a 'special relationship' and 'healing' for both of them (Howard, 1996). The member may believe the leader to be ethical and righteous and doing God's work, and therefore, rationalise and excuse the behaviour, arguing to themself that it must be acceptable, or that they are somehow to blame if they view the behaviour negatively. They may also have doubts, but be unable to express these because of the leader's status and mystique.

The difference between the leader's status and their behaviour creates cognitive dissonance in the member. In order to remain a member, any doubts have to be suppressed (milieu control, M10.1) and rationalised away (M11.2). The member assumes that they are the one who is wrong and must change.

MI2.3.2 Hidden puppet masters

Some leaders are hidden authority figures who act like puppet masters, controlling from behind closed doors. For example, some groups are controlled from a distance by a guru, body of elders or governing body. Most members rarely meet them, but have them 'on a pedestal' as they do their leading from afar. Their character, personal lives and activities are hidden in the shadows.

This secrecy enables the leader to create a mysteriously ideal image. The members, knowing no different, then introject this ideal image and project it back onto the leader, even when the leader is untrustworthy. Sometimes personal information has come out about these leaders, showing them to be greedy and cruel, not saintlike and ethical as their projected image implies. Unfortunately, the members may not believe this new information and may continue to idealise them.

These puppet master leaders usually have a structure of leadership beneath them to do their bidding and maintain the smooth running of the group. This can make it more difficult for former members to recognise their group as cultic. The local elders or leaders may not seem particularly powerful, although they may be controlling and abusive when carrying out orders from the hidden leader above.

It is important to look at the whole structure of the group, to identify where power and control are located. Each layer of leadership needs to be unmasked. We will return to this at M12.5 below.

M12.3.3 Narcissistic powerful leaders not endorsed by society generally

In other cases, the leader wants to be seen and elevated for their assumed power and gifts. These leaders may promote themselves as having special insight into such issues as life coaching, business, wellness, mental health, spirituality, existential concerns or politics. They often give the impression they are the only one who has such incredible insight. They will impress their followers through mystical manipulation (M10.2).

Brian, one of the leaders of the Community, fitted this category of narcissistic leader. He thought the local church leaders (including Bishops in the Anglican Church) should come and 'sit at his feet' and be taught by him. Little did he realise that they were very concerned about him, and that he was the last person they wanted to consult!

Destructive leaders that subjugate (conquer, subdue, defeat or overpower) their members are what Daniel Shaw calls 'traumatising narcissists'. These are the most extreme types of narcissist, on the far right side of the continuum of self-love (M9.2). They have an overinflated, entitled and grandiose sense of self to cover their inadequacies, seeing themselves as far more important than anyone else, and thinking they have the right to dominate others. Shaw says:

> This narcissist ... is so well defended against his developmental trauma, so skillful a disavower of the dependency and inadequacy that is so shameful to him, that he creates a delusional world in which he is a superior being in need of nothing he cannot provide for himself. To remain persuaded of his own perfection, he uses significant others whom he can subjugate.
>
> (Shaw, 2014, pp. 10–11)

Zeiders and Devlin describe this category of destructive leaders as 'malignant narcissists' who "inflict untold psychic damages upon anyone at any stage of development, regardless of their ego strength": that is, no one exposed to them, however 'strong' they may be, remains unscathed. Such "mad leadership" embodies "narcissism, criminality, sadism, and paranoia ... hurting friends and enemies alike" (2020, p. xv). Their inadequacies and mental health problems, combined with a position of power, make them dangerous to those around them. They may well be grandiose, antisocial, psychopaths, sociopaths and/or criminals.

It is not possible to diagnose your cultic leader in a medical sense through the information contained in this book, and that is not the purpose here. But understanding about such leaders, and their impact on those around them, may help you identify your leader and why they had such an impact on you.

M12.3.4 Hidden subtle narcissists

There are some leaders who hide their narcissism. They appear relatively normal and to be benign, good leaders, but they mask their true nature. They may be what Craig Malkin refers to as "subtle narcissists". Subtle narcissists "are more difficult to detect, more common, and more likely to wreak havoc in our lives" because of their manner: they can be "quiet, charming, capable of warmth, and even occasional empathy" (2015, pp. 12–13). We may be won over without recognising the danger.

Signs of narcissism can be hard to spot, but they are still there. For example, subtle narcissists may be "bad listeners, endlessly preoccupied with how they measure up to everyone else", have a high level of "entitlement" (Malkin, 2015, pp. 87, 89) and probably deny reports of abuse.

I have observed that a narcissist is easier to handle if they get what they want, and if they are in the limelight. The threat may come if they are challenged, or someone else tries to become 'top dog'. In these circumstances, a hidden narcissist may be exposed – and those near them are at risk of harm.

M12.3.5 Historical founders

There are groups where the followers still adhere to rules and regulations laid down by their, now long-dead, founders. These leaders still exert much influence over the group because members continue to comply, and have not chewed over their teachings or perhaps even updated or modernised them. Sometimes subsequent generations of leaders are from the founder's family, implying they have an inborn right to lead.

If your group fits this category, it might help you to investigate its history, so you can view the leader and their family more clearly, as suggested in P3.2.3.

M12.3.6 Dominant individuals in intense one-to-one

There are coercively controlling relationships that amount to a one-to-one cult. The leader may be a partner in a relationship involving coercive control or narcissistic and psychopathic partner abuse; a therapist in a one-to-one relationship with their client; a church minister with a member of their congregation, etc. In these cases, the member is intensely involved with that leader, and may have little objectivity or space to reflect on their true nature – they are too close to get a perspective.

M12.3.7 Dominant individuals in small family groups

There are some families which are ruled over by one or both narcissistic parents, or another family member, entrapping the family in what amounts to a coercive cult. The 'leader' is well placed to control the others, who are too close to get a perspective.

M12.3.8 Which category fits your leader?

In Worksheet M12.2, you have an opportunity to reflect on the category or categories of leader in your situation – you may find that more than one applies.

Worksheet M12.2: Which category fits your leader?

Date _____

1. Which category or categories fit your leader/ship?

_____

_____

_____

_____

_____

_____

_____

_____

2. Would you like to say more about how they fit these categories?

_____

_____

_____

_____

_____

_____

_____

_____

M12.3.9 Was your leader 'evil'?

In your cultic setting, the word 'evil' may have had a specific, loaded language (M10.6), meaning, or may have been used in a spiritual sense. For example, it may have been used for those opposing the leader and their aims, or linked to ideas about 'the devil'. It may be helpful to consider Philip Zimbardo's "simple, psychologically based" definition:

> Evil consists in intentionally behaving in ways that harm, abuse, demean, dehumanize, or destroy innocent others – or using one's authority and systemic power to encourage or permit others to do so on your behalf.
>
> (2007, p. 5)

Whilst all leaders are different, many seem to fall within this definition of 'evil'. There are some, including members who become leaders, who set out with good intentions, but as they become more powerful, they become abusive and end up fitting this definition.

Worksheet M12.3 is an opportunity to consider whether this definition applied to your leadership.

Worksheet M12.3: Was your leader 'evil'?

Does Zimbardo's definition of 'evil' apply to your leadership? You could reflect on this here or in your journal.

Date _____

_____

_____

_____

_____

_____

_____

_____

In this next section, we will look at former members' perspectives on cultic leaders.

M12.4 Understanding and unmasking the leader

We have identified various types of dangerous leaders. We now need to address the vital task of understanding and unmasking them, which is an essential part of the recovery process.

It is helpful to hear the voices of others who have gone through the process of finding, or growing up with, a leader they thought was perfect or worthy of utmost respect, and coming in time to see their deceitful, controlling and abusive nature. This section is adapted from my Doctoral research (Jenkinson, 2016), and the quotes are from my interviews with former members who participated in it.

Although most of the quotes are from those who joined a cultic setting, and therefore bought into the leader's claims, some are from those born and/or raised. Many of these also idealised their leader growing up and as adults, before becoming sceptical about them. All former members needed to unmask their leaders to move forward.

The nature of the leadership is crucial to members' experience of life in the cultic setting because they held the power and status. Former members' experiences vary; some were in personal contact with the leader whilst others followed from afar, sometimes via the internet or TV.

All the research participants were affected by the leader as members, sometimes positively, but mainly negatively. For most, the leader was the centre of their mental universe and their motivation for joining, although the success and reach of the leaders varied across different cultic settings.

The participants variously came to believe that their leader:

- was the embodiment of a god
- had a special power to point them to a higher spiritual being
- had the power to transform their life
- could heal them and/or fulfil their needs
- could give them purpose and direction for their life

A new member may, therefore, initially be filled with optimism, thinking that they have found the answer to life's problems and that:

> ...the world is wonderful and I'm enlightened or I'm working towards enlightenment, I have the perfect teacher. [Lavinia]

The member becomes convinced that what has been promised is real, the 'Truth' (sacred science and doctrine over person), and that the leader is central to this. The projection of perfection onto the leader, and belief in their actual, perhaps miraculous, power (mystical manipulation), can lead to the member accepting everything else:

> Once you see something that's miraculous you buy into every other thing very, very easily. [Maribel]

For some, their leader was gifted and charismatic, and had positive qualities which attracted them and contributed to the idealisation (putting them 'on a pedestal'):

> But on the other hand he was quite brilliant. And he could talk a blue streak, he had a sense of humour, he laughed, um, was a performer, he would sit in his chair and he would suddenly just start talking and there were of course tape recorders or videotapes, and [they would] transcribe it, and then there would be an article or a book or a whatever. [Reginald]

Sean's aim on joining:

> ...was to get closer and closer to the guru [in order to] replace myself... because the old me was just worthless.

Members hope that the leader's power will rub off on them:

> One of the magical ideas... is ... to be near a so-called Avatar, you know that kind of rubs off on you. [Reginald]

Getting close to the leader is risky because becoming confluent means that there is no differentiation, no assertive anger (M8), no protective boundary in place whereby the member can judge what is healthy and what is not; and so:

> When the member's openness, and let's say vulnerability, your protective shields go down, then unfortunately manipulative leader or leaders take advantage of that. [Lavinia]

Abusive leaders may publicly present a charismatic, idealised and saintlike mask, attractive to outsiders (including potential new members), but like most abusers, they hide their abuse behind closed doors. Sean suggests that abuse happens because some cultic leaders need to maintain their narcissistic belief in their absolute power:

> Keeping [members] enslaved one way or the other is sort of necessary for the leader or else they can't sustain their own delusion of omnipotence.

For many participants, as they grew closer to the leader, the idealised view was challenged and they began to see them for the human they were. This can lead to confusion as to why the perfect leader, the "lover of all lovers" [Max], who is also viewed as a god by some, would treat the member in such an abusive manner. In order to maintain the illusion, the member is likely to self-suppress the doubts (milieu control) and assume some wrong or impurity in themself (demand for purity and confession).

Lavinia suggests that:

> The arbitrariness of abuse ... has so often so much more to do with the abuser and the abuser's mental state or let's say, on unworked through issues that get projected onto the member.

Once the leader shows "cruelty and deception and corruption" [Sean] then the inner conflict may begin in the member, leading to cognitive dissonance (M11.2) and doubts. This confusion, as to what sort of person the leader is, may only be resolved by concrete evidence and can take time. Maribel expresses this dilemma:

> This man was either a pathological narcissist, a sociopath, anti-social personality disorder, or he was a God.

Unmasking the leader entails bringing them "down to earth" so the former member can "dissect their persona, ...take them down; and understand their psychology" [Nigel]. It is helpful, therefore, to humanise them, to understand who they are as a person, their psychology and their developmental background. As long as these aspects remain a mystery, recovery is likely to be hindered.

The idealisation and beliefs about the leader need to be "debunked" [Lavinia]. When one participant heard that the leader was dealing in drugs, a fact that had been obscured from her for decades, she left immediately. She needed to "unpick the person and see that he absolutely wasn't what he said he was".

Fred came to see his powerful, abusive leader as a weak human being who was "messed up with a lot of problems". These problems resulted in him, apparently unconsciously, treating his followers in an abusive manner. Eventually, Fred came to see that the abuse and control became conscious and deliberate, although none of the other members realised it at the time:

> I believe that there is only one person that was conscious about what he was doing.

If the leader is not unmasked then it will be difficult for the former member to recover and move forward in their life, because the leader's power has seemed so real, mystical – and frightening (mystical manipulation, sacred science and doctrine over person):

> It just reinforces the magic and the power, it's a very scary power. You don't want to betray that power, or go against that power because … for me he was God-like, and, and um the threat of his disapproval was horrible. [Maribel]

Even the death of the leader may not be enough to free the former member from their beliefs about them. They may believe the power will continue beyond the grave, as shown by Dolores, whose leader had died a few years prior to the interview:

> I constantly struggle with this, the sense we got, that there's a presence there. He always would say he's inside you, he's around you, he's above you, whatever. Ah, you know, if there is an empty chair that would be where [the cult leader] would sit, you put the chair out, you put a place for him at the table.

Without unmasking them, a living or dead leader may continue to haunt the former member for years to come.

It is important to remember all the cultic dynamics we have looked at on this journey. The leader is the key person who has used and maintained these. The former member is a victim of the leader's abuse, and should not blame themself. Maribel uses graphic terms, which you may find distressing, but which powerfully express her experience:

> It was important for me to see him for what he was. I really saw myself as a victim, not as a willing victim, I don't see myself that way. I see myself as someone who was a victim, who was psychologically raped. Spiritually and psychologically raped and um, it would be the same as if I was walking down the street and he came out of a dark corner and grabbed me. Yeah, he had me emotionally captive for 10 years.

Unmasking him helped Maribel recognise her pseudo-identity and connect with her authentic identity:

> As soon as I realised he had no power over me there was just me left.

Understanding and unmasking the leader helps us to reinstate our boundaries, activate our assertive anger (M8), stop being an echoist (M9) and establish our authentic identity. We may have complex emotions, including for some a sense of loss of the leader, or of the idealised image of the leader. Although this may be painful and disillusioning, it is a necessary and ultimately helpful stage on the way towards recovery.

Note: If your leader is dangerous or has committed crimes, you may wish to consider reporting them to the police. Cultic leaders have occasionally been convicted and imprisoned. If you are considering this, I encourage you to seek support from safe others or a therapist, and ensure you look after yourself (P3.1 and P5).

You now have an opportunity to think about the structure of your cultic setting.

M12.5 The structure of your group or relationship

The structure of your group or relationship is likely to have an impact on your experience as a member and with the leadership. If it was a small group or a one-on-one, you probably knew the leader personally, and it may have been a straightforward and simple structure. If it was large, you may have followed from afar, and the structure may be complex and multi-layered. It can, therefore, be helpful to organise your thoughts by setting out the structure, and where you and the leadership were placed within that.

You could create a diagram or a description of the leadership and structure of your cultic setting in Worksheet M12.4, or your journal, being as creative as you want to be! It may be that the leadership structure changed during your involvement. If so, you could draw several different diagrams.

Understanding the structure will help clarify the category of leader in your situation; where you fit into the structure; and the implications of this. For example, I was never in leadership in the Community and always felt at the 'bottom of the pile'. (I suspect most of us were made to feel like this, but because we did not speak with each other about it, we never knew what others felt.)

There is no right or wrong way to set out the structure, but I have given an example in Figure M12.1. This uses a pyramid approach, showing layers of leadership and membership. This is a fairly complex structure, loosely based on various cultic settings. There is a main leader, L1, a second in command, L2, and five sub-leaders. Below them are many members: the dotted lines indicate their broken boundaries. The members take part in various activities: recruiting visitors, leadership training, study (indoctrination) groups and a music group. The public image of the group comes from various businesses. The general public may not know these are affiliated with the group, but they earn money for the leader and the group.

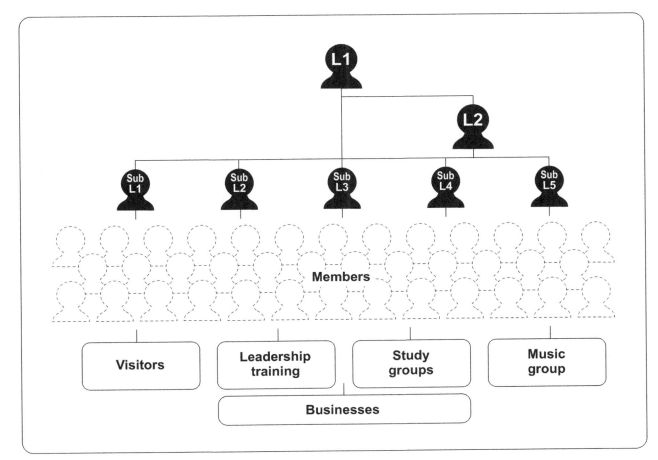

Figure M12.1 The structure of a cultic and spiritually abusive group

Worksheet M12.4: Draw or describe the leadership structure of your group

You could create a diagram or a description of the structure of your cultic setting in the box below, or in your journal, showing the leadership and your own position.

Date _____

What does this tell you about the setting and your relationship with the leader? You may like to reflect on this in your journal.

In the next section, there are some more Worksheets to help you chew over your experience of the leader.

M12.6 Unmasking your leader

In this section are some Worksheets to help you unmask your leader. You may have had more than one leader, and these can be used to analyse each one. They can also be used to review your leadership at different stages of your time as a member. You could photocopy the sheets for the different leaders or stages, or use your journal.

Reminder: If any of these are difficult to do or become overwhelming, please remember to take care of yourself and perhaps have a break and return to them later. You could revisit P3.1 or speak with a trusted friend or therapist (P5).

Worksheet M12.5: Attributes of abusive leaders

In this Worksheet, you have an opportunity to look through a list of attributes and characteristics of an abusive leader. You can reflect on whether your leadership fits any of these.

This section quotes, and is adapted from, *Feet of Clay* by Anthony Storr (1996, pp.xi-xvi). (Some attributes refer to religious and spiritual situations, but if you were in a different kind of setting you may well find parallels.)

So, thinking about your experience, you could mark to what extent each attribute was present for your leader: 0 = not present, 10 = fully present; or simply tick the box. You might like to go through this quickly at first; and revisit it later, spending more time reflecting, and see if you come up with the same responses.

Date _____

Was your leader...	Scale 0–10	
1. Self-selected (Storr comments that "anyone can become a guru" or leader if they have "the hubris" (excessive pride, arrogance, self-confidence and narcissism) to claim they have special gifts)		
2. Claiming possession of "special, spiritual insight" based on personal revelation (e.g. from God, angels, spirits, aliens, etc.)		
3. Believing that their special insight applies to all humanity and is 'the Truth' (sacred science)		
4. Believing "all humanity should accept their vision" or face destruction		
5. Teaching about a world crisis (the end of the world, the Rapture, nuclear holocaust, Armageddon, etc.) when "their own followers will be saved, whilst the majority of mankind will remain unredeemed" and/or die		
6. Promising "followers new ways of self-development, new paths to salvation" (maybe psychotherapeutic, political, spiritual, religious, etc.)		
7. Deceitfully wielding power to exploit their followers in various ways		
8. "More interested in what goes on in their own minds than in personal relationships" or friendships (many are introverted, self-absorbed and narcissistic)		
9. "Intolerant of any kind of criticism, believing that anything less than total agreement is equivalent to hostility"		
10. "Isolated", leading to lack of exchange of ideas		
11. "Elitist and anti-democratic" or paying only "lip-service to democracy" (e.g. implying everyone has a say, but actually pulling the strings)		
12. Valuing status and dominance over friendship		
13. Imposing ideas rather than discussing them		
14. Exhibiting "fervent certainty" and "intensity of conviction", which explains their powerful effect (their excessive confidence convinces others)		
15. Compelling and able to quickly impress and influence others, and attract devoted followers		
16. Directing "every aspect of ... followers' lives" e.g. where to live, sexual relationships, how to spend money and what to think		
17. Seeing themselves as exceptions who are "entitled" to act and live in different ways from their followers		
18. Exercising power by "making their followers perform meaningless and unnecessary tasks, ostensibly as spiritual exercises, but in fact as a proof of the guru's power over them"		
19. Assuming they are above the law and can do as they wish		
20. Inventing a mysterious background or life story		

(Storr, 1996, pp.xi–xvi)

Once you have completed this table, you could review how you have marked each aspect, and reflect on each in case you have any blind spots.

Let's look at Worksheet M12.6 to further assist you in unmasking and humanising your leader.

Worksheet M12.6: Humanising the leader

In this Worksheet, you have an opportunity to think about your leader *as a human being*, and to answer some questions, if you think that would be helpful. The purpose of this is to continue to 'unmask' them and 'bring them down to earth' – and down to size!

You could answer these questions about aspects of your leader in your journal:

1. Can you describe your leader as an ordinary human being, including their birth name (not 'guru' name, if there is a difference); gender; what they looked like and wore; what age they were when you met them?
2. What do you know of their life history, family of origin and psychiatric history?
3. What led them to become the leader they became, for example, a crisis such as mental illness, or what they claimed to be a special revelation?
4. Did your leader present one image of themself to the outside world and another behind closed doors? How did these differ?
5. In what ways did your leader set rules and then not follow them?
6. In what ways was your leader abusive or controlling?
7. Did your leader have any good attributes?
8. Do you have any reason to still fear or look up to your leader?
9. Can you now see your leader as an ordinary human being, and describe them apart from their 'guru' or special status? (One way to humanise them is to imagine them on the toilet!)

Worksheet M12.7: Personal experience of the leader

This Worksheet is designed to help you reflect in greater depth on your *personal experience* of and contact with the leadership. You could answer as much as you want here or in your journal.

Date _____

1. Were you in personal contact with the leader; did you ever (or often) meet them, or were you worshipping/following from afar, including online?

   _____

   _____

   _____

2. What difference did this contact make to your experience?

   _____

   _____

   _____

3. How were you affected by the leader, positively and/or negatively?

   _____

   _____

   _____

4. Was the leader the reason you joined, or stayed, and what was it about them?

   _____

   _____

   _____

5. Did you believe the leader was the embodiment of God, or had special powers, for example, to point you to a higher spiritual being, transform your life or fulfil all your needs?

_____

_____

_____

6. Did you believe they could heal you physically, psychologically or emotionally?

_____

_____

_____

7. Did you believe that being close to the leader meant their power and 'goodness' would rub off on you?

_____

_____

_____

8. Did the sense of 'awe' around the leader (mystical manipulation) mean that spiritual, sexual, emotional, psychological or physical abuse was rationalised and explained away?

_____

_____

_____

9. Were you confluent with the leader (M4), and how did this affect you?

_____

_____

_____

10. As you got closer to the leader, did you begin to see them differently from their public image? If so, how did this affect you, for example, was it confusing?

_____

_____

_____

11. What did you do with your doubts about the leader?

_____

_____

_____

12. Is there anything else you want to say about your personal experience of the leader?

_____

_____

_____

13. How do you see them now, for example, as powerful or ordinary?

_____

_____

_____

Worksheet M12.8: Do you fear you have become like your cultic leader/ship?

Living in a cultic setting means that you may have closely identified with the leadership. This could lead to a fear that you have taken on some of their harmful attributes. This Worksheet is an opportunity to reflect on these aspects and chew them over.

For example, when I left the Community, I had been so hurt by the leader's abuse that I became afraid of being like them and hurting others. I feared that others would experience me as abusive if I set my boundaries and used my assertive anger. This made it difficult to protect myself and maintain healthy boundaries. Eventually, I realised that I had those fears because I had been so confluent with the leader – I had lost the sense of where I began and they ended.

I wonder if you can relate to this in any way, and if you think you are like the leader? It is important to chew over the ways you may think you are like them, and to assess if this is true or not. You could reflect on these questions here or in your journal.

Date _____

1. Did you introject attributes of the leader, and did these aspects become part of your pseudo-identity? (For example, are you a kind person who became cruel and judgemental, like the leader?)

   _____

   _____

   _____

2. Do you fear you are like the leader? If so, how does this show itself in your life? (See my own example above.)

   _____

   _____

   _____

3. If you consider what you have learned about your authentic identity, is it true that you are like the leader, or are you different?

   _____

   _____

   _____

Worksheet M12.9: Compare your view of the leader to your view of a 'God' or higher spiritual being

Has your image of 'God', or of a higher spiritual being, merged with the leader's personal traits: that is, are you confusing God's, or the higher spiritual being's, character with the character of the cultic leader? If so, you could reflect on this and compare the two in this Worksheet. I have provided an example to help:

Aspect of the leader	Projection from leader onto God or higher spiritual being	Can you challenge these projections?
The leader was terrifying, always criticising me and telling me off, and I believed that they were watching me all the time and knew what I was thinking and doing.	I think [God/spiritual being] is terrifying, always criticising me and telling me off, watching me all the time and knowing what I am thinking and doing.	Now that I have left, the leader has no influence over my life and so why would I still fear their criticism? I don't even respect them anymore. I can see that my view of [God/spiritual being] is skewed and a projection of the leader and so I don't need to be fearful! I will spend time investigating how others see [God/spiritual being] and chew over what I am learning. I will decide for myself what I believe and learn to see things in my way.

You could add your examples in the table below or your journal.

Date _____

Aspect of the leader	Projection from leader onto God or higher spiritual being	Can you challenge these projections?

We have now completed Milestone 12, and I hope you have unmasked your leadership, or at least started to! We are making great progress and have completed all the tasks in Region 2. You may want to revisit some of the Milestones, or you may feel ready to move into Region 3, and reflect on emotions and emotional healing.

Region 3

Heal emotionally

We are making great progress on the Walking Free journey and have now entered a new Region on the map where we will address emotional healing needs.

All the Milestones in Region 2 have focussed on psychoeducation and *understanding* what happened in the coercive, cultic and/or spiritually abusive setting. This includes facing doubts, diagnosing your cultic setting, recognising confluence, chewing over and challenging introjects and beginning to unlayer the cultic pseudo-identity and to identify what belongs to your authentic identity or 'real me'. We have looked at what happens to us during traumatic stress, at assertive anger, and at healthy and unhealthy self-love. In the thought reform hills, you have had an opportunity to relate each of the eight components to your experiences. We have also looked at other controlling dynamics and unmasking the leader.

It is important to keep all you have learned in mind when it comes to facing emotions, which is the focus of this Region. We will also discuss the experience of joining, for those who did so.

One reason we address the *psychoeducation* contained in the previous Milestones *before* we focus on and address the emotions is that the cultic experience changes and affects our emotions, inducing some and suppressing others. We need to *understand the cultic dynamics*, what has been done to us, and where our emotions are coming from – so we accurately assess our experience and do not inaccurately blame ourselves.

DOI: 10.4324/9781003305798-19

For example, if we try to address fear, a feeling induced in the coercive cultic setting, before we understand that the setting taught us to fear, we may think we are a fearful person – but perhaps we are not! It is more productive to first challenge the cultic dynamics which created that fear, for example, the teachings (sacred science) and the resulting introjects, so we *understand where our feelings are coming from.*

There is a similar reason why we have not previously addressed the question of why you joined, if you did. The cultic setting distorts and confuses our understanding of who we were before joining. Also, after leaving, there is a risk that we quickly blame ourselves and our pre-membership vulnerabilities, including emotional issues from childhood, for the decision to join.

It is, therefore, important first to understand how the cultic setting, including its deceptive recruitment methods, has affected and changed us and our view of ourselves. It then becomes easier to accurately interpret our reasons for joining, and to see whether, and how, any previous emotional issues played a part in that.

So, let's think a bit more about emotions in Milestone 13.

Emotional healing

In order to Walk Free and complete the journey to recovery and growth, we need to address the subject of emotions and emotional healing and unpack any related baggage. The terms 'feelings' and 'emotions' mean the same thing here, and I use them interchangeably.

M13.1 Your emotions matter

There are many, varied feelings, as illustrated in Figure M13.1.

We feel feelings all the time, and they are all significant and interesting: "Each of our emotions has its own individual message, its own wants and needs, and its own purpose in the psyche" (McLaren, 2010, p. 27).

Steve Biddulph says feelings are a "response on the inside to something that happens on the outside" (2021, p. 79) and that "they mean something, something important to figure out. Emotions – fear, anger, sadness and joy – tell you the deep truth about something, usually right here and now. They also energize you in a certain way that will help you get through a situation. Emotions are a kind of intelligence, and they are especially important for relating to others" (2021, p. 30).

Our feelings are essential for our survival and safety, and they connect us to our unconscious awareness (M7.2). They take place within our body, so they connect us to our body. They also connect us to others and the world around us.

DOI: 10.4324/9781003305798-20

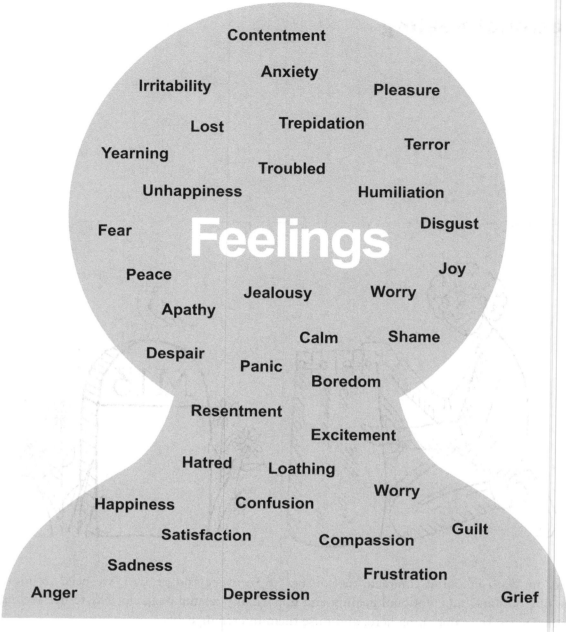

Figure M13.1 The range of feelings

We cannot know who we really are until we are in touch with our feelings, and they are vital if we are to discover our authentic identity and complete the Walking Free journey.

Your feelings or emotions matter, they are part of you, they are you, they have something to say - about you, others, and the environment! It is a fundamental human right to be allowed your feelings, and vital that you listen to them.

Self-care is very important, and if you become overwhelmed, you could remind yourself of Oasis Lake, and revisit your Safe Enough Space (P3.1.1) or the tips for grounding (P3.1.2). Or you might need to find another person, such as a trusted friend or therapist (P5), to talk this through with.

Let's look at what happens to emotions as a member.

M13.2 What happens to emotions in a cultic setting?

In a thought reform environment, we learn to suppress our feelings (alongside our thoughts) and are likely to be disconnected from our body – in a state of 'freeze'. This results from all the components of thought reform, but especially milieu control and demand for purity (M10).

However, for many, feelings may also spill out, unprocessed and unregulated, and can't be controlled or packed back in. The pressures of the cultic setting, perhaps combined with trance and/or drug-induced states, make self-regulation virtually unattainable.

For most members, there is probably a mixture of suppression and of feelings spilling out. Let's think about these in turn.

M13.2.1 Suppression of feelings

In a cultic setting, feelings are likely to be categorised into 'good' and 'bad', 'positive' and 'negative', 'pure' and 'impure'. So, we may be taught that certain feelings are acceptable, 'good' or 'right' (perhaps joy and happiness); and others unacceptable, 'bad' or 'wrong' (maybe anger or fear). This leads to suppressing certain feelings and allowing others (demand for purity).

Many former members report that in the cultic setting they were not in touch with their feelings because they were virtually never allowed to express their authentic feelings, or they were punished for doing so. Within a thought reform system, members learn to suppress feelings and to think that is the right thing to do. But it is not – it is harmful!

Cultic settings often tell their members that they have personal problems which can only be resolved in that setting – such as being 'sinful', 'unenlightened', 'mentally unstable', 'egotistical', 'too attached' or 'uncleared' (or whatever the loaded language was). This can lead to members believing that there is something deeply wrong with them and their feelings, which are assumed to be 'bad' and perhaps toxic to others. This baggage can carry on influencing them long after leaving – and their fears may even become phobias (M5.3).

Whilst fear is an emotion, it also drives other feelings underground, especially when it overwhelms us. There are many things to be afraid of in a cultic setting: teachings about hell, 'Armageddon' and 'the rapture' (the idea that 'true believers' will be rescued from the earth leaving unbelievers behind to suffer); the consequences of disobeying; discipline, beatings, threats and humiliations; and many more. Fear can petrify us, and we suppress our feelings – they go cold as we move from 'fight or flight' to 'freeze and submit' (M7).

We may simply not know what to do with our feelings and so suppress them. We may fear they will overwhelm us, kill us or cause us to act irrationally. I was like this: feelings seemed so very scary and I didn't know what to do with them. I thought I was toxic because of them, and that I would harm others if I expressed them. I believed this because I was punished for having feelings. For example, when I cried, I was told that was 'self-pity' or 'attention seeking' (loaded language) when I needed some kindness, empathy and understanding. I had no one to provide emotional support, and I had been stripped of my natural human authentic coping strategies, so I became overwhelmed and went into freeze.

Peter, multigenerational born and raised, now in his 50s, and who left at age 17, says:

> I think at 18, I would not even have understood the concept of thoughts, emotions, feelings. Our feelings and emotions were always numbed, and we were not allowed to express them. To understand that we are in control of our own thoughts and feelings was huge for me, and a big shift from believing it was God or the Devil putting thoughts in my head.

Max, who joined as an adult, agrees:

> To me it's actually pretty horrible because cult members are not feeling, but you can't even think straight unless you pay attention to your feelings.

As Karla McLaren says, "The state of being emotionless is not something to celebrate" (2010, p. 28). It is not a good thing to have no emotions, and we can't think straight (or critically, M5.2) without paying attention to our feelings.

In Worksheet M13.1, you have an opportunity to reflect on how you suppressed, or still suppress, your feelings.

Worksheet M13.1: How did you suppress your feelings?

What did you do within yourself to suppress your feelings? For example, I physically swallowed when I wanted to suppress my feelings – literally 'swallowing my feelings'; I held my breath; I hid behind a chair in meetings, to hide my feelings from others and myself; I dissociated and 'zoned out'; but I also often got frustrated and wanted to hit things, which was my attempt at expressing some of those pent-up emotions! You could reflect on this in the space below or in your journal.

Date ______________________

I suppressed my feelings by:

It may be helpful to think now about which feelings were judged 'good' and which 'bad' in the cultic setting. It is important to keep in mind that no emotions are actually 'good' or 'bad'. They each have their place and are connected to one another – as Karla McLaren says, they come as a "boxed set" (2010, p. 27)!

Worksheet M13.2: Which feelings were judged to be 'good' and which 'bad', and why?

In Figure M13.1, there was a list of feelings in the head and shoulders shape. You could have another look at that and choose some feelings you want to think about. In the table below, you have the opportunity to reflect on whether a particular emotion was seen as 'good' or 'bad' in the cultic setting. You might also like to consider *why* you were taught this. For example, if anger was considered 'bad', it may be because the cultic setting wanted to keep you compliant and confluent.

Date _____

Feeling	Assumed 'good'?	Assumed 'bad'?	Why do you think this was?

The next Worksheet gives you an opportunity to choose a particular emotion, and to think in more detail about why your cultic setting taught that it was either 'good' or 'bad'.

Worksheet M13.3: Why were you taught a feeling was 'good' or 'bad'?

Here, you can choose an emotion, perhaps one from the last Worksheet, that seems significant. You might like to reflect on these questions here or in your journal.

Date _____

Emotion/Feeling: _____

1. What do you think their motivation was for teaching that this emotion was 'good' or 'bad'?

_____

_____

_____

2. In what ways was the suppressing or expressing of this emotion a part of the thought reform, control and manipulation?

_____

_____

_____

3. What were they trying to achieve through getting you to suppress yourself or overly express yourself (see below)?

_____

_____

_____

4. How do you view this emotion now?

_____

_____

_____

There are times when we cannot contain our feelings, and we will look at this next.

M13.2.2 When feelings spill out

There are several reasons why members may be flooded and overwhelmed with feelings in a cultic setting.

This may be because they cannot control or regulate their feelings in a pressurised environment with no support, as in my own example in the last section.

However, in some cultic settings, this overwhelm is purposely induced and encouraged. It may, for example, be taught as a spiritual practice or 'worship', or as necessary for 'enlightenment' or 'cleansing'. The member is expected to be overly emotional, but may be left discombobulated and living in a state of hyperarousal and confusion, unable to think straight because there is too much feeling which cannot be regulated or packed back in. This, of course, means they are more easily controlled.

In a state of overwhelm, we are unable to move through the feelings, process them and recover. We will revisit this later in this Milestone.

M13.2.3 Introjects about emotions

The cultic setting does more than just categorise emotions as good and bad, acceptable and unacceptable. It also provides introjects about emotions that we, as members, take in, and that help to form our cultic pseudo-identity.

We, therefore, need to chew over and challenge these introjects in order to connect with our authentic identity and our authentic feelings. This includes introjects that tell us that it is wrong or 'impure' to have certain feelings. Worksheet M13.4 can help with this.

Worksheet M13.4: Highlight and challenge introjects about feelings

Can you identify introjects that might stop you from facing your feelings? Here are two examples:

Identify an emotion/ feeling	Identify introjects about emotions/ feelings	Challenge
Sad	Feeling sad is selfish [so I suppress sadness]	I have a right to feel sad and process my loss and grief until I have resolved it – that is much healthier than suppressing it or pretending I am not sad
Happy	Feeling 'happy' all the time is 'good' and the only way to live [so I aim to be 'happy' all the time but suppress all my other feelings]	No one feels happy all the time and it is unrealistic to expect this of myself – there is no value judgement as to whether I should be happy or not

You could highlight and challenge your own introjects in the table, or in your journal. If you need to remind yourself of different feelings, you could refer back to Figure M13.1.

Date _____

Identify an emotion/ feeling	Identify introjects about emotions/ feelings	Challenge

M13.3 Coping with emotions after leaving

Before we look at how emotional healing can happen, I will briefly mention two issues that may arise after leaving.

M13.3.1 Struggling to identify or name feelings

In order to face our feelings, we need to be able to identify and name them, but many people struggle to do so. There is a word for this: alexithymia, which is derived from Greek words that literally mean "having no words for emotions" (Muller, 2000). This condition is not limited to those who have been in cultic settings, but the cultic experience may make it harder to identify and name feelings.

If you are finding this difficult, it may help to start by using a visual representation, like emojis (or emoticons) on mobile (cell) phones, to identify your feelings. These are digital images that express and communicate emotions. Worksheet M13.5 provides a way of experimenting and playing around with different emojis and names for feelings.

Worksheet M13.5: Emojis for feelings

I have provided some head and shoulder shapes for you to fill in with eyes and mouths to express feelings. You can either start by thinking of a feeling (for example one from Figure M13.1), or by looking at your phone and picking out an emoji that shows a feeling. Then draw that face into the shape and write the name of the feeling on the line underneath. Alternatively, you could find faces in a magazine, cut them out and stick them on.

Date _____

Feeling _____ **Feeling** _____ **Feeling** _____

Feeling _____ **Feeling** _____ **Feeling** _____

Feeling _____ **Feeling** _____ **Feeling** _____

M13.3.2 Society and emotions

It is not only a cultic experience that may cause us to suppress feelings, or think our emotions are 'bad'. In society, generally, there is an unhelpful perception that "good emotions are the ones that make us easy to be around, while bad emotions are the ones that shake things up" (McLaren, 2010, p. 26). After leaving, we may have to challenge some of these expectations, as well as those from the cultic setting.

Instead of splitting emotions into "good or bad things that happen *to* us" (McLaren, 2010, p. 29), it helps us if we learn not to judge our feelings, but to approach them with curiosity and compassion, and to see that they all have a vital role to play in our life and health.

In the next three sections, we will look at some ways in which emotional healing can happen.

M13.4 Learning to self-regulate

One thing that helps us cope with feelings is **self-regulation** – we learn to regulate, soothe and calm our feelings for ourselves, and remain grounded in our authentic identity and the window of tolerance (M7).

When we are little, we need adults and caregivers to give us attention, to make us the 'centre of their world'. This helps us to know we are important and special. They are also there to help regulate us and teach us to regulate ourselves. A key person is our main caregiver, also known as a 'primary attachment figure' (Chen, 2019). If there is no such person, and we grow up in a family or setting where we are not attended to, listened and responded to, then we are likely to grow up not knowing who we are and how to self-regulate. This is the case for many who are born and/or raised.

A caregiver helps us self-regulate by cuddling and soothing us when we are upset; or helping us to calm down if we are over-excited, or having a tantrum or panic about something. Self-regulation can be challenging when we have had no one to help us do it in the past, but it can be learned in adulthood, with the right help and support around us. Former members, especially those who have lost contact with their family who remain members, may struggle to find this kind of relationship – but it is something a kind therapist or counsellor may be able to provide (P5).

There is, therefore, a challenge for those, including many who were born and/or raised, who did not learn to self-regulate in early life. But there is another issue for everyone who has experienced a cultic setting, which is that the setting disrupts the process of self-regulation, even for those who had previously learned it.

Ideally, in 'normal' life, when people are free from controlling influences, they process feelings as they go along, they face them and work through them. If you imagine a wavy line, like hills and valleys, indicating the highs and lows of life; then imagine a little pot, full of emotion, at the top of each hill and the bottom of each valley. As we live life, we inevitably go through these highs and lows, but ideally, we process the emotions as we go along, that is we empty the pots, so the emotions do not build up and overwhelm us.

But in a cultic setting, we may not be able to process these feelings and empty the pots, and so we could imagine the feelings instead being stored in a big tank. When the tank gets full, the complex unregulated feelings may spill out over the top in depression, overwhelm, hot rage, panic attacks, etc. – many feelings and many symptoms of trauma – causing us pain, shame and distress.

This overflow of unregulated feelings may happen while still in the cultic setting, as we have already discussed (M13.2.2), but it is also likely that you left the setting with a full tank. This may cause unregulated feelings to spill out from time to time. And since the feelings are perhaps scary to face, you may try ever harder to keep a lid on the tank.

To recover, we need to empty the tank in a purposeful way, with compassion and care, rather than leaving the feelings to spill out everywhere!

One way to start emptying the tank in a more controlled way, and to soothe and regulate ourselves, is to imagine a water tap (faucet) attached to the tank. In time, we can learn to turn this on and off as we need to (at least, most of the time!) – and this helps to empty the tank and process the stored-up feelings from years of cultic abuse and control.

We begin the process by identifying the feelings in the tank; naming them; connecting with them; understanding why they are stored in the tank and not processed; and finally moving through them (see M13.5).

We need to aim to process one stored-up emotion at a time. This is more helpful than having all the feelings explode out together, unprocessed, or continuing to try to suppress those feelings (and filling up the tank again). Going forward, it is important to learn to process these feelings as they happen rather than storing them up.

To help with self-regulation, let's look at the feelings tank!

Worksheet M13.6: Feelings tank

In the illustration below, there is a water tank. There are three kinds of shapes shown:

- circles on the tank represent suppressed and unprocessed, stuck feelings
- explosive shapes coming through the top are unregulated, uncontrolled feelings breaking out
- drops coming out of the tap show feelings being released and processed in a more regulated, calm way, as we face, process and move through them

You could write on the diagram and name the feelings that are stuck in the tank; those that explode out; and those that you face and let out in a regulated, calm and controlled way.

   If you are struggling to name the feelings, you could have another look at Figure M13.1.

   If you have more to say, you could write in your journal.

Date _____

In the next section, we will look more closely at how we can process and move through emotions.

M13.5 Face and move through emotions

In considering facing and moving through emotions, it may help to look at an example. Although this does not involve a cultic setting, it provides valuable insights on engaging with and processing emotions.

Richard Lannowe Hall, a psychotherapist, sailor and former addict, who says he used his addictions to avoid feelings, finally came to realise he had to face them if he was to recover and heal. This is what he says about his process as he started to feel his feelings:

> I alternated between feeling enormous gratitude and pleasure and experiencing dark and painful days and nights, full of tears and doubts. I realised that by staying longer connected to these painful sensations I could explore them more deeply. At times they were accompanied by physical sensations; aches and pains cropping up in one part of my body and then moving onto somewhere else. ...If I allowed these aches and pains to exist and accept[ed] them, they would morph into some other sensation, probably somewhere else in my body (2021, p. 37).

It is interesting that his emotions were linked to physical symptoms. It is not unusual for strong feelings to affect the body in this way. Richard allowed both his emotions and their physical impact to make themselves known to him:

> As I became more adept at doing this, I accepted them for exactly what they were. I was not trying to make them mean anything, just maybe accepting them as something important, as though I was being shown something. I was being prised open like an oyster to reveal the luscious fruit within. As this process continued, I began to sense that it was a battle going on, a battle raging within me... some part of me was resisting with everything I had not to go there, not to feel this or that...
>
> (2021, pp. 37–38)

As a result of his being able to be in touch with his feelings, both emotionally and in his body, he says:

> I began to recognise that a different, an alternative personality was emerging, enhanced by this way of being.
>
> (2021, p. 38)

Once we stop being afraid of our emotions, perhaps we will find relief.

This can happen as we start to just accept that they are there. There is nothing to do about them necessarily – they are just part of us and, like everything else about us, deserve to be 'heard' and accepted as they are.

If we can accept all of our feelings with *curiosity, not judgement*, and with *compassion*, then maybe we can move through them and heal emotionally!

You could refresh your memory of the 'noticing brain' (M7.8).

It was noticeable in my research that none of those participants who indicated they were recovered was afraid of their feelings. They faced their suppressed and painful feelings (whatever the source) and were (mostly) in touch with them day to day, moment by moment, emptying the 'pots' as they went along. This is a sign of recovery – you could remind yourself what recovery looks like by revisiting P1.16.

Facing suppressed feelings and the emotional pain related to the cultic experience, with the right strategies, support and conditions, can lead to integration and healing. It helps put us in touch with our authentic identity, which can then emerge, breaking through the tarmac of the cultic pseudo-identity (M6).

Worksheet M13.7 provides a way to reflect on what your feelings are saying to you.

Worksheet M13.7: Two chair work – talking to your emotions and learning from them

Date _____

To help you hear what your emotions are saying to you, you could try the 'two chair' exercise. This can help one emotion speak to another emotion, or just help you to speak to your emotions – either way, it is a dialogue between parts of yourself. It can also help raise awareness of the polarisation or splitting of emotions, so you can challenge the idea that some feelings and parts of you are 'good' and some are 'bad'.

You could:

Step 1. Place two chairs opposite one another.

Step 2. Pick an emotion and place something on one chair to indicate it. It could be a piece of paper with the name of the emotion written on it or something to symbolise the emotion, such as a soft toy or object. For example, a child's dinosaur toy might symbolise rage or fear; or a happy-looking dog could symbolise joy.

Step 3. Sit in the other chair.

Step 4. Start to talk to that emotion. For example, if you chose 'fear', you could ask fear why it is there, what purpose it is serving, when it first started, and whether it is trying to remind you of another time in your life for a reason. You could ask fear if it is a symptom of a memory, rather than related to the present (M7.7); and whether it is from your pseudo-identity (the cultic you!) or your authentic identity (the real you!).

Have fun with this, if you can. It is not meant to be overly serious but is to help you understand and move through your emotions and become more aware of your authentic identity.

You could reflect in your journal what each emotion 'tells' you about itself.

In the next section, I want to say something about letting ourselves and others off the hook.

M13.6 Letting ourselves (and others) off the hook

After experiencing a cultic setting, there may be many reasons to blame ourselves and others.

In a thought reform environment, where individuals are expected to obey the leadership and the doctrine, it is inevitable that each person's actions will have an impact on others, often in an abusive and harmful way. The abusive cycle is therefore maintained, not only by the leader but also by members. In some cases, they victimise one another, and "spy and report on one another" (Lalich and Tobias, 2006, p. 39). Maribel views herself as a victim/accomplice of her leader, which led to regret, guilt and shame post-cult:

> But you know some psychopaths don't have partners, they have victims and accomplices - I REALLY regretted being an accomplice to this man.

The cultic experience is filled with injustice and abuse. Some things that happen, and the resulting painful emotions we are left with, are hard to move on from. We can also be left with so many regrets, guilt and so much pain and sorrow related to many losses, including lost opportunities, lost years, lost relationships and so much more.

> In a cultic setting, family life, including relationships between parents and their children, is usually compromised, since parents are likely to put the needs of the leader and the setting before the well-being and safety of their children (Goldberg, 2017, p. 242).
>
> This can be really difficult for all parties after leaving. Parents who have recognised and understood the abusive nature of the setting are likely to experience much guilt about the harm caused to their children, and the children may feel deep hurt and rage towards their parents who neglected them and did not protect them.
>
> There are, therefore, some difficult but potentially healing actions and conversations to be had – but how do we even begin to approach these? Lorna Goldberg suggests that parents who neglected their children in the cultic setting should initiate the process by simply apologising for being unable to protect them from harm. It may be best to avoid long explanations to start with, as these may sound like excuses. This is not for the parents to process their own guilty feelings, which they need to work on separately, but it is a step towards reconciliation and being able to be a comforting parent, even if their children are now adults (2017, p. 251).
>
> Each individual member of the family needs to go through their own process of recognising what they have been through and understanding themselves and their feelings. But perhaps, in time, the children can find a way to understand their parents, and to some degree let them 'off the hook'. That will be up to them.

So the challenge is, what do we do about the injustices and the losses, the things we have done and the things that were done to us? We have addressed some of these issues already, but another way to approach this is the idea of letting ourselves off the hook (and letting others off the hook too)!

The idea of 'forgiveness' is one way of attempting to resolve this difficult matter. But the word and concept of 'forgiveness' can be triggering because it is also loaded language for many former members. In the Community, it implied, "Let the abuser off the hook in spite of their abuse because 'God' requires it, and if you don't you will be punished severely – and, by the way, don't ever think about that abuse again." I do not agree with that interpretation at all! I would also emphasise that when I refer to forgiveness, this does not mean resuming a relationship with someone, or necessarily having any contact with them at all.

In spite of these challenges with the word 'forgiveness', approaching the concept from a psychological perspective might be worth considering. It might help to see forgiveness as both a *decision* and a *process* to help us move forward (Toussaint and Worthington, 2017, p. 30). *It is not denying that wrongs or injustice were perpetrated.* Perpetrators of abuse need to take personal responsibility for their wrongdoings. Where crimes have been committed, punishment is appropriate as "it acknowledges the seriousness of the harm done to the victim; it acts as a deterrent to others" (Parkinson, 1997, pp. 157–158).

Forgiveness can help us 'let go' of some of our painful feelings about the past and, *in (our) time*, to look to the future. It goes in two directions – towards ourselves, and towards those who have wronged or harmed us.

Understanding is key to forgiveness. It is vital that we understand the dynamics of what happened to us, as addressed throughout this journey, and that we face our past experiences with understanding and compassion towards ourselves first and foremost. We may need to forgive ourselves, let ourselves 'off the hook', both for simply being a member and for what we have done in the cultic setting, especially if we victimised or hurt others. Once we understand ourselves and let ourselves off the hook, it is perhaps easier to understand those who have wronged or harmed us and let them off the hook.

Toussaint and Worthington identify two sorts of forgiveness. The first is what they refer to as "decisional forgiveness", which is the "intention to not seek revenge and to treat the offender as a valued and valuable person" (2017, p. 30). This means we may make a *decision* to forgive someone, but still *feel* "emotional unforgiveness" and a whole mix of emotions about them. Making the decision to forgive does not mean we ignore or suppress our feelings of injustice and symptoms of trauma, but we make this choice for our own sake – it's a choice, probably an emotionally messy one, but still a choice! If we have been abused by a leader or partner, we may choose to 'forgive' but still feel rage – it's not all neatly resolved, but it is healthier for us in the long run.

The second type is what Toussaint and Worthington refer to as "emotional forgiveness", which is when we (at least try) to replace the "unforgiving emotions" with "emotions such as empathy, sympathy, compassion or love". It may help the process if we also feel "gratitude, humility and hope" (2017, p. 30). Emotional forgiveness can therefore help us feel better! It is a process which takes time and patience.

I have seen clients show great courage in making the decision to forgive, and in starting their process of emotional forgiveness. Some were ostracised and shunned by their member family and felt a huge mix of feelings ranging from rage to grief to dejection, but they also deeply understood that their families were victims of the leader and cultic dynamics.

It is important that you do not see forgiveness as a rule or requirement, and I am certainly not saying that you should, or must, forgive those who have abused you. If you have been in a Bible-based setting, the emphasis on forgiveness can be a heavy weight, and there is a danger that you have introjected the requirement to forgive. You may then feel you 'must' or 'should' forgive before you are ready, and suppress your feelings about the abuse and the abuser. It is important that you can chew it over, making the decision and the process your own, in your own time and for your own benefit. If we choose to forgive, it needs to be authentic and real, our choice and our process, not someone else's!

It is also important we do not confuse this encouragement to 'forgive' with having to trust the perpetrator; to be friends with them (or in any contact); or to pretend that the abuse never happened (self-suppression). It also does not mean that they will or should be exempt from punishment for any crimes.

There is an opportunity to highlight introjects about 'forgiveness' in Worksheet M13.8.

Worksheet M13.8: Introjects about 'forgiveness'

In this Worksheet, you might like to consider what 'forgiveness' meant in your cultic setting, and what you have introjected in relation to the concept; then chew it over and challenge it.

For example, if you have introjected the idea that forgiveness means you cannot be angry with the person who has abused you, and that you have to stop feeling the anger, you could put that in the first column. In the second column, you could put your challenge, such as, "It is my human right to have my feelings and I feel angry! I decide to let go of my rage, but that does not mean that what happened was not serious. It shouldn't have happened, and I will use my assertive anger to protect myself."

You could add your examples in the table below. You may want to say more in your journal.

Date _____

What have you introjected in relation to the concept of 'forgiveness'?	Can you challenge this?

Worksheet M13.9: 'Letting go'

In this Worksheet, you might like to reflect on what you want to 'let go' of. If you have more to say you might like to use your journal.

Date _____

1. Is there anyone you want to decide to forgive (even if you do not emotionally forgive them yet)?

    _____

    _____

    _____

2. Is there anyone you want to 'emotionally forgive', in other words, to start a process of replacing unforgiving emotions with forgiving ones?

    _____

    _____

    _____

3. Is there anyone you are not ready to forgive, and why?

    _____

    _____

    _____

4. What do you need to forgive yourself for?

    _____

    _____

    _____

Emotional healing is complex and takes time, so be patient with yourself, and get support when you need it. Sometimes, issues that we think have been laid to rest pop up in our lives again, and healing is never 100%. But emotions can and do heal, even after terrible times. I have seen this in myself and many other former members.

Before leaving emotional healing and this Region, we will look at the issue of why people join cultic settings.

M13.7 Why did you join?

Another area that impacts the issue of emotions is how and why we joined. If you are first generation, or if you were born and/or raised in one cultic setting and joined another as an adult (cult hopping), you may find it helpful to reflect on your motivation for joining, and even what made you vulnerable to joining. Others who are born and/or raised could consider your parents' or ancestors' motivation for joining, if you know about this.

Some joiners simply (and reasonably) believe the group or relationship is representing itself in a truthful and honest fashion. For example, the potential recruit may think it is a genuine political movement, church, business, spirituality, mentor or loving partner, with worthwhile or even noble aims. Unbeknown to them, hiding behind a mask of respectability, and apparent kindness and concern, there were other intentions. From the recruiter's point of view, these can be to control, for financial gain, to groom for sexual abuse, to promote the leader, etc.

Since its true nature is obscured, the individual joins without knowing the potential consequences until it is too late. They may not fully withdraw from the confluence and loss of boundaries until they leave physically and psychologically – and that may be many years later.

When someone is considering joining such a setting, the leader and other members are likely to appear loving and accepting (and on their best behaviour!). A genuine, heart-warming relationship seems to be established very quickly, promising a happy, healing and worthwhile future (Jenkinson, 2016). In reality, it is a form of grooming, seducing the individual into joining without giving them all the information needed to fully understand what they are joining. This is referred to as 'love bombing'.

Once they become a member, the apparent acceptance from the leadership and other members usually does not last long, and a different set of expectations is imposed – and thought reform and abuse follow. This results in the joiner becoming enmeshed, confluent (M4) and dependent, as the boundaries between them and the cultic setting blur.

I have noticed that many feel deep shame and judge themselves harshly for having joined a cultic setting (I certainly did). This is not helped by myths in society that people join cults because they are mentally unstable, or there is something wrong with them or they made an informed decision (Jenkinson, 2016). These assumptions do not recognise the subtle coercion and deceitful techniques used by groups or individuals who are out to recruit or groom.

The cultic setting may also take advantage of the joiner's idealism and desire to make the world a better place. It presents itself as the answer to the world's problems, and the individual projects their desire for a better world onto the cultic setting and leadership, believing they have the same aims.

Although it is a myth that everyone who joins a cultic setting does so because of pre-existing emotional issues, it is also true that everyone has issues of some sort, and they may be involved in our recruitment. Cultic settings can be clever at sniffing out our vulnerabilities, whatever they may be, and using them against us. Again, it is important that we are compassionate and patient with ourselves as we face these issues.

M13.7.1 Motivation for joining

In my research, I discovered that the motivation for joining differed amongst participants, and it appears that each joined for a variety of multi-layered reasons (Jenkinson, 2016). Worksheet M13.10 sets out what drew participants to join. I have listed these in a table, for you to tick those categories that apply. There is also space to say more if you wish and add any other reasons that apply to you. You could also reflect on this in your journal.

Worksheet M13.10: What was your motivation for joining (as an adult)?

Date _____

Which fits with your motivation for joining?	Could you say more?
seeking friendship (e.g. because lonely, in a new city, etc.)	
seeking a sense of place/home	
wanting to belong/felt lost	
looking for a service (e.g. to bless a forthcoming marriage, political information, meditation, yoga, etc.)	
seeking to do voluntary work (e.g. charity work, help the poor, etc.)	
seeking a solution to emotional problems (e.g. to address emotional pain, low self-esteem or depression, etc.)	
seeking spiritual enlightenment	
wanting help from a 'normal' organisation (e.g. a local church or therapy practice)	
a desire to join what seemed to be a genuine church or spiritual centre	
wanting to start a business	
seeking an alternative lifestyle	
seeking adventure (e.g. travel, gap year, new experiences, etc.)	

Whilst some participants (out of those who joined and those cult hopping) said they joined in order to address their emotional problems, they nevertheless had normal, healthy reasons for joining and, in most cases, their decisions were intended to lead to a sense of health and well-being. That is, joining was an attempt to make their life better on a practical, spiritual and/or psychological level.

They did not knowingly become a member of a coercive, cultic and spiritually abusive setting, and none said they were looking for or expecting abuse. They believed they were joining an organisation that was trustworthy and that had accurately represented itself to the public. Daphne poignantly explains that she:

> …never wanted to be a part of…you know, a group that wasn't doing the right thing…I was sold a bag of goods that I never received.

It is vital, therefore, to recognise the deceit and influence. Try not to take a blaming or shaming approach to joining, but be compassionate with yourself.

It may also help those born and/or raised to think about this in relation to your parents or ancestors joining. They may not have been aware of the deceitful recruitment techniques that trick people into joining, as noted above. I realise this may be hard to consider because of all the harm that has likely been caused, but it is perhaps something to consider at least (see M13.6).

You can reflect on why/how you joined in Worksheet M13.11.

Worksheet M13.11: Why/how did you join?

You could use the questions in this Worksheet as a springboard to reflect on the issue of joining and how it impacts you. You could answer these here or in your journal.

I suggest you explore the reasons for your joining, or your parents/ancestors joining, with *curiosity and not judgement* towards yourself or them. Thinking about why and how you joined may raise some strong emotions, so I encourage you to take care of yourself, revisit the earlier sections in this Milestone if that would help, and find the support you need.

Date _____

1. What age were you when you joined?

   _____

2. How and why did you join?

   _____

   _____

   _____

   _____

3. Were you at a life transition or vulnerable in some way, e.g. grieving, feeling lost, going through changes in your life, etc., when you joined?

   _____

   _____

   _____

   _____

4. Did you join to resolve psychological or mental health issues? Can you say more about this?

   _____

   _____

   _____

   _____

5. Were you deceived by an organisation or relationship that misrepresented itself?

_____

_____

_____

_____

6. Anything else?

_____

_____

_____

_____

We have now reached the end of Milestone 13 and Region 3, and are nearly at the end of our Walking Free journey! We can now move into the last Region, and the final two Milestones.

Region 4

Walking Free

We are nearly at the end of our Walking Free journey! You have visited all the Milestones in Regions 1, 2 and 3, and had an opportunity to complete the tasks set out in this Workbook as you unpacked your baggage one Milestone at a time. Well done!

I hope you have:

- left both physically and psychologically
- learned many things and made (more) sense of your coercive, cultic and/or spiritually abusive experience
- identified and challenged many introjects
- learned to activate your assertive anger and begun to love yourself (more)
- begun to unlayer your cultic pseudo-identity and to build up your authentic autonomous identity
- been able to recognise, face and process many feelings along the way, perhaps with support from a safe other
- begun to move on with your life, without the cultic setting or leader 'haunting' you (as much)

DOI: 10.4324/9781003305798-21

To complete your Walking Free journey, in this Region 4, you are invited to reflect on whether you have recovered, at least enough to 'move on'. In Milestone 14, we will reflect on the idea of 'post-traumatic growth' to help you establish what you have learned from your cultic experience. If you feel ready, then you can finish your Walking Free journey by visiting Milestone 15 and Moving On. This suggests some recovery tips to keep in mind as you Walk Free into the next stage of your life.

Let us visit Milestone 14!

Milestone 14

Reflections

At Milestone 14, you have an opportunity to sit and reflect on your cultic experience, and whether you learned and grew from it. You can also reflect on whether you have achieved the focus and aims you set at the beginning (P1.17), and how much you have resolved your baggage. The Milestone raises the possibility of pulling everything together by writing up your life story, before concluding with some final reflections.

M14.1 Reflections on what you learned – post-traumatic growth

Many of us who leave coercive, cultic and spiritually abusive situations notice that we have grown *in spite of* the trauma and abuse. This is the concept of 'post-traumatic growth' (PTG).

It is generally accepted in psychology that humans have a natural tendency towards health, growth and 'self-actualisation' (Perls et al., 1951). Self-actualisation refers to a desire to fulfil our talents and potential, and provides evidence of our authentic identity. It can lead to PTG (Tedeschi and Calhoun, 2004).

PTG:

- challenges the idea that trauma inevitably leads to a damaged and dysfunctional life, and is therefore a hopeful concept (Joseph, 2011)
- is "an accepted facet" of post-traumatic stress disorder (Turnbull, 2011, p. 413)
- is not a measure of someone's character, that is, if they have not achieved PTG, they are NOT in some way failing (Joseph and Murphy, 2014)

DOI: 10.4324/9781003305798-22

- is not an expectation or a requirement, especially as it arises from trauma and suffering (Jenkinson, 2016)
- is not (necessarily) a measure of being recovered, because growth and personal distress often co-exist (Tedeschi and Calhoun, 2004).

This is what Harriet has to say about it:

> So certain kinds of life experiences make people really examine who they are, you know and this was one of them, because people either have to completely invent themselves or reinvent themselves and do so much self-examination to figure out who they are, who they wanna be. There aren't very many life experiences that push you to do that like this does. So that's a good thing, I mean, I wouldn't wish it on anybody but I don't regret it.

Lavinia acknowledges that, after leaving, we can become:

> ...more and more grounded in the new me, the post-cult self, having a positive sense of self - the resilient self.

For some, there is a sense of genuine healing rather than the false "quick fix transformation", which Lavinia says is promised in cultic settings. Fred realised he didn't need the leader and says:

> I know that I am healing myself, that I am now making real progress, as opposed to the fictitious - lack of - progress in the cult.

Others express a sense of freedom in being in touch with their authentic identity. Their life belongs to them now, they are autonomous; no longer expected to be dependent and beholden to others. This is what Fred had to say about this when I interviewed him:

> And I've arrived here today having gone through the whole cleansing process. It feels like this interview is the final piece of the puzzle - I'm now free of that experience. It feels like I am myself again! It feels like my life is mine and that I'm autonomous again and that I'm not beholden to anyone else's wishes.

There is self-acceptance for some. A new sense of their authentic identity as well as joy, exhilaration and relief at being free. This is what Sean has to say about this:

> I am who I am and who I want to be, that's what makes me happy [he laughs], or a feeling of fulfilment. I have learned to leave behind the most depressive part of myself, the most self-deprecating, the most empty part of myself. I have learned to manage that part and not to be trapped and enslaved by it, and I've allowed myself to enjoy and take pleasure and pride in things I've done and accomplishments, relationships.

These next sections are an opportunity for you to reflect on the ways in which you might have grown and changed – PTG. You can think about what you might take away from your experience. There may be nothing – and that is fine, it is for you to say, not me or anyone else – but there may be things, even small things. You could consider personal changes, philosophical changes and relationship changes. You will see these overlap to some degree. I will give a short explanation for each and then provide questions for you to reflect on.

M14.1.1 Personal changes

This category broadly relates to "finding new inner strengths, achieving greater wisdom or becoming more compassionate" (Joseph, 2011, p. 73).

You have an opportunity to reflect on this category by answering the questions in Worksheet M14.1 or in your journal.

Worksheet M14.1: PTG and personal changes

Date _____

1. Have you been able to see your experience as an opportunity to invent or reinvent yourself, and can you relate to Jane's experience?

    One good thing is that actually you are getting a second chance to really decide who you wanna be and what you are going to do. I know it's a bit of a consolation prize but, but actually that's really quite exciting, you know, you, you can start again.

    _____

    _____

    _____

2. What new inner strengths are you now aware of?

    _____

    _____

    _____

3. Are you aware of having developed more inner wisdom?

    _____

    _____

    _____

4. Have you learned that critical thinking and being sceptical are better than introjecting what others have to say? Can you relate to what Marjorie says, that it is better to be

    …willing to rethink, reconsider, ask questions, be persuaded, always reading, always wanting to know more[?]

    _____

    _____

    _____

5. Has finding more autonomy, more of a sense of your authentic autonomous identity, resulted in a sense of freedom and joy (at least sometimes)?

_____

_____

_____

6. Have you learned to take control of your life in a balanced and new way?

_____

_____

_____

7. Do you feel you are allowed to take responsibility for your own life? Do you allow yourself to do this, and do you experience this as freedom?

_____

_____

_____

8. Have you been able to make decisions about the quality of life you want?

_____

_____

_____

9. Have you discovered what you now want to create in and with your life?

_____

_____

_____

10. Have you realised that when such (cultic) people approach you again, you can say to yourself, like Fred,

> …no I've been there, thank you, and I don't want to go there again!

_____

_____

_____

11. Have you learned that you don't have to be 'pure' or perfect, and that being human is good enough?

_____

_____

_____

12. Have you learned to have compassion for yourself?

_____

_____

_____

13. Have you explored what you are going to do to become the person you want to be?

_____

_____

_____

14. Do you accept that, despite what happened, your motivation for joining (if you joined) or for remaining was genuine and good, and that you can now build on this motivation?

_____

_____

_____

15. Have you learned to accept what happened? This is what Sean says about his process:

> So, so, you know I'm not indifferent, I'm not forgiving, but I am not obsessed and I am not filled with hate or rage, I've gotten on with my life and tried to make my life good and the life of people in my world better or good enough.

_____

_____

_____

16. Have you been able to build on aspects of what you learned, such as the work you did? Fred, a successful therapist in his cultic setting, says this about continuing to see the types of clients he helped when he was a member. Can you relate to Fred's experience?

> It gave me a confidence that otherwise I would never have had. And that, that meant that I could immediately translate all the negative experiences in the community into things that I had to go through in order to become this therapist that I had become in order to help people.

_____

_____

_____

17. Have you (like Fred, above) been able to 'translate' the negative experiences into things you went through to become the person you have become?

_____

_____

_____

18. Have you discovered that what you were told about bad things that would happen when you leave, was not true, and that you can be more successful than you expected? Can you relate to Cheryl's experience?

> [I believed] all those bad things would happen [after leaving] until I finally had more successes and then I, when I had more successes, better outcomes, I felt better about myself and I look at it now as a disconfirmation of those inaccurate self-limiting beliefs.

_____

_____

_____

19. Did you learn anything from the leadership, despite everything?

_____

_____

_____

20. Did you learn practical skills that you have taken with you, such as a writer, plumber, electrician, carpenter, etc.?

_____

_____

_____

21. Have you used your cultic experience to support a career, such as training as a therapist or psychologist, writer, educator, advocate or activist?

_____

_____

_____

M14.1.2 *Philosophical changes*

This category broadly relates to being "unexpectedly gifted with a new-found sense of what is really important in life" (Joseph, 2011, p. 75).

You have an opportunity to reflect on this category by answering the questions in Worksheet M14.2 or in your journal.

Worksheet M14.2: PTG and philosophical changes

Date _____

1. Have you found that you have had to challenge every area of your life?

   _____

   _____

2. Have you figured out who you want to be?

   _____

   _____

3. Have you held onto your idealism, the part of you that wanted to make a difference, to be compassionate, help others and make this a better world – but for yourself now and not a cultic agenda? This is what Marjorie and Lindsey had to say about this – can you relate to their experience?

   Idealism is a wonderful thing and although it may be what got us involved we need to hold onto it and after [I left] I had a BURNING hatred of injustice and misuse of power. And it makes very little people able to do very big things and that is how it should be.

   As I understood the ridiculousness of the cult doctrine, that was completely 'not me', such as the elitism, arrogance, oppression and disregard for autonomy and individualism, I was able to hold onto the idealism, the enthusiasm, the compassion, the love, the fun etc. that was also very much part of my cult experience.

   _____

   _____

4. Is a desire to make a difference, be compassionate, help others and make the world a better place, a new thing arising out of your own suffering?

   _____

   _____

5. Have you found a healthy, balanced and boundaried way to make a difference by not giving all of your life over to others?

_____

_____

_____

6. Have you learned that in future you need NEVER forsake your own value system?

_____

_____

_____

7. Can you reflect on who you admire and might like to emulate, without giving your whole life over to an authority figure?

_____

_____

_____

8. For some, the cultic experience is the "best of times and the worst of times". This is what Ginny had to say about this aspect – can you relate to her experience?

> I promised myself to have that perspective in mind, later on in life too - so that I wouldn't paint everything black.

_____

_____

_____

9. Are you able to remember some good times as a member?

_____

_____

_____

M14.1.3 Relationship changes

This category broadly relates to taking a new approach to our relationships. Many people become more empathic and understanding, more readily feeling the pain others feel (Joseph, 2011, p.77).

You have an opportunity to reflect on this category by answering the questions below or in your journal.

Worksheet M14.3: PTG and relationship changes

Date _____

1. Has your experience helped you to see the difference between healthy and unhealthy relationships? This is what Matt had to say about this aspect – can you relate to his experience?

   > That's the mirror image isn't it? My relationship with [my partner] is this strong healthy, adult relationship and there's no controlling, manipulation, there's none of THAT going on...um, and it makes me much more able to see and feel how damaging the cult was.

   _____

   _____

   _____

2. Have you learned that it is important to belong, and to be involved in society and others' lives, but not at the cost of your integrity or individuality?

   _____

   _____

   _____

3. Are you now able to approach relationships with balance: without becoming confluent and introjecting, but holding onto your critical thinking and boundaries?

   _____

   _____

   _____

4. Have you changed in positive ways in how you relate to others, for example, are you less shy, can you relate to many types of people, etc? Can you say how?

_____

_____

_____

5. Are you able to remember any good relationships when a member?

_____

_____

_____

6. Have you been able to retain any relationships you had in the cultic setting, but without harmful cultic dynamics?

_____

_____

_____

We are now at the end of our reflection on PTG. Let's reflect next on whether you have fulfilled your aims for this Walking Free journey and resolved your baggage – and what, if any, you are still left with.

M14.2 Reflections on your initial focus and baggage

Healing and recovery are not all-or-nothing processes, and you will almost certainly need to revisit the previous Milestones again if something emerges or triggers you. Integration, recovery and growth are the aims – that is, we don't forget the experience, and we don't suppress or dissociate from it either – but we have (on the whole) processed it!

In this part of Milestone 14, you have an opportunity to reflect on your initial focus and what you set as your recovery aims. But first, you might like to think about how much of your baggage you have processed and resolved.

Worksheet M14.4: Have you resolved your baggage?

In P1.17, Worksheet P1.1, you labelled or noted the baggage you wanted to resolve. Can you look again at this, and reflect on what has been resolved or processed, and what might still be left to deal with?

In this Worksheet, or in your journal, you can write down the issues you noted at the beginning, and any you want to add from the journey so far, say what has been resolved and what hasn't, and consider what may help to resolve them.

Date _____

Issue	Yes	No	Partly	What will help to resolve any remaining issues?

If there are still issues you need to resolve, you could consider revisiting the relevant Milestones by following the footpath on the Roadmap, and stopping at those you need to – you could make a note of these in the table above or in your journal.

I have suggested that recovery and growth are the aims and destination for the Walking Free journey – but what about *your* aims? You may find it encouraging to remind yourself of what you put down at the beginning of the journey, and to see how far you have come!

Worksheet M14.5: Reflect on your focus – have you fulfilled your aims on this journey?

In P1.17, Worksheet P1.2, you had an opportunity to reflect on your chosen focus, aims or destination for this Walking Free journey. You might like to revisit these aims and consider whether you have fulfilled them, or if there are still some left to fulfil. If there are, you could consider revisiting the relevant Milestones. You could reflect on this in the table below or in your journal.

Date _____

What were your stated aims or destination?	Have you fulfilled these, and if not, what will help you to do so?

Having reflected on PTG, and your baggage and focus, you might like to consider your story as a whole. Let's briefly address this before making some final reflections.

M14.3 Writing your life story

Now you have nearly completed the Walking Free journey and reflected on your life experiences from different angles at the Milestones, you could consider pulling your whole story together into a clear narrative. A narrative is a spoken or written account of connected events. This would be for yourself initially, so you have a clear, ordered overview of your own history. The exercises in P3.2, where you had an opportunity to reflect on your family tree, timeline and the history of your group, may help with this.

If you create a narrative, it is up to you how long, detailed and polished it is. You do not have to write a book or use perfect language. This is for you, and you can always go back and work on it later if you want.

I suggest that you stay aware of how you are expressing yourself and what you are saying. For example, are you confessing, or reiterating introjects? Are you allowing yourself to say how strong you are in surviving? The process of writing can help us to chew over our introjects. If we allow it, telling our story can take us forward in our life, because it makes a difference to our identity and how we see ourselves.

M14.4 Final reflections

And so, we come full circle, back to the beginning and the purpose of this whole Walking Free journey, which is to know our story, understand our story and accept our story; to heal from the coercive, cultic and spiritual abuse; and to address its impacts and ripples down the years.

I will end this Milestone on a hopeful note – that recovery is possible, and that, as we have seen, it is possible to grow in spite of, and sometimes because of, a coercive, cultic and/or spiritually abusive experience and the resulting trauma. It is a journey, sometimes a long journey, and certainly a personal journey, but with Milestones that help along the way. For some, therefore, their life is enriched by, and they learn from, the experience. They are changed either way – it is inevitable – and so the end of this journey is, or can be, positive. Life can be rich and we can flourish.

I have been on this long journey. I cannot say what my life would have been like if I had not been deceitfully recruited into a cultic setting and spiritually abused, but it would have been very different. My years in the Community were terrible ones that I did not deserve and would not wish on anyone. Even after leaving I spent another 15 years with cultic thinking still dominating my life, struggling to find my way towards authenticity and fulfilment. And then came the deeply painful process of facing what had happened to me, and all the grief, rage and confusion involved in that.

But that was not the end of my story, it was a new beginning. Out of that pain, confusion and grief, I was able to find something authentic, the 'real me'. Not the 'me' that I was before I joined, but 'me' with new clarity, strength and wisdom, even though the experience has inevitably left its mark – and that is okay too. This did not happen overnight, it all took much time, work and patience. But it did happen and I am here to tell the story!

I leave the last words to Sean (joined) and Gloria (born and raised):

> You know, this is a horrendous, really kind of insane and evil guru - the group is very destructive - but they were selling and I was buying, and I learned a lot, and for a time it felt good until it didn't, and coming out of it gives me knowledge and experience that many people don't get to have. And being able to bear the traumas of life, because everybody has them, is in the end where I am left, which is a good place.

> Oh yeah...it's like I can be a whole person!! It, its, I, I AM A WHOLE PERSON!

We have now completed Milestone 14!

On the Roadmap, you will see you have reached the roundabout. You have a choice of directions – either to go along the footpath and revisit the previous Milestones, or to turn left to Milestone 15 and Moving On.

Moving on and Walking Free!

We have now reached Milestone 15, the final Milestone! As we come to the end of your Walking Free journey (hooray!), you might like to consider some 'recovery tips' and things to hold in mind as you journey on.

You will see that our traveller is no longer kneeling and sorting baggage, but is walking freely with a manageable rucksack which is no longer weighing them down, holding them up or causing discomfort.

You might like to look back over the Milestones and remind yourself of all you have learned. Perhaps some meant more to you than others. You could pull out certain points that were helpful at each stage, and summarise them.

Before looking at the list of recovery tips I have compiled over the years, perhaps you would like to reflect on what you find helpful and inspiring in your life. What keeps you going, encourages you and builds you up?

You could summarise these ideas in Worksheet M15.1 or in your journal, and keep them so you can remind yourself of them in future.

DOI: 10.4324/9781003305798-23

Worksheet M15.1: What are your recovery tips?

Date _____

What helps you heal and what are your recovery tips?

M15.1 Recovery tips

Below is my list of recovery tips. They are in no particular order and are included for you to chew over and decide what speaks to you and what does not! You might like to use a coloured highlighter, or mark those that mean most, or change the wording if some are not quite right. Any new ideas you have can be added to Worksheet M15.1 or your journal.

1. It is important to *identify what gives you pleasure* as this can help you flourish in your life and continue to build your authentic identity, your 'real me'! The word pleasure means enjoyment with a happy satisfied feeling! Different things give us pleasure at different times. For example, tasting coffee (or tea for me!), food, music, singing, dancing, acting, owning a pet, creating things, hobbies, cinema and theatre, walking, beauty in nature, attending to our needs, helping others, volunteering, being generous or expressing gratitude can all cause us to feel pleasure. You could revisit your Safe Enough Space at P3.1.1 and remind yourself of things you love or that are helpful to you.

2. Let your brain 'rewire' itself. Did you know that your brain has 'neuroplasticity', which means you can change your neural pathways and how you think? Knowing and learning about this can help change the effects of the coercive, cultic and spiritual abuse – it is possible.

3. Eat well, sleep well, keep fit – it really helps us in every way including our mental health!

4. Do what makes you stand out as different from others: this is in part what defines you as you and builds your authentic identity.

5. Keep challenging the introjects and the negative cultic voice – it's really worth doing!

6. You can change your mind if you want to.

7. You can change the course of your life if you want to.

8. You can take your time over things.

9. You can rest as and when you need to.

10. You can make your own choices for your life.

11. It is important to use your critical mind and develop your ability to analyse and critique.

12. Remember about the window of tolerance zone and aim to live a grounded life, where you can think and feel at the same time.

13. Anticipate if you are going somewhere or doing something that may remind you of the past, so you can self-regulate, hold yourself and remain (as much as possible) in the window of tolerance.

14. Remember to keep visiting Oasis Lake and your 'Safe Enough Space'.

15. Remember the grounding tips.

16. Remember it is normal to ask for help when you need it.

17. Remember to keep journalling if you find it helpful.

18. Remember how it feels being in the fight and flight (hyperarousal) and freeze (hypoarousal) zones, so if you are triggered you are aware of what is going on in your body.

19. Break triggers down into manageable symptoms and memories so that you can then notice your reactions with curiosity and not judgement, and ground and soothe yourself.

20. Use your healthy boundary setting assertive anger to define your boundaries and do what is right for YOU.

21. Transform your hot and/or cold rage into a positive energy, for your good and the good of others.

22. Love yourself and keep yourself in view all the time, it is healthy and normal to do so.

23. Remember we put the oxygen mask on ourselves first on an airplane!

24. Resist being an echoist and use your voice to speak YOUR truth. Say what you need and how you see things.

25. Listen to and welcome your feelings, they are your friends and part of you. Learn how to process and move through them.

26. Talk about your feelings with trusted others. Let the hurt heal – it is normal to have feelings and to need support.

27. Remember your autonomic nervous system is constantly shifting zones. Use the Worksheets in M7 as tools to track your nervous system.

28. Approach life with curiosity – notice what is new to you. What have you learned about life that you didn't realise before?

29. Try to learn something new every day or week or month.

30. Think of at least one thing each day that you can be grateful for – it can help build hope!

31. Be curious about society and other people, how they live their lives and how they do things.

32. Be curious about yourself, your feelings, your body and your mind.

33. Educate yourself. Keep reading, learning and studying!

34. Keep in touch with your dreams and ambitions – can you allow yourself to fulfil them?

35. Don't give up on your dreams, keep going – if you stop, they'll never happen.

36. What haven't you done that you would love to do?

37. Do you have a 'bucket list' – a list of things you want to do before you die? If you don't, you could consider compiling one and working through it. Some people want to travel to certain places, while others want to achieve things such as a degree or Doctorate, or set up a business.

38. Oh and did I say, do what gives you pleasure, this helps build your authentic identity or the 'real you'!

39. Search for sayings, memes and quotes that inspire you, and compile a list in your journal, or print them and paste them into a scrapbook.

40. Listen to challenges from trustworthy kind people because we benefit from criticism and can grow through it – it helps us recognise blind spots about ourselves and our past – but only from those who have our best interests at heart and who are prepared to be open to discuss what they have said.

41. Learn to play! It is a great way of expressing your authentic identity and being creative, so give yourself permission to play and be playful.

42. Give yourself permission to have fun. If you already have fun, revel in it!

43. Give yourself permission to develop a sense of humour. If you already have one, then enjoy it!

44. Keep laughing and be silly!

45. Keep colouring the illustrations (here and in colouring books) as this is playful and grounding.

46. You have a right to be happy.

47. You have a right to be free!

48. If it helps, see the coercive, cultic or spiritually abusive experience as a chapter in your life, one that you can leave behind, like leaving school or university.

49. Remember all you have learned so far, not just on this Walking Free journey but in your life in general.

50. Don't identify with the abuser or abusive leader – separate yourself from them in your mind so you do not blame yourself. (If you eat a bad shrimp, it is not your own stomach that poisons you, it is the shrimp!)

51. Remember that others need to prove themselves worthy of your trust.

52. Oh and did I say, get support when you need it and ask for help if you can – it is normal to need and get help!

53. Exercise your right to make your own choices, and to say what you want and what you think.

54. Remember you have your own inner sense of what is right – learn to trust it. Check out with trusted others if you are not sure *but still make up your own mind*.

55. Affirm to yourself that you are a good person.

56. Remember to speak kindly to yourself, and resist 'confession' and reiterating the introjects.

57. Put the responsibility that belongs to others onto them – it is not always your fault!

58. Affirm to yourself that you are strong, you can survive and even thrive – you have survived so far!

You have now had the opportunity to visit all the Milestones and we have completed the Walking Free journey!

You can always revisit the Milestones whenever you need to, but for now, our journey is complete – WELL DONE, this is a HUGE ACHIEVEMENT! You might like to add your name to the medal to mark this occasion!

has completed the
Walking Free Journey!

Part Five

Seeking therapy

While you are Walking Free, you may want to investigate accessing professional support from a psychotherapist, psychologist, counsellor or therapist. I will refer to all these as 'therapists' who offer 'therapy' for simplicity here.

Finding a therapist can be a baffling journey. This section will introduce you to the area and help you begin an investigation so you can decide for yourself what you need.

P5.1 Why seek therapy?

There are various reasons why we might seek therapy. We may feel overwhelmed, anxious or depressed. We may have a specific problem we want to address or just want to understand ourselves better. Former members often seek therapy because they find they are overwhelmed by emotions, memories and triggers of their experience in the cultic setting and cannot seem to move on in their lives. Sometimes they need help to understand where difficult emotions come from, and may not, at first, link these with their experience (M7 and M13).

One problem for former members is that therapists are generally not trained to work with cultic issues and so might miss them altogether, or assume they understand when they do not!

To help you think a bit more about this, I will briefly introduce you to some of the many different types of professionals and theoretical approaches to therapy.

DOI: 10.4324/9781003305798-24

P5.2 Who offers therapy?

There are many different titles that describe mental health professionals who offer therapy and who may work in many varied settings. There are private practitioners who work for themselves, those who work in government-funded services or private companies, and those who volunteer or work for mental health charities. The level of training and experience, and the setting in which they work, are likely to affect the cost.

To help you decide who might offer you the support you need, here are some general categories of mental health providers to get you started. You will see that there are crossovers between these types, but differences in the level of training received and the issues they are equipped to consult on.

The summaries below reflect the UK position. You can check professional websites that clarify the terminology in your country, as this can vary.

Clinical psychologists train in psychology and work with people who are experiencing mental health problems, emotional difficulties, behavioural issues or physical health problems that have a knock-on effect on mental well-being. Some also work with people who have learning disabilities.

Counsellors and psychotherapists train specifically in counselling and psychotherapy and help people resolve emotional, psychological and relationship issues. Clients may be experiencing general underlying feelings of anxiety, depression or dissatisfaction with life, or they may have difficult and distressing events in their lives, such as bereavement, divorce, health problems or job concerns. The terms are often used interchangeably, but counsellors more usually work short term (from a few sessions up to a year), while psychotherapists may work long term to allow time to explore past and developmental issues that may be impacting the client's current life. Both usually offer weekly sessions.

Coaches help motivate people to develop the skill sets required to achieve their goals in settings such as sports, fitness, business, leadership and well-being. They generally offer shorter-term, and less regular, sessions than a counsellor or psychotherapist. In the UK, some accredited counsellors and psychotherapists are also trained coaches, usually referred to as therapeutic coaches. Those who do not have counselling training are not necessarily trained to work with mental health issues and so you need to tread cautiously. An ethical coach will know the limits of their expertise and refer you to others when appropriate.

Psychiatrists are medical doctors who specialise in mental health and can diagnose and treat people with mental illness, as well as dispense medication, such as anti-depressants. Some psychiatrists are also psychotherapists.

P5.3 Theoretical approaches

There are many different theoretical approaches or 'modalities' to working with clients, and therapists may train in one or more of these. I have trained in a number:

My initial training, Pastoral Counselling, was 'eclectic', meaning we looked at many modalities, including 'Person Centred' therapy, based on the work of Carl Rogers, and 'Cognitive Behavioural'. We learned to apply these in our clinical work whilst also reflecting on pastoral and spiritual issues.

For my Master's degree, I trained in 'Gestalt Psychotherapy', which is a 'humanistic' modality. Humanistic approaches value and emphasise subjective experience and the need to understand it. We also studied 'Object Relations', which helps people understand their relationships with others and is a more developmental and 'psychodynamic' (or 'Freudian') approach.

There are many other modalities and offshoots from these. A more recent development is 'Pluralistic Therapy', which is humanistic and assumes that each client is different and will benefit from different therapeutic methods at different times.

You can check out more about modalities and approaches to therapy where you live because these can vary by country.

There is no 'right' or 'best' modality: they all have their pros and cons and may suit different people. Generally, therapists are not trained to help with the specific issues of those who have been abused in cultic settings. That doesn't mean that they can't help you in some ways, and some do have relevant training and experience, but they will need to be flexible in their approach to address cultic dynamics.

P5.4 Challenge introjects about therapy

Many cultic settings warn their members against any sort of professional support outside the group or relationship, including therapy, perhaps implying the therapist is 'worldly', an outsider not worth listening to or even someone with malign intent. Or they tell members it is selfish, self-centred or egotistical to spend time thinking and talking about themselves. This is not true and needs challenging!

There are also some cultic settings that use a distorted form of therapy or counselling as a way of recruiting, or of creating and maintaining coercive control. If you were in such a setting, you will have understandable caution about seeking therapy.

You may, therefore, have introjects about therapy, or about yourself in therapy, that it would be helpful to challenge. You could have another look at M5 to refresh your memory about introjects.

If you do not challenge these introjects, then the fears and phobias that you still hold about this issue may make it much harder to access the support you need and deserve. Before looking at some tips to keep you safe in therapy, you could reflect on what you believed about therapy as a member and what you think now, so you go into the search with less baggage! You can do this in Worksheet P5.1.

Worksheet P5.1: What were you told and what did you believe about therapy?

In the table below, or in your journal, you could note down your introjects related to therapy. For example, if you have introjected the belief that spending time talking to a therapist about yourself is selfish, you could put that in the first column. In the second, you might challenge this, for example, "I have to be able to talk about myself, otherwise I cannot make relationships or get support with the things I am struggling with. So, I need to spend time talking about myself and it is NOT selfish!"

Date _____

What were you told about 'therapy'? What did you believe about 'therapy' and 'therapists'?	What do you think now, and can you challenge the introjected beliefs?

P5.5 Choosing a therapist and keeping safe

While it is important not to fear therapy, it is also important to keep safe, so I offer a few tips below to help you as you seek support following a coercive, cultic and/or spiritually abusive experience.

Most therapists work safely and ethically, but there are some who make inflated claims about their expertise and results, and a few who may be recruiting for a cult. It is important that seeking therapy does not lead to 'cult hopping'.

It is important to check out the therapist's training and experience. The types and levels of training vary, so I suggest you be cautious and investigate carefully. Also, find out whether they are a licensed or accredited member of a professional body with a code of ethics: a set of guidelines for professional and safe practice that all members should follow. If not, I suggest you avoid them! I recommend that you read the statements of ethics and good practice on the professional body's website, so you know what you have a right to expect.

Many therapists have websites and these can be useful sources of information about their background, training and specialism. I suggest that you do not rely on these alone, but also check the listings on their accrediting or licensing body's website.

> Another question is whether you should try and find a therapist who also experienced abuse in a cultic setting, and perhaps now specialises in helping former members. I think the answer is usually, 'Yes, if possible'! But this is not an all-or-nothing situation. Not every therapist who has had a cultic experience will be helpful, especially if they have not fully understood cultic dynamics and addressed their own issues: they may not then be able to help you identify your own blind spots, and may be triggered by your story. And some therapists who have not personally experienced a cultic setting may be helpful, if they are honest and realistic about the extent of their own knowledge and are willing to listen, investigate and learn. So it may be worth keeping an open mind on this while you consider your options.

This Workbook started life as a series of Worksheets that I used with clients, and it can be used with a therapist. If you want to work through this book with your therapist, then I suggest you show it to them and discuss whether they are prepared to support you on the journey set out here.

Before going through some questions to ask a potential therapist, let me tell you a bit about my own experience of receiving therapy.

I love receiving therapy, and I have chosen to have access to a therapist for virtually all the time I have been a therapist – which is a long time! After receiving the exit-counselling which helped me begin to understand the cultic dynamics, I saw a wonderful Gestalt therapist for over 20 years. It was because of her that I decided to train in the Gestalt modality. I do not regret spending the money and time getting to know myself better and to heal in a safe space – in fact, I am a far richer person, in every way, as a result!

But, before meeting my Gestalt therapist, I had a few experiences which helped me to work out who was right for me and who was not. For example, I was seeking a new therapist and went to her house. We met in her very untidy sitting room with old boots and kids' (smelly!) sports kit lying around, and children shouting outside the door. Most therapists have a dedicated private space but she did not offer this and I did not feel safe or relaxed. I never went back, even though she had (very) good credentials!

Another therapist I saw used to fall asleep in sessions and somehow managed to blame me for it, saying I was not in touch with my feelings, and this was why she fell asleep! Because of my vulnerability at the time, I accepted this. She later admitted that her friends told her that she also fell asleep with them! Now I am more assertive and understand how therapy works, I would say that it was unethical for the therapist to be falling asleep in my session (whether paid for or not) and unethical to blame me!

While most therapists are well meaning, I have heard many stories from clients, including former members, about unhelpful situations they have encountered while seeking therapy. It is important to use your assertive anger (M8), have a voice (M9), walk away if you are not happy, and report them if they are abusive.

There is nothing wrong with asking questions of a therapist, in fact, it is to be encouraged! A well-trained ethical therapist will expect it. It is also usual to try a session or two before considering a longer-term therapy relationship. You do not have to continue with the first therapist you see. Don't be afraid to interview them to make sure they will be the one most likely to meet your needs.

Below are some points to consider when choosing a therapist.

As mentioned above, do some initial research, including checking their and their professional body's website, covering their training and experience, location (or whether they work online, if you are happy with that), charges, etc.

In the first session, the aim is 'mutual assessment': both you and the therapist need to consider whether they can help you.

The areas I would cover in the discussion include:

- Their background, training, experience, specialism(s) and accrediting or licensing body.
- Are they a former member of a cultic setting? (Some therapists prefer not to disclose much about themselves, and this is not obligatory, but it can be helpful.)
- What experience do they have with clients from cultic settings?
- What approach or modality do they take, with clients generally and/or with clients from cultic settings? (Don't hesitate to ask them to explain anything you don't understand. If there are any aspects of their approach that you are unsure or unhappy about, or that are triggering, are they prepared to offer alternatives?)
- Are they interactive in sessions? (By interactive I mean a two-way discussion or dialogue. It is usually more helpful for trauma survivors and former members to have a therapist who interacts – offering a relationship whilst also being psychoeducational – rather than sitting with long silences.)
- If you want them to support you in the Walking Free journey set out in this book, are they happy to do so?
- Do they have specific expectations on how long therapy should last?
- Practical and cost issues, including charges, length and frequency of sessions, availability in a crisis, etc. (Ask about anything you are unclear or unhappy about.)

It is of course important to discuss what you hope to get from therapy, the issues that most concern you and whether they can help with those.

I suggest that *how* they answer is at least as important as *what* they answer. You want someone with the right expertise, but not someone who thinks they know it all! They are there to help you find your way forward, not to tell you what to do.